Indian Intelligence
Missing in Action

INDIAN INTELLIGENCE
Missing in Action

M.K. Singh

PRASHANT PUBLISHING HOUSE
DELHI-110094

Published by :
Prashant Publishing House
C-34, 28 Foota Road, Gali No.-3,
West Karawal Nagar, Delhi-110094
Phone : 011-22963970, Mob. : 9810396373

Indian Intelligence

First Published 2012

ISBN 978-93-80565-28-6

PRINTED IN INDIA
Published by Mr. R.K. Jha M/s Prashant Publishing House and Published at **Dynamic Printers, Delhi**

Preface

India's intelligence community is divided into a traditional structure that separates military and civilian, and foreign and domestic intelligence. Though each agency is charged with its own mission, the government has provided a means to facilitate the sharing of information between members of the intelligence community. The Joint Intelligence Committee (JIC) processes and analyzes data gathered by both civilian and military intelligence agencies and coordinates joint operations. The National Security Council acts as liaison between the government's executive branch and the intelligence services, advising leadership on intelligence and security issues.

The main civilian intelligence agency in India is the Intelligence Bureau (IB). The IB focuses on domestic intelligence, but the exact structure and operations of the agency are largely unknown. Political espionage is illegal in India, and police gathered wiretapping information is inadmissible as evidence in court proceedings. However, the IB conducts regular electronic monitoring of telephone communications, and mail surveillance, despite occasional admonitions from Parliament. The Central Bureau of Investigations handles most criminal investigations, often acting on initial information provided by one of the IB's many departments. Increasing political tensions with neighboring Pakistan altered the focus of IB operations in recent years, with increasing attention paid to the protection and surveillance of national borders.

The Research and Analysis Wing (RAW) is India's primary agency responsible for foreign intelligence. RAW operations are largely focused on espionage against Pakistan. With the addition of both India and Pakistan to the growing cadre of the world's nuclear powers, India's RAW conducts counter-intelligence operations, as well as technological and remote espionage, against Pakistani defense and military interests. The RAW is not subject to Parliamentary review, and its actions are highly secret. The Indian government also used RAW resources to aid predominantly-Hindu Bangladesh's 1971 quest for independence from Muslim Pakistan. Most recently, the RAW aided international antiterrorism efforts by providing the United States and British governments information on the al-Qaeda terrorist network and its strongholds in Pakistan and Afghanistan.

Military intelligence is conducted by the Army Directorate of Military Intelligence. The agency is the weakest of India's intelligence community, but often aids civilian intelligence operations. The Army also maintains the Joint Cipher Bureau, the main code breaking department of Indian intelligence. To the northwest, the independent Muslim nation of Pakistan claims the Kashmir region of India. The two nations have never resolved the border dispute, and tensions recently reached a climax when both nations declared themselves nuclear powers and began testing weapons of mass destruction. The nuclear programs of India and Pakistan raise interesting questions about the efficacy of current non-proliferation measures and the increasing global prevalence of industrial and scientific espionage. The increasing instability of the region has aroused the concern of the international community and the United Nations Security Council.

This book concludes that the only way to bring about a lasting peace and prevent more insurgencies rising up in the future is to build a state that attends equally to the interests of Indian Intelligence.

Contents

1

Introduction

AWAITING STILL ITS TRYST WITH DESTINY

Indian Intelligence is frequently in the news, often for the wrong reasons. It is a favourite kicking target for a large number of those who compulsively articulate, like the media, political leaders, academics etc. Why should it be so when its stellar contributions to national security have quite often been praised by different Prime Ministers at different times in India's history? A public acknowledgement of the services rendered is also indicated by the Padma awards, bestowed on Intelligence personnel from time to time.

But there is no denying that the system suffers from many fault lines, some systemic, some a legacy of the past but most due to reluctance, express or implicit at various levels in the power structure of the country, to bring about a change. It is the cumulative mindset, operating at the cutting level in the country which is mostly responsible for this dismal state of affairs.

Also, the mindset does not or perhaps cannot change in a few short decades. National security has never been a hot issue with the people at large as evident from several public polls conducted in the country. Removal of the fault lines, therefore, remains a low priority. The episodic prominence the subject receives now and then has proved incapable of influencing the frozen channels in the subconscious.

For any State, Intelligence is a prime necessity, not only to know about adversaries but also about friends, so as to remain fore warned about their intentions and capabilities and to prevent surprises. It is a multidimensional complex activity but its basics remain the same, collection, analysis, counter intelligence and covert actions. A fair idea about the functioning of Indian Intelligence can be made by examining how well it is equipped for handling these four sectors.

Collection is a three pronged exercise, each arm performing a distinct role. Published information provides the bulk of intelligence, close to 80%. Well researched articles and books and field journalists not only prove invaluable source of key facts, they also provide reliable insights into any situation a country maybe interested in. Advent of computers now makes recording, indexing and retrieval of such information a lot easier but if the organization is not computer savvy, a good part of such information would fail to get stored. One suspects that such skills are still to be universally acquired and mastered in the world of Indian Intelligence. If this is correct, it bespeaks of a handicap at the starting level itself.

Technological and scientific means invariably produce intelligence of high accuracy. The gadgetry required for technical collections is very expensive and the state of art equipment is not available in the market. Investigations into Mumbai 26/11 events reveal that intercepts of Voice over Internet Protocol conversations between the terrorists in Mumbai and their handlers in Pakistan had to come from foreign agencies.

States share intelligence in absolute self interest and not for considerations of ethics, morality or law. Imagine, if foreigners had not been the victims of 26/11 carnage, the requisite information in all probability have remained hidden from Indian authorities. Selective concealment is an acceptable reality of the Intelligence world. At no stage in the past India's collaborating partners had disclosed to India anything about Pakistan's ongoing nuclear weapon development programme and China's stellar role in it when it was widely known that this programme directly targetted India.

The solution lies in having an in-house research and development capability with an extremely high powered technical staff, second to none, that can work on dedicated technical requirements of the Intelligence. It calls for a very high level of funding; something which is not very kindly looked upon by the fund managers of the country. The alternative is to tie up with governmental and non governmental hi-tech institutions to look for answers.

The key to the highest grade of Intelligence is held by human sources to raise whom a great deal of focused attention, ingenuity, daredevilry and deep pockets are necessary. It is not a job of a run of the mill kind which can be performed by anyone. A successful operator, capable of recruiting high net worth human agents, has to belong to a rare breed. Identifying such potentially gifted operators and enrolling these into Intelligence then becomes a matter of incentives and competitive remunerations.

This area has been a long standing weakness of Indian Intelligence. The problem dates back to the dawn of Indian Independence when many of the legacies of the British colonial rule were uncritically accepted and passed on down the line. The British had created a steel framework to rule the country and a police system which, among other things, kept watch on nascent political trends. The steel frame attracted gifted individuals, scholars and thinkers because of the extraordinarily high compensation package. The prime tool made available to the police was repression. There was no comparable incentive for a bright Indian to join its ranks, except that of getting employed. The steel frame had lorded over British India. The legacies continued after the British left. Even today the rule exists that ensures that no member of any other service can overtake his IAS colleague of the same seniority in emoluments or rank even if he is a genius. Then why should the Indian Intelligence attract the best when it is required to exist at an inferior level? In point of fact it does not. The results that get produced, therefore, are matching the caliber that is to be found in such establishments today.

This problem can be fixed only by the political managers of the country. India now finds itself in a very complex national security environment, requiring intelligence to become the first line of defence. Men who work in it must have the capacity to develop the highest levels of professional values and solid leadership qualities.

Centuries ago a Chinese sage, Sun Tzu, admonished: "Nothing should be as favourably regarded as Intelligence; nothing should be as generously regarded as Intelligence; nothing should be as confidential as the work of Intelligence". To produce Intelligence of this order, service in Intelligence must be made as attractive as the British had made their premier colonial service in India. Intelligence organizations of other countries run their establishments on this paradigm. They often are the best paid organizations in their own country. The CIA is reputed to attract the highest number of PhDs from the best schools into its ranks, as compared to other US organizations.

The terms and conditions of service, apart from the opportunities of work, serve as a magnet to pull the talent of supreme quality among whom will be engineers, management specialists, scholars, bankers, scientists, economists, sociologists and academics. In India, unfortunately, it is only the second grade that thinks of gravitating towards Intelligence. In recent times, even this category is not offering to look at Intelligence as a career. A revolving door policy as in the US should also not be ruled out to draw in expertise and eminence.

Another negative factor is that Intelligence in India has no locus in law, especially for those who work in foreign Intelligence. India's Intelligence agencies have not been created by Acts of the Parliament. The entire range of foreign operations is covered by just executive instructions. An instruction to operate in a foreign country ipso facto implies a requirement to break the local laws but no legal authority exists for issuing such instructions or indemnifying the would be violator under the laws of the home country. This is a very serious lacuna which does not seem to have caught the attention of anyone in authority. As the law stands today all those who issue such executive instructions and those who carry out these instructions in a foreign country to spy and steal secrets can be held accountable under the Indian laws. Foreign Intelligence is the only organization directed by the Govt. to violate the local laws of the country of operation but the Govt. does so without enjoying any legal authority to do so. This state of affairs is reflective of the apathy in which Intelligence is held in India.

Analysis comes in the picture to make a sense from collected raw intelligence in juxta position with publicly available data. It interprets the pooled information and comes up with likely scenarios of what may happen. This exercise has to be meaningful because Government's policy decisions could be based on them. In fast moving contexts like an ongoing terrorist engagement, speed of the analysis becomes a key determinant to catch the action. However, the process as it takes place has serious flaws.

These arise from a mistaken apprehension that intelligence will seek to overtake the role of policy making or even replace it. In fact intelligence has no commanding part in the making of policy. On the other hand the policy maker has to set the agenda for intelligence to work on so that intelligence becomes custom produced. However, intelligence support to policy makers becomes more meaningful if it is allowed participation in policy debates, told about gaps in knowledge and encouraged to disclose constraints on intelligence capabilities to close these gaps, and focus its analysis on policy issues and options under scrutiny. If such opportunities are missing, intelligence works in the dark, benefiting no one.

Years ago in an article by me the role of the analyst was described in the following words: "A good intelligence analyst is an asset to the national security apparatus. In the intelligence organizations in India, analysts work for several years at the same desk and are therefore able to develop a much better insight and expertise in their fields than those serving other wings of the Government. Although not infallible, sound analysis can often point to the likely course of events. It takes into account all the information available, secret or published, mentions what remains unknown if it is relevant to the issue under study, describes the reality of the facts stated, indicating guardedly of how they were obtained, and transparently and cogently explains the logic of the conclusions and estimates it projects.

The analyst's expertise serves as the backdrop to the inferences drawn; the deeper his experience, the more value he can get out of the data assembled to make his submissions of likely scenarios of the future. When the analyst is tasked in the context of national security by the policy maker, his study is lifted out of the academic realm and becomes a basis for choosing a course of policy".

Indian Intelligence can boast of having in its ranks many excellent analysts with deep expertise and insights but it is not certain if full use has been made of them. There is hardly any culture in the country requiring policy papers to be prepared on national security issues, with participation from intelligence, diplomats, military specialists, scientists etc., detailing likely scenarios and examining the pro and con of each. Kargil and Mumbai 26/11 demonstrated the pitfalls of absence of coordinated analysis. Where coordination is called for between the centre and the states to deal with an internal security problem in a cohesive manner, the Indian Constitution can become sometimes the stumbling block as powers stand delegated to the states some of whom may disagree with the Centre's approach. In the face of such differences the tasks of Intelligence become even more difficult. Dealing with Naxalism is an issue which proves this assumption.

The quality of Indian Intelligence analysis has been applauded by foreign intelligence partners. Senator Claiborne Pell, former Chairman of the US Senate Foreign Relations Committee, is on record, stating that Indian analysis of developments in Afghanistan in the late 1980s was the only accurate indication available to the West, of what was happening there. In the Indian system the operations officer and the analyst often double up for each other. In small outfits this may not be a serious handicap but as organizations grow larger, the two streams of intelligence should have their own dedicated cadres for best results.

Counter intelligence prime functions are identifying operations and agents of foreign intelligence organizations, and protecting the secrets of the State from penetration through use of human agents and technical means like bugs, monitoring, surveillance from space, interception of communication channels etc. Lack of national awareness generally for the needs of security makes the task of counter intelligence more difficult. Dangers arise equally from hostile and friendly agencies, driven by the operational necessity of discovering protected information.

Results from counter intelligence have been a mixed bag of successes and shame. Over the years counter intelligence has been able to unmask several of the Indian agents of all the major intelligence organization of the world. The shame lies in the fact that it could not prevent foreign penetration even into their senior ranks. Actual truth may be more hurting. There is a general belief in the country that the influence of foreign intelligence organizations has reached deep into the civil society. Suspicion was cast once even on a Prime Minister. Due to various reasons exposures of highly placed Indian moles has always proved to be a daunting task. The field of counter intelligence has exponentially grown with the advent of international terrorism. This phenomenon poses a multidimensional threat of mass destruction through acquisition of a nuclear device, mass disruption of communication systems through cyber attacks, ideological brain washing through selective interpretations of religious doctrines, and jehadi military style attacks at random on people and key sites. Countering such terrorism has to be a composite exercise requiring participation, apart from intelligence, of other organs of the state such as armed forces, state police, crisis management groups, paramilitary directorates and science and technical communities among others. Countering ideological indoctrination in a sustained manner is perhaps yet to kick start in the country. It is not that the dangers are not realized but extraneous factors like vote bank politics relegate the issue to the lowest priority.

Since terrorist organizations which work on the cell system are extremely difficult to penetrate, good preventive intelligence may not be easily forth coming, despite the best efforts of the intelligence agencies. Because of large numbers of what can constitute a target it may not also be possible to provide effective perimeter security to every single target. If terror attacks like Mumbai 26/11 continue, sooner or later the authorities will have to decide and declare the policy steps which should compel their sponsors to weigh the costs involved. A new counter terrorism architecture in the country, aiming at better analysis, coordination and prevention, can at best remain a good defensive exercise but the need of the hour may turn out to be offensive rather than defensive tactics. In offensive counter terrorism, the intelligence and armed forces will have distinctive and definitive roles. They may have to work together on the lines of the CIA and US military command that have been jointly handling Iraq and Afghanistan.

Nations are no longer squeamish about employment of covert techniques though specific operations may continue to be shrouded by the mystique of deniability. Nations seem willing to use any tool of statecraft to strengthen national security though the arm chair liberal or the abstract human rights activist may raise objection on grounds of ethics and morality. The Indian State in the past was not hesitant in using such instruments. This is widely known. But one cannot switch to covert actions overnight. Long preparations are necessary. If "all options" are being kept open to deal with the vicious terrorist threat from across the borders, it will be proper to give a green signal to the intelligence now to make its covert plans. Pakistan is proving to be an enduring threat. A redefinition of national interests will bring out that India needs to move out of its self created soft image and to entrust the Intelligence with a new range of responsibilities to become more secure.

Even otherwise Intelligence needs to develop new perspectives as globalization advances, defining a new permissiveness in political environment, creating opportunities for newer forms of economic penetration and triggering fast technological changes which render borders meaningless. After the demise of the Soviet Union the World has been left unipolar but the equation of balance of power remains far from settled. In Asia, the rivalry between three rising entities, China, Japan and India, each of whom will be competitively looking for new markets and new sources of resources, can become acute. The national security architecture worldwide remains shifting in a kaleidoscopic pattern, recreating all the time, newer axes of conflict and conciliation. Add to them the hunger for land and water, symbolized by refugee flows and mass migrations, and differing international concerns for climatic changes and ecology. Correct analysis and assessment of trends over a vast spectrum has become a national necessity to keep the country's interests safe and secure. Knowledge now is the new coefficient of power and Indian Intelligence must keep step with such knowledge.

The current systems are unlikely to match the challenges that have emerged. Drastic reforms are necessary to unshackle Intelligence from its rigid bureaucratic mould and to invest it with a dynamism and innovative spirit which should be the hallmark of an unconventional organization. The very first step of reform should begin by giving Indian Intelligence the backing of legislative enactments. The laws should provide a degree of autonomy which frees intelligence from all bureaucratic restraints and controls relating to financial management, administrative functions, pay scales, recruitment, posting and promotions, hire and fire policies and enforcement of discipline. The laws should spell out the charter and authorize the Central Government to fix broad targets within the charter. This will prevent misuse of the institutions by those in authority. The laws should hold intelligence accountable to the Cabinet or its committee for security but also create a parliamentary committee for oversight. Detailed rules can be worked out to determine the parameters of oversight and areas of intelligence work over which it will be exercised, in consultation with the parliament. The laws should give the right to the Govt. to authorize any kind of covert action and keep all such activities outside the ambit of oversight. The process of oversight and accountability can be expected to keep intelligence on its toes. However, even after such reforms, errors due to human frailties and intellectual stubbornness will not all disappear but their numbers can be expected to be far less.

There is a new area of activity which Intelligence must consider if it has not already done so. Outsourcing which globalization has promoted has a good potential for intelligence work. The Japanese corporate world and intelligence have cooperated with each other over the past several years with both reaping good dividends out of such collaboration. The US is believed to have taken major steps in this direction. According to one estimate the US Intelligence community invests 70% of its budget on its joint ventures with American Industrial Complex. The Indian corporations are also traversing the multinational route. One may expect overtures to them will be rewarding to intelligence.

One last word. Is there any way that can measure the depth of devotion and commitment of Intelligence to the national cause? The following anecdote can be a revealing guide. At the height of Afghan resistance to Soviet Union in 1989, the situation in Kabul became so dangerous that the

US, British and other Western countries withdrew their Ambassadors and staff from the country. Our foreign office and Ambassador wanted to follow suit, Intelligence included. Intelligence refused. While others came back to Delhi, Intelligence remained at Kabul to continue to fly the Indian flag over the Embassy in Kabul.

INDIAN INTELLIGENCE AND THE PROSTITUTES OF INDIAN MEDIA

This is one of the finest articles that has come out of the amazing B. Raman himself (by far my favourite commentator). Here he describes the details of two amazing stories in the Indian intelligence history-one a failure and one an outstanding success... and the frivolous and downright idiotic media that is in India. You just have to listen to the news to know how nonsensical the Indian media news coverage is. Journalists in India are no more than prostitutes. I have had personal experience with them during my stint while starting my company's Corporate Communications department and I don't have any more opinion of them. That is why thankfully there is blogging. Where, hopefully, you can read or listen to some sane and intelligent voices like Atanu Dey etc.

Read B. Raman's latest book "The Kaoboys of R&AW-Down the memory lane".

I wrote the first article on this subject for The Hindu in 1996, after the detection of the penetration of the Intelligence Bureau by the Central Intelligence Agency at a high level. Since then, I must have written at least 20 articles on this subject One of the past cases mentioned by me in the book is the penetration of the Prime Minister's Office by the French intelligence in the early 1980s. I was surprised by the kind of excitement or scepticism this evoked among the anchors of our TV channels and journalists from our media.

'Prime Minister's Office penetrated by French Intelligence, says an ex-R&AW spy', screamed the headlines. 'A claim without corroboration,' commented an anchor of NDTV. A commentator of the same channel sarcastically compared my reference to this to Jaswant Singh's claim of a mole in P V Narasimha Rao's office.

'Is he trying to embarrass the prime minister?' asked the Jumping Jack anchor of another channel. 'Has he violated the Official Secrets Act?' wondered another. My dear friends in the world of journalism, this sensational case of penetration — considered one of the most sensational anywhere in the world — was detected in 1985 shortly after Rajiv Gandhi had taken over as the prime minister. The penetration had taken place when Indira Gandhi was the prime minister and was detected after Rajiv Gandhi succeeded her.

The whole world was shocked by the ease with which two French intelligence officers, assisted by their Polish counterparts, had penetrated the PMO and removed tonnes and tonnes of documents. It was alleged that they were so sure that nothing would happen to them that they used to go to the office of the PMO on Sundays and other holidays, go through all the files and papers, take out what was of interest to them and took out photocopies using the photocopying machine of the PMO using the photocopying paper of the PMO.

It was a scandal of unbelievable proportions. It was found that these people had not only penetrated the PMO, but also the office of President Zail Singh and other sensitive ministries of the Government of India. The scandal and the speculation about it created such a furore in the Lok Sabha that Rajiv Gandhi had to make a statement on the subject on the floor of the house and Dr P C Alexander, who was Principal Secretary to Indira Gandhi and Rajiv Gandhi, had to resign. He did not accept responsibility for the shocking state of negligence in his office, but attributed his resignation to high moral principles.

The investigation brought out that the French and other collaborating intelligence agencies operated through Yogesh T Maneklal, then managing director of Maneklal Industries

Limited of Mumbai, who had extensive contacts at the lower levels of the PMO, the President's office and other ministries and persuaded many government servants to work for the French intelligence. He was sentenced to 14 years rigorous imprisonment on July 18, 2002.

The spy ring consisted of S Sankaran, then senior PA in the President's Secretariat; Jagdish Chandra Arora, then PA to the then Secretary, Defence Production; Jagdish Mittar Tiwari, then senior PA to then Additional Secretary, Ministry of Defence; Amrik Lal, then senior PA to erstwhile Joint Secretary (Supply) MoD; V K Palaniswamy of the Ministry of Shipping and Transport, H N Chaturvedi, then Assistant, Ministry of Commerce; T N Kher, then PS to Dr P C Alexander; P Gopalan, then senior PA and K K Malhotra, then PA to Dr Alexander; Swaminath Ram, UDC in the office of Dr Alexander; K C Sharma, then PA in the Planning Commission, and S L Chandra (official position not known). All of them were sentenced to 10 years RI each.

The court found all of them guilty of the charge that 'they had entered into a criminal conspiracy with foreign agents, including Lt Col Mexi Morvan and Lt Col A Bain Bioley of the French embassy and some officials of the Polish embassy and the embassy of the then German Democratic Republic here and collected, obtained and communicated secret official codes, secret and classified documents and information pertaining to defence, shipping, transport, finance, planning, Research and Analysis Wing and Intelligence Bureau reports, official codes and other classified top secret and confidential information and passed the same to foreign agents.'

They had communicated to the French intelligence not only copies of a large number of classified documents, but also the code books used by the Government of India. All these details are available in the records of the Lok Sabha and the court of the additional sessions judge, R K Gauba, before whom they were tried. One is surprised and disturbed that within 25 years of this disgraceful betrayal, most of our national security managers and so-called strategic analysts have forgotten about it. When I draw attention to this, some in the media accuse me of disseminating claims without corroboration, others ridicule me by comparing me with Jaswant Singh, and some others attribute motives to me. This is why we face national security disasters again and again and again. A nation, which has no memory for the past, is bound to repeat its mistakes in the future.

The other comment, which has amazed me, relates to my mention of an alert received from a mole of the R&AW in Yahya Khan's office regarding a pre-emptive air strike planned by the Pakistan Air Force on the forward air bases in the Western sector. An anchor of NDTV said this air strike was meant to divert attention from the fighting in the Eastern Sector. Manoj Joshi, the journalist, pooh-poohed my statement and said when the Indian Army entered East Pakistan it was expected that the PAF would make a diversionary air strike in the West. According to him, a general alert was, therefore, sounded. He implied that the R&AW was trying to take credit for this.

Well Mr. Anchor, well Mr. Joshi, you apparently do not remember or know how the 1971 war started. In 1967, the Israeli Air Force had launched pre-emptive air strikes on the Egyptian Air Force planes parked in its Air Force bases and destroyed them on the ground. Then, the Israeli Army went into action. The Egyptian Army had to fight without air cover. It surrendered.

The Pakistanis studied what the Israeli Air Force had done and decided to emulate it. Their calculation was that if they destroyed a large number of IAF planes on the ground, it could affect the operations of the Indian Army in the East by damaging the air cover available to it. The R&AW got advance intimation of this plan and the IAF was alerted. The intended pre-emptive air strike failed. Indira Gandhi, who was then in West Bengal, flew back to Delhi and in a midnight broadcast declared war on Pakistan. She let the world know that the war was started by Pakistan through its failed pre-emptive air strike and not by India. Mr. Joshi asked: If it is true that the R&AW had a mole as claimed by me, why the mole did not give information about Pakistani plans in the Jammu area? Mr.Joshi, a mole can give only that information to which he has access. This is a basic principle of the craft of intelligence — no access, no information.

The information that the R&AW got advance intelligence about the planned pre-emptive strike was known for over 30 years and acknowledged by Indira Gandhi herself. I had referred to this in my past writings too. All I have done in the book is to identify for the first time the R&AW officer who raised this source and got the information through him so that there is public knowledge of the role played by him.

MUMBAI BOMB BLASTS - INTELLIGENCE AND COUNTER-INTELLIGENCE

While addressing to a press conference on Saturday, Mumbai Police Commissioner A.N. Roy accused the ISI of masterminding the Mumbai train bomb explosions on 11th July this year resulted in killing 200 people. The commissioner provided the details of the plot with names, locations and whereabouts of the people involved in the attacks. He also provided information about the explosives which were kept as RDX packed in the pressure cookers. The commissioner told the newsmen about the interrogation procedure 'narco-analysis', through which the suspects are questioned under the influence of drugs to get the correct answers. He said, ISI agents began planning the attacks in March, and later provided funding and training for the bombers in Bahawalpur to plan that professional, precise and well-planned operation. He added that police had found no evidence of the involvement of Al Qaeda in the attacks.

On the other hand Pakistan Foreign Office spokeswoman Tasnim Aslam completely rejected Indian claim by calling it baseless, irresponsible and (done) out of habit. In his statement Mr. Tariq Azim Khan, the Minister of State for Information said that India had always chosen the path of pointing fingers at Pakistan without evidence. The allegation has appeared at a sensitive time to enhance the stress of President Musharraf who had already spent the previous days of a lengthy overseas trip persuading against Afghan and British implications that the members of his security apparatus were secretly supporting the Taleban revolt intensifying in the Southern Afghanistan. Moreover, it was only two weeks before when Musharraf managed to get India resuming a peace process, which had frozen after the Mumbai blasts.

In the era of a neo-globalisation with multiple actors on the stage to shaping up the future image of the global village, this becomes very important for the regional actors like India and Pakistan to immediately agree on an agenda of regional cooperation for progress, prosperity and better facilities for the people of the two nations. ISI which had been a much stronger power in the past is currently engaged in its revitalisation process with much of its energy being consumed in keeping the fine balance maintained between its modernist and conventional parts. In these difficult times it simply can't afford the sooper adventures like this. If we compare the capabilities of the Regional Analysis Wing (RAW) and the Inter Services Intelligence (ISI) both are complexly rooted in their targeted segments of the respective countries. If one agency has the advantage of entrenching profoundly into the socio-national structure of the targeted country, the other one has the advantage of being deeply ingrained into the religio-sectarian segment of the targeted country. In this complex situation there is always a chance of entry of a third international player to reshape the geo-political structure of the area into its own favour.

The story of making and remaking of the regional map starts from the late seventies when the CIA drafted a map of defeating the USSR in Afghanistan with the help of ISI. The then Pakistani President Gen Zia knew only about the half part of the plan while knowing nothing about the second half of the agenda. Only very few officers within ISI like Brig

Irshad Tirmazi could notify the presence of strange phenomena within the Mujahideen's camps in Afghanistan in form of Arab nexus. These were the operative groups mainly belonging to the Middle East, the European countries and the countries like Indonesia. The main features of the nexuses were; having massive 'foreign currency', their daily march towards Russia and the areas bordering China-with their passionate concentration in training of the religious elements for the sectarian (Shia-Sunni) violence.

During the Zia regime the tension between India and Pakistan remained alive especially on the issues of Kashmir and the Eastern Punjab. Well before successfully implementing his type of regional agenda, Gen Zia passed away in a mysterious plane crash and right after his death there started the second half of the international agenda for regional reshaping. It was a time when the unseen hands brought India and Isreal closer for defense and intelligence cooperation after a no relationship history of more than 40 years. Although Israel provided India with the devastating artillery weapon, 160 mm mortars and modern ammunition during 1971 war against Pakistan yet the deal remained secret as a condition by Mossad. Even after the 71's war the defense relations had not been adequately established between the two countries.

It was in 1992 when the formal diplomatic relations established between India and Israel with the visit of the Deputy Director of Israel Foreign Ministry Moshie Yaeger. Following the establishment of formal diplomatic relations in 1992, India and Israel had signed a number of agreements on economic, scientific, agricultural and cultural cooperation. In December 96 Israeli President Weizman visited India that became the first ever visit by any Israeli President to India with a 24-member business delegation.

Although the relations between India and Israel kept on developing after 1992 with strong ties on defense and economics yet 1998 can really be considered as the revolutionary year in the history of the Indian intelligence. In this year the

Mossad transferred to India the most sophisticated intelligence techniques to penetrate deep into religious/separatist groups. Before that point the ISI clearly superceded the RAW in terms of making networking within socio-political systems while after acquiring the newer techniques the RAW not only got the capability of breaking the networks but also to exert the counter-intelligence through religious grouping. During this year Indian Home Minister L. K. Advani visited Israel with his delegation comprising the heads of Indian intelligence agencies like RAW, IB, and central police organizations for their training on the latest intelligence techniques. Followed by these developments the Israeli intelligence agencies opened offices in New Delhi on the lines of United States FBI.

It was the time when the international plan was simply ready to be implemented to shape up the new world diagram. Maulvi Masood Azhar a 30-year old Sunni cleric from Bahawalpur was in BSF custody at 'Papa II' interrogation center in India. Here he meets Omar Sheikh with a history of being infiltrated into India and participated in some acts of terrorism. He was arrested and jailed by the Indian authorities to meet Maulvi Maood Azhar and to plan the drama of hijacking the Indian plane. Omar Sheikh belonged to the Arab-European Nexus of 200 UK Muslim citizens with natively linking to Pakistan, hired by some agency in the UK and sent to Pakistan to get training in the camps of Harkat Ul Ansaar (HUA) and joined the HUA's contingent in Bosnia with full complicity of the British and American intelligence agencies. These intelligence agencies had masterminded the Arab Nexus, a large corps of jihadi personal of Arab origin to mix up with Afghan Mujahideen in their war against the Soviet troops.

Maulvi Masood Azhar met there a number of 'jehadi' persons some belonging to Jamiat Ulma E Hind (JUH) and some to Arab Nexus where they planned the Hijack of Indian plane and made their future agenda to be implemented in Pakistan. On 24th December 1999, an Indian aircraft flight

IC 814 carrying 174 passengers and 18 crew (Kathmandu-Delhi) was hijacked on its way to New Delhi at about 1730 Hours IST. It landed at Amritsar and was refused fuel and ultimately landed at the Kabul airport. Three arrested jehadi persons Masood Azhar, Omar Sheikh and Mushtaq Ahmed Zargar had been handed over to the Taliban militia at Kandahar. The five hijackers had left the aircraft and had been taken to an undisclosed location by the Taliban.

On 11th September 2001, the tragic incidence of the World Trade Center took place followed by the announcement of President Bush to start a long-term global war against terror to bring the perpetrators to justice. It was the time for India to inform the US about the involvement of Pakistan in the attack. It is said that Prime Minister Vajpai personally presented a copy of the cheque to President Bush which was given by the then ISI chief Gen Mehmud to one of the terrorists of the 9/11 attack. In this way, India played a key role in providing the US authorities the HOT information about Pakistan as the funding source for the September 11 attacks. The Times of India first reported on October 10, 2001 that India told the US that some $100,000 had been wired to the leader of the hijackers, Mahmud Atta, by British-born terrorist Omar Sheikh.

John S Pistole, deputy assistant director of the FBI's counter-terrorism division confirmed about the information, however, did not specify how those accounts in Pakistan were funded, how those found their way to Omar Sheikh and how the copy of the cheque reached to the Indian Prime Minister. Nobody knows about the secrets behind that deal but everybody knows about the immediate acceptance by the Pakistani government of the 7 point US agenda to role back Islamism, Talibanism and terrorism from Pakistan and Afghanistan.

Indian authorities also told the US that the trail led back from Omar Sheikh to the then Chief of ISI, Lt Gen Mahmud Ahmad who was subsequently forced to retire by Pakistan resident Pervez Musharraf. The Indian authorities provided the FBI with the details, including Omar Sheikh's mobile numbers.

Later the same Omer Sheikh was found guilty in the murder of the Wall Street Journal reporter Daniel Pearl. The case was highlighted around the globe and once again became the cause of embarrassment for Pakistan around the globe. Maulvi Masood Azhar established Jaish E Mohammad (JEM) and remained involved in the activities of sectarian and religious terrorism. Another example of 'international intelligence cooperation' is the information of the suicidal attack against Gen Pervez Musharraf. Very recently, the former Indian Defense Minister George Fernandes has said that India was aware of an assassination attempt on Pakistani President three years ago. He said that he had warned Islamabad two days before the attack in December 2003. The above-mentioned examples simply highlight the capabilities of the Indian intelligence agencies in masterminding intelligence and counter intelligence operations.

We are living in the post cold war era when the super power has nothing to do with the Pakistani abilities of running or winning a war. Knowingly or unknowingly, Pakistan can be pushed back to the post 9/11position by the 'international cooperation of intelligence'. It is for the broader interests of the 2 countries in specific and the South Asian Region in general to establish the long-term socio-economical relations and peace treaties between the regional players to ensure better living conditions, better education and medical facilities for the inhabitants of the region. Otherwise the intelligence and the counter intelligence adventures between the two countries will give the international players the opportunities to implement their global agenda which is nothing but the 'Bandar Bant'.

2

Indian Intelligence Agencies

Soon enough, there appeared to be a convergence of interests between the newly-independent nation India and its former rulers Britain when it came to intelligence assessments. MI5 Deputy Director General Guy Liddell and TG Sanjevi, the first head of India's intelligence agency, which was curiously called Delhi Intelligence Bureau (DIB), were "united in their deep distrust of the first Indian high commissioner in London, VK Krishna Menon, the Congress party's leading left-leaning firebrand," writes Professor Andrew.

Menon, an old friend of Nehru's, was a flawed man of protean talents: he studied at the London School of Economics (LSE), was the first editor at Pelican Books, Penguin's famous non-fiction imprint, and somebody with whom Nehru could discuss, according to a diplomat who knew both the men well, "Marx and Mill, Dickens and Dostoevsky." He is also remembered for a record-busting eight-hour-long speech on Kashmir at the United Nations, and as a federal defence minister who presided over the Indian rout in the hands of China during the 1962 war. Most of the service's special liaison people appointed to Delhi were "gregarious people, fond of India and good at getting on with both the DIB and their high commission colleagues," writes Professor Andrew. Even a chill in Indo-British diplomatic relations after the Anglo-French invasion of Suez which Nehru roundly condemned "had little impact on collaboration between the DIB and MI5."

As the 1960s arrived, the relationship evidently grew feebler. There was mounting frustration inside MI5 over how it was losing out to the Soviets as India became a key ally of the Soviet Union. "In the view of the security service," writes Professor Andrew, "the DIB was increasingly unequal to coping with the Soviet intelligence presence in India, greater than in any other country in the developing world."

Two decades later, the service was taking note of the "increasing danger" of Khalistani extremism in the UK. It had, Professor Andrew writes, become a major threat during the summer and autumn of 1984. The Operation Blue Star at Golden Temple in Amritsar by Indian troops to put down a separatist rebellion and the anti-Sikh and Khalistani riots in 1984 triggered off by the killing of premier Indira Gandhi by her khalistani bodyguards had produced an upsurge of support within the Khalistani community for the creation of an independent Khalistani state of in India.Prof Andrew reveals "plots" to kill prime minister Rajiv Gandhi during a state visit to Britain in October 1985 were unearthed by MI5. "Good intelligence, combined with the arrest of Khalistani and Kashmiri extremists, was believed to have frustrated plots to attack Rajiv Gandhi during the state visit," Professor Andrew. Real Sikhs are not wanting khalistan writes.

Directorate of Revenue Intelligence

Functions under the Income Tax Dept, in the Ministry of Finance, Department of Revenue. Headed by Director General in New Delhi, it is presently divided into seven zones, each under the charge of an Additional Director General, and further sub-divided into Regional Units, Sub-Regional Units and Intelligence Cells with a complement of Additional Directors, Joint Directors, Deputy Directors, Assistant Directors, Senior Intelligence Officers and Intelligence Officers. For more information, click here.

National Technical Reconnaissance Organization

The country's prime civilian technology intelligence agency.

Modelled on the American NSA. Works in very close coordination with the Aviation Research Centre.

Defence Intelligence Agency (DIA)

This agency was established on 5 March, 2002 with the appointment of Lt. General Kamal Davar as the first Director General (DG). The DG reports to the Chief Of Defence Staffs (CDS). It is supposed to be the nodal agency for all defence related intelligence, thus distinguishing it from the R&AW. Much of the agency's budget and operations are classified. The DIA has control over some of the Army's prized technical intelligence assets – the Directorate of Signals Intelligence and the Defence Image Processing and Analysis Centre (DIPAC). While the Signals Directorate is responsible for acquiring and decrypting enemy communications, the DIPAC controls India's satellite-based image acquisition capabilities. The DIA also controls the Defence Information Warfare Agency (DIWA). DIWA handles all elements of the information warfare repertoire, including psychological operations, cyber-war, electronic intercepts and the monitoring of sound waves.

Joint Cipher Bureau

The Joint Cipher Bureau works closely with the IB and R&AW. It is responsible for cryptanalysis and encryption of sensitive data. The inter-services Joint Cipher Bureau has primary responsibility for cryptology and SIGINT, providing coordination and direction to the other military service organizations with similar mission. Most current equipment providing tactical intelligence is of Russian origin, including specialized direction finding and monitoring equipment.

The Joint Cipher Bureau is also responsible for issues relating to public and private key management. Cryptographic products are export-controlled licensed items, and licenses to India are not generally available for products of key length of more than 56 bits. The domestic Indian computer industry primarily produces PCs, and PC-compatible cryptographic products have been developed and are being used commercially. More robust cryptologic systems are not commercially produced in India, and progress in this field has been slow due to the general unavailability of technology and know-how. Customised cryptographic products have been designed and produced by organizations in the defense sector are engaged in the implementation of cryptographic techniques, protocols and the products.

All India Radio Monitoring Service

The Central Monitoring Service of All India Radio monitors all radio broadcasts in India as well as all foreign radio broadcasts which can be received in India. Central Monitoring Services based in New Delhi, Jammu and Kolkata is taken over by NTRO, National Technical Research Orgnisation in 2005 and now working as open source intelligence unit.

Signals Intelligence Directorate

The Signals Intelligence Directorate is a joint service organisation, manned by personnel from the Army, Navy and Air Force. It has a large number of WEUs (Wireless Experimental Units) that carry out the task of monitoring military links of other countries. The Central Monitoring Organisation (CMO) is directly under the Ministry of Defence. It has several monitoring companies, located at different locations around the country. Task is to monitor use of radio spectrum by all users, such as Defence, Police, AIR, Railways, PSUs etc.

Directorate of Air Intelligence

The DAI is responsible for air and satellite reconnaissance missions.

NATIONAL INVESTIGATION AGENCY (INDIA)

National Investigation Agency (NIA) is a federal agency approved by the Indian Government to combat terror in India. The agency is empowered to deal with terror related crimes across states without special permission from the states. The

National Investigation Agency Bill 2008 to create the agency was moved in Parliament by Union Home Minister on 16 December 2008. NIA was created after the Nov 2008 Mumbai terror attacks as need for a central agency to combat terrorism was realised. The current Director General is S.C Sinha who succeeded first Director-General of NIA R.V Raju as he retired.

Bill

A Bill for the formation of the much-talked about National Investigation Agency was cleared by Parliament in December 2008. As per the Bill, NIA has concurrent jurisdiction which empowers the Centre to probe terror attacks in any part of the country, covering offences, including challenge to the country's sovereignty and integrity, bomb blasts, hijacking of aircraft and ships, and attacks on nuclear installations. The ground staff of the agency in the national capital could be drawn from existing central staff and security organisations while in the states, permanent deputation from the state police could be taken. Other than offenses of terrorism, it also deals with counterfeit currency, human trafficking, narcotics or drugs, organised crime (extortion mobs and gangs), plane hijacking and violations of atomic energy act and weapons of mass destruction act.

The National Investigative Agency Bill and Unlawful Activities (Prevention) Amendment Bill on Tuesday, 30 Dec, 2008, became a law as President Pratibha Patil gave her assent to the legislation which were passed in the last session of Parliament.

Some of the Salient Features

- This is applicable to whole of India, citizens of India outside India and persons on ships and aircraft registered in India.
- Officers of the NIA have all powers, privileges and liabilities which the police officers have in connection with investigation of any offence.

- The police officer in charge of a police station on receipt of the report of the offence shall forward it to the state government which in turn will send it to the Centre.
- If the Centre feels the offence is terror related, it shall direct the NIA for investigation.
- Provision for transfer of investigation and trial of offences to state government with Centre's prior approval.
- A state government shall extend all assistance to NIA for investigation of terror-related offences.
- Provisions of the Act with regard to investigation shall not affect powers of the state government to investigate and prosecute any terror crime or other offences.
- The Centre shall constitute special courts for trial of terror-related offences.
- For speedy and fair trial, the Supreme Court may transfer any case pending with the special court to another special court in the same state or any other state, and the High Court may transfer such cases to any other special court within the state.
- Offences punishable with imprisonment for less than three years may be tried summarily.
- Special court to have all powers of the court of sessions under CrPC for trial of any offence under the Act.
- Proceedings to be held 'in camera' if special court deems it necessary.
- Trial to be held on day-to-day basis on all working days and to have precedence over the trial of other offences.
- State governments empowered to constitute one or more special courts.
- No appeal shall be entertained after the expiry of 90 days.

UNINTELLIGENT INTELLIGENCE: INDIAN INTEL AGENCIES

One institution in India – apart from the political one – that has kept up with constant failures and rare successes is our intelligence. Since 2005, the onslaught of terror has claimed 550 lives and now the *aam aadmi* wonders each day where the terrorists will strike next. And the sheer incompetence of our security and intelligence agencies, added to our inefficient political and judicial setup, apparently encourage the terrorists further. In 1947, IB and the Military Intelligence (MI) were the only two intelligence agencies in India. Post-independence the Central Intelligence Bureau had the sole responsibility of internal and external intelligence in India. After its inability to foresee the Sino-Indian war of 1962 and India-Pakistan war of 1965, the IB was bifurcated in 1968 to create RAW (Research and Analysis Wing) as the external intelligence agency.

Today we have eight such agencies: the IB, Directorate General of Security, the RAW, Directorate General Of MI, Air Intelligence, Naval Intelligence, the Defence Intelligence Agency and the National Technical Research Agency. Ironically, this multiplicity of intelligence agencies hampers efficiency as our agencies are nowhere near well-coordinated; rather they don't see eye to eye when it comes to information sharing.

Each time India bleeds at the hands of terrorists, the nodal domestic intelligence agency, the IB is made the scapegoat. But there are certain hurdles that need to be overcome for efficient functioning of the bureau. Firstly, it is terribly short of manpower. It has no more than 100 IPS officers as against the 250 posts sanctioned. Since state police forces offer swifter means of promotion and career advancement, most prefer to don *khaki* over the stressful IB jobs.

The lack of motivation is compounded by lack of skill. Intelligence gathering as a specialized skill has not yet been recognized in India. So state level branches of IB that gather information and intelligence are staffed with dissatisfied, unenthusiastic workers-often the leftover useless lot. Besides the bureau's resources are also taken up by additional responsibilities like counter intelligence operations, security in the states and routine monitoring of state governments.

Thirdly, IB and RAW do not quite hang together. RAW's unwillingness to share information with IB, which it sees as a political agency spying on political rivals, is legendary. One fiasco includes the neglect of available intelligence provided by the RAW to the IB, and the negligence and weak supervision by the IB and Tamil Nadu police which led to the assassination of ex-Prime Minister Rajiv Gandhi.

RAW too is no less responsible for successive intelligence debacles. Noted former RAW additional secretary B.Raman has criticized the agency for its "asymmetric growth" and it being "...strong in investigation, weak in prevention; strong in crisis management, weak in crisis prevention".

In his controversial book 'THE KAOBOYS OF R&AW', released in 2007, Raman has exposed the political pressures exerted on the agency, apart from highlighting the need to reassess the functioning of the agency. For example he tells us about the former PM Narasimha Rao's request to RAW to provide him a secret recording device to be used at his discussions with LK Advani during the Babri Masjid demolition crisis.

Another controversial book by Retd. Major General VK Singh, former secretary general of RAW alleges that political interference and corruption in the agency has made it vulnerable to defections. As a case in point, despite all precautions Rabinder Singh, Joint Secretary and head of RAW's South East Asia Department, managed to defect with 'sensitive' files from RAW's headquarters in Delhi to the US in June 2004.

RAW has also drawn flak for not providing information to defence intelligence agencies which might have altogether prevented the Kargil War with Pakistan in 1999. To blot our intelligence history further there are at least half a dozen instances of foreign penetration of many Indian agencies under the garb of intelligence cooperation.

But it is no use splitting hairs as the problem which tops the list for our agencies, politics and citizens is terrorism, which no longer is a "foreign-hand" thing but a pan-Indian phenomenon. In the last decade or so, unlike the *jehadis*, our intelligence agencies haven't improved much.

Today terrorists have a common command and control; the investigative agencies do not. There is also no central mechanism for coordination and monitoring of data which can be stored in a central database. Investigations are conducted in an isolated and piecemeal manner, as the police and investigative agencies do not want to share information. The solution lies in a model similar to one followed by the US. Post 9/11, all agencies were brought under a single Department Of Homeland Security and information sharing became a norm rather than the exception that it was.

More than a few top intelligence officials and most former officers feel that structural changes, along with a change of attitude in our polity are necessary for effective revamping of our intelligence.

Our short-sighted leaders and statesmen should give party politics a backseat where national security is concerned. Apart from those in power, citizens too must become vigilant and contribute to local intelligence. The need of the hour is motivated individuals, well-coordinated agencies which are not under the thumb of transient governments (especially in this era of coalitions). And this involves a strong will: political and otherwise at all levels of our society.

RAW: INDIAN INTELLIGENCE AGENCY, A TERRORIST ORGANISATION

The role of an intelligence agency should be different from that of a terrorist organization. The CIA, the Mussad, the ISI and the Raw must not be mixed up with LTTE, the Black Water Force and particularly the detracted groups of Taliban & Al-Qaida which are defaming not only Islam but also the Muslims all over the world. If an intelligence agency is trying to forget its prescribed aims and objects by surpassing its limits, it should not be ranked as an intelligence agency but a terrorist organization.

A few days back the Federation of American Scientists FAS issued a report which confirmed that the Research and Analysis Wing RAW, was directly involved in the secession of East Pakistan into Bangladesh, and is currently engaged in similar activities in Balochistan. The FAS is a group which is engaged in analysis and advocacy on science, technology and public policy concerning global security, especially about the countries having nuclear capability. It is a privately funded non-profit policy organization whose Board of Sponsors includes 55 American Nobel laureates. The report says "'The assistance provided to RAW by the Russian KGB enabled RAW to arrange terrorist attacks in Pakistani cities throughout the Afghan War.

The defeat of the Soviet Union in Afghanistan did not end the role of RAW in Pakistan, as it established training camps in East Punjab, Indian Held Kashmir, Uttar Pradesh and Rajasthan where agents are trained for terrorist activities." Pointing towards the role of Raw in the formerly East Pakistan the report says, 'The involvement of Raw in East Pakistan started in 1960s when it began with promoting dissatisfaction against Pakistan. Later on Raw funded at a large scale Mujeebur Rehman's general election of 1970. This organization not only funded Mukti Bahini but also trained and armed the workers of Mukti Bahini.' There is another shocking revelation in the report that Raw staged the drama of hijacking a plane of Indian Airlines proceeding to Lahore in 1971. The hidden aim behind this hijacking was to put all blame on the Kashmiri Freedom Fighters and to introduce them throughout the world as terrorists. In the light of the above disclosure it won't be wise to rank Raw as an intelligence agency. Hijacking of airplanes, massacre of innocent citizens and patronizing training camps of terrorist are certainly never the job of an intelligence agency. These are the actions of a terrorist organization. It is not only Pakistan which has been suffering from the childish misdeeds of Raw since long; the list of the afflicting countries is endless.

A few months back, in one of its editorials the leading newspaper of Sri Lanka, Daily Mirror criticized RAW by saying that this agency is playing a heinous role in the regional countries to destabilize them.. Commenting on the RAW's role in Sri Lanka, the editorial said: "The RAW in Sri Lanka has a pretty colorful record. Having raised, nursed and fortified the Liberation Tigers of Tamil Eelam, it later went through phases where it adopted 'rock the baby, pinch the baby' approach towards the LTTE." The paper is of the opinion that Raw never works on serious grounds because this organization is nothing more than a vase weeded with bitter thorny and discolored wild flowers. Its workers and employers are morally bankrupt and spiritually barren. The newspaper wrote: "In 2007, ripples were created in the spy agency when one of its Colombo-based officers, Ravi Nair of 1975 batch, was found allegedly carrying on an affair with a woman working for another country's spy agency. The 'crime' was considered only second to what was committed by the RAW Joint Secretary, Rabinder Singh, in 2004 when he escaped with copies of several highly-confidential documents and is believed to have passed them on to the CIA. This was after Singh's superiors confronted him with evidence that he had spent time with a Delhi-based female US embassy officer at a resort down the New Delhi-Jaipur highway."

According to the sources RAW and the Indian Ministry of External Affairs are provided Rs. 250 million annually as "discretionary grants" for foreign influence operations. These funds are meant for supporting the organizations fighting Sikh and Kashmiri separatists in the UK, Canada and the US. An Extensive network of Indian operatives of Raw is controlled by the Indian Embassy in Washington DC whose covert activities include the infiltration of US long distance telephone carriers by Indian operatives, with access to all kinds of information, to blackmail relatives of US residents living in India. In 1996, an Indian diplomat was implicated in a scandal over illegal funding of political candidates in the US. Under US law foreign nationals are prohibited from contributing to federal elections. The US District Court in Baltimore sentenced Lalit H. Gadhia, a naturalized US citizen of Indian origin, to three months imprisonment. Gadhia had confessed that he worked as a conduit between the Indian Embassy and various Indian-American organizations for funneling campaign contributions to influence US lawmakers. Over US $46,000 from the Indian Embassy were distributed among 20 Congressional candidates. The source of the cash used by Gadhia was Devendra Singh, a RAW official assigned to the Indian Embassy in Washington. Now Raw is adopting the same philosophy and mode of action in Balochistan by patronizing the so called 'separatist elements' which originally do not belong to the 'soil'.

Talking to the media men, Balochistan Chief Minister Jam Mohammad Yusuf said that involvement of external elements; including the Indian intelligence agency Research and Analysis Wing in the current acts of terrorism in Balochistan could not be ruled out. As long as Kashmir issue is not settled these elements will continue to create difficulties for Pakistan. Jam Yusuf referred to various training camps in which, according to him, terrorists were being harboured and paid huge sums to create trouble. He said that none of the Baloch 'waderas' had the capacity to finance such an operation. RAW had been running terrorist camps in Iran and Afghanistan since long and now it has set up 30 to 40 such camps in Balochistan, each with training facility for 30 people who are paid Rs10,000 monthly.

If we compare the East Pakistan episode and the present situation of Balochistan with reference to the report issued by the FAS, we can very easily analyze the scenario. Raw is repeating the same story of 'divide and disperse' in Balochistan which was once employed in the formerly East Pakistan. The situation calls for a very serious attitude on the part of Pakistani politicians. They must not waste their time and efforts in digging old graves.International forces are trying their best to divert the attention of the Pakistani politicians to some very trivial and valueless issues so that they may not be able to concentrate upon the worsening situation in Balochistan. Raw is craving for giving birth to another 'East Pakistan' out of its old barren and out worn womb. The Pakistani politicians must keep in mind like sensible fathers that we can no more afford another pregnancy.

INDIAN SPECIAL FORCES-CAPABILITIES AND SHORTCOMINGS

India, like any other country does have its own Special Forces – the Army has Para Commandos, which are elite airborne units and the Ghatak Platoons which are attached to each infantry battalion of the Army, the Navy has the Marine Commandos (MARCOS for short), and the Air Force the Garud. Besides, India has the National Security Guards (NSG), a Special Response Unit which is primarily tasked with counter terrorism activities, the Special Frontier Force whose one squadron is responsible for counter-terrorism duties and the various state police have their own Special Task Force for special operations, like for instance Jammu and Kashmir Police has the Special Operations Group to tackle terrorism. Opinion seems to be divided if we really have the intelligence and military capabilities to emulate the operation carried out by the US Navy SEALs in Abbottabad on May 2, 2011 to neutralize Osam bin Laden. In the backdrop of Osama bin Laden's killing in Abbottabad, India's Air Chief Marshal P.V. Naik and Indian Army chief General V.K. Singh declared their forces have the capability and competence to carry out a commando operation outside the country to target terrorists.

'There is no doubt about it. The army, navy and air force are paid to be ready. None of the services chiefs is going to say he does not have the capability,' says retired Commodore C. Uday Bhaskar, director of naval think-tank National Maritime Foundation, when asked about the services chiefs' comments. Brigadier Gurmeet Kanwal, director of army think-tank Centre for Land Warfare Studies, concurs with Uday Bhaskar. 'We virtually have the same capability (as the US Navy SEALs),' Kanwal told IANS, pointing out that the army itself has over half-a-dozen special forces battalions trained to carry out such attacks on strategic targets. Brigadier Kanwal, however added that India should look at energising its external intelligence agency Research and Analysis Wing (RAW) for getting its wanted, rather than use its armed forces.

'To be very honest, it is not possible to disclose if we have these capabilities or not. But, yes, we have the joint strategic capability for any special task that the government assigns to the armed forces, not necessarily in the neighbourhood, but anywhere around the globe,' Air Marshal P.K. Barbora, former Indian Air Force (IAF) vice chief, told IANS.

'But the decision on such operations is not taken by the uniformed personnel. It is taken by the political leadership after receiving all inputs including the implications and fall-out, and after planning for all exigencies, be it a nuclear conflict,' Barbora said.

The Contrary View

According to Lt. General R. K. Nanavatty, who has been involved in planning aspects of Indian Special Forces and has been studying the subject for years, India does not have the capabilities of executing an operation similar to Operation Neptune's Spear. Nanavatty said "We are not capable for a variety of reasons. Political understanding of special operations is very important then only you can commit money, time and technology for nurturing such a force. "Special Operations today are controlled by men who do not understand them".

Lt Gen P C Katoch, a former SF officer and a leading expert on Special Operations, said major operations by Indian troops have at various stages demonstrated what was wrong with them. "There are problems of intelligence, logistics etc. Our SF forces are doing what conventional troops can do and there is an overall lack of political willpower to nurture the capability with long term vision," said Katoch, who led an SF unit in Sri Lanka with the Indian Peace Keeping Force in the 80s and has also been involved in planning of Indian SFs. "Our men are ready, but minus intelligence, support etc," Katoch pointed out.

General Katoch pointed out that many of the mistakes of 1988 when Indian troops carried out an unsuccessful operation to capture the top leadership of the LTTE including its supremo Prabhakaran from Jaffna University were there to be seen in November 2008 in Mumbai when NSG commandos were deployed to take on the Pakistani terrorists. A decade back in 1999, a team of NSG commandos tailed hijacked IC814 aircraft to the Gulf region but returned. They couldn't also think of carrying out a surgical operation in Kandahar for a host of reasons including lack of airlift and political will.

According to Colonel Anil Athale, the Indian State does not have the will to carry out such operations and hence has not created the wherewithal to carry out strikes like Operation Neptune's Spear.

The Essentials

The two essential pre-requisites for conducting a successful special operation are availability of hard intelligence and sophisticated technical support. To elaborate, the planners and executors of this type of operation must be fed with concrete real time intelligence about the mission or objective to be accomplished. For instance, when the Israelis executed the raid at Entebbe in 1976, the commandos and the senior military commanders sitting in Tel Aviv were fully aware of the location of the hostages, the number of terrorists, the layout of the terminal building, etc. The commandos knew where their targets were, where precisely the Ugandan troops were stationed and how reinforcements, if any, were to be neutralized. There were no loose ends. In the absence of human intelligence (HUMINT), it may be impossible to carry out a successful operation. America's Central Intelligence Agency maintained a safe house near Abbottabad town for a small team of spies who conducted extensive surveillance on slain Al Qaeda chief Osama bin Laden's compound for months before President Barack Obama signed an order to kill the most wanted terrorist on April 29. It is estimated that the US has had about 3000 operatives active in Pakistan at the time of the Abbottabad raid.

The second essential is the availability of technological support such as satellite imagery of the target area, stealth technology for the purpose of infiltrating and exfiltrating of the operatives undetected and secure communications. India's Imagery Intelligence (IMINT) capabilities are quite limited. India, in April 2009 launched its first dedicated radar reconnaissance satellite Radar Imaging Satellite 2 (or RISAT-2). The radar has an Israeli-built primary sensor which allows RISAT-2 to return images at any time of day, and in any weather conditions. India also has Cartosat-2 launched in 2007, which according to some experts may be used for military purpose. India needs to augment its space-based intelligence gathering capabilities.

Another important essential for carrying out special operations is political will. India lacks the political will to carry out any type of surgical strikes against non-state as well as state actors, notwithstanding the fact India has repeatedly been subject to terror strikes sponsored by Pakistan. In 1999, when IC 814 was hijacked and flown to Kandahar, Indian commandos merely tailed the hijacked aircraft but did not attempt a hostage rescue mission. Again in 2001, in the aftermath of the attack on Indian Parliament, the political masters could not muster the political will to carry out surgical operations against Pak-based terror outfits. It was the same story in 2008. Israel on the other hand, has displayed considerable amount of political will in striking back at its adversaries and has the unique distinction of having struck against non-state actors far from its borders.

India's past experience of special operations (involving its Special Forces) have been limited in its scope. Barring Operation Cactus (1988) in Maldives, the failed mission to nab the leadership of the Tamil Tigers in Jaffna in 1988 and Operation Khukri (June 2000) in Sierra Leone all Special Forces' operations have been carried out within the country, mostly in Jammu and Kashmir and in the North-East. In Operation Cactus a battalion of the Parachute Regiment was air-dropped to rescue and assist the government of Abdul Gayoom against the mercenaries belonging to the People's Liberation Organisation of Tamil Eelam (PLOTE) and Operation Khukri was a daring rescue mission conducted by the Para Commandos in Sierra Leone resulting in the rescue of 21 hostages. In Operation Blue Star (June 1984), commandos of the 1st Battalion of the Parachute Regiment were unsuccessful in reaching the edge of the sacred pool to the Akal Takht. The National Security Guards (NSG) was established pursuant to an Act of Parliament called the National Security Guard Act, 1986. It was set up in the aftermath of the infamous Operation Blue Star wherein apart from the high casualties suffered, the shrine itself suffered severe damage. The operation necessitated the need for setting up a highly specialised and efficient force for counter-terrorist operations. Thus, NSG was deployed initially to combat the militancy in Punjab. In Black Thunder I (April 1986) about 300 National Security Guards commandos stormed the Golden Temple along with 700 Border Security Force troops and captured about 300 separatists. Two years later, in May 1988, the Golden Temple was again besieged and the security forces conducted Operation Black Thunder II and were successful in eliminating about 40 militants and forced the surrender of 200 militants. Operation Ashwamedh was an operation conducted in April 1993 when NSG commandos stormed a hijacked an Indian Airlines aircraft with 141 passengers on board at Amritsar airport. The lone hijacker, Mohammed Yousuf Shah, was killed in the operation. In September 2002, again the NSG carried out Operation Vajrashakti to flush out two heavily armed LeT terrorists who had caused carnage in the Akshardham Temple, Gandhinagar. In this operation, while the terrorists were killed, nearly 29 devotees and two commandos and one state police officer were also killed. About 79 devotees were also injured in the terrorist attack.

It is important to remember that all operations carried out by Special Forces have not been successful. The US which is lauded today for its operation against the terror mastermind Osama bin Laden had to face embarrassment and political backlash in April 1980 when the then US President Carter authorized an operation to rescue fifty-three American citizens held hostage in Iran ended in disaster. Operation Eagle Claw, as the ill-fated rescue mission was called resulted in the death of eight US servicemen. The fireball in the Iranian desert took the Carter presidency with it.

Concluding Observations

In conclusion, it must be said that though India has Special Forces, they have been largely used as a kind of super-infantry-employing them on missions which the regular army would baulk at. India does not lack brave men and officers, but what it does not currently possess is the right blend of political will, politico-military-intelligence integration and specialized technology that make these operations possible. As former Intelligence Bureau chief Ajit Doval says "What we need is to have a national political will accepting active national self defence as a doctrine to neutralise the enemies of India". "The nature, instrumentalities and deniability quotient of covert actions should be determined by our mission objective, intelligence capabilities and requirements of consequence management," he added.

By their very nature, all Special Forces operations are fraught with not just physical danger, but grave political consequences may ensue from failure. A goof-up in Abbottabad would have led not only to the possible capture and death of the US Navy Seals, but a possible sinking of Barack Obama's presidency as in the case of Operation Eagle Claw.

INDIA, INTELLIGENCE AND SECURITY

Espionage and intelligence appears in the recorded history of the Indus Valley as early as the fifth century. The modern nation of India gained its independence from Britain in 1947. The withdrawal of the British colonial government left India with little governmental infrastructure, and the nation embarked on an ambitious plan to create a new national government. Indian independence, however, also sparked resistance from ethnic groups on the Indian Subcontinent, such as the large Muslim community. As a result of the developing conflict, India quickly established military and intelligence forces.

India's intelligence community is divided into a traditional structure that separates military and civilian, and foreign and domestic intelligence. Though each agency is charged with its own mission, the government has provided a means to facilitate the sharing of information between members of the intelligence community. The Joint Intelligence Committee (JIC) processes and analyzes data gathered by both civilian and military intelligence agencies and coordinates joint operations. The National Security Council acts as liaison between the government's executive branch and the intelligence services, advising leadership on intelligence and security issues.

The main civilian intelligence agency in India is the Intelligence Bureau (IB). The IB focuses on domestic intelligence, but the exact structure and operations of the agency are largely unknown. Political espionage is illegal in India, and police gathered wiretapping information is inadmissible as evidence in court proceedings. However, the IB conducts regular electronic monitoring of telephone communications, and mail surveillance, despite occasional admonitions from Parliament. The Central Bureau of Investigations handles most criminal investigations, often acting on initial information provided by one of the IB's many departments. Increasing political tensions with neighboring Pakistan altered the focus of IB operations in recent years, with increasing attention paid to the protection and surveillance of national borders.

The Research and Analysis Wing (RAW) is India's primary agency responsible for foreign intelligence. RAW operations are largely focused on espionage against Pakistan. With the addition of both India and Pakistan to the growing cadre of the world's nuclear powers, India's RAW conducts counter-intelligence operations, as well as technological and remote espionage, against Pakistani defense and military interests. The RAW is not subject to Parliamentary review, and its actions are highly secret. The Indian government also used RAW resources to aid predominantly-Hindu Bangladesh's 1971 quest for independence from Muslim Pakistan. Most recently, the RAW aided international antiterrorism efforts by providing the United States and British governments information on the al-Qaeda terrorist network and its strongholds in Pakistan and Afghanistan.

Military intelligence is conducted by the Army Directorate of Military Intelligence. The agency is the weakest of India's intelligence community, but often aids civilian intelligence operations. The Army also maintains the Joint Cipher Bureau, the main code breaking department of Indian intelligence. To the northwest, the independent Muslim nation of Pakistan claims the Kashmir region of India. The two nations have never resolved the border dispute, and tensions recently reached a climax when both nations declared themselves nuclear powers and began testing weapons of mass destruction. The nuclear programs of India and Pakistan raise interesting questions about the efficacy of current non-proliferation measures and the increasing global prevalence of industrial and scientific espionage. The increasing instability of the region has aroused the concern of the international community and the United Nations Security Council.

3

Central Bureau of Investigation

The Central Bureau of Investigation (CBI) is a government agency of India that serves as a criminal investigation body, national security agency and intelligence agency. It was established on 1 April 1963 and evolved from the *Special Police Establishment* founded in 1941. Its motto is "Industry, Impartiality, Integrity". The CBI is controlled by the *Department of Personnel and Training* in the *Ministry of Personnel, Public Grievances and Pension* of the Union Government usually headed by a Union Minister who reports directly to the Prime Minister. While analogous in structure to the FBI, the CBI's powers and function are severely limited to specific crimes based on Acts (mainly the *Delhi Special Police Establishment Act, 1946*). The CBI is the official Interpol unit for India.

As of November 30, 2010 the director of CBI is former Indian Police Service officer Amar Pratap Singh. He replaced Ashwani Kumar.

Introduction

The Central Bureau of Investigation traces its origin to the *Special Police Establishment* (SPE), which was set up in 1941 by the Government of India. The functions of the *SPE* were to investigate cases of bribery and corruption in transactions with the War & Supply Department of India during World War II. The superintendent of the SPE was vested with the War Department. Even after the end of the War, the need for a Central Government agency to investigate cases of bribery and corruption by Central Government employees was felt. The *Delhi Special Police Establishment Act* was therefore brought into force in 1946. This Act transferred the superintendence of the SPE to the Home Department and its functions were enlarged to cover all departments of the Govt. of India. The jurisdiction of the SPE extended to all the Union Territories and could be extended also to the States with the consent of the State Government concerned.

Founder director

The founder director of the CBI was D.P. Kohli who held office from 1 April 1963 to 31 May 1968. Before this, he was Inspector General of Police of the Special Police Establishment from 1955 to 1963. Before that he held responsible positions in police in Madhya Bharat, Uttar Pradesh and Govt. of India. He was Police Chief in Madhya Bharat before joining the SPE. Kohli was awarded 'Padma Bhushan' in 1967 for his distinguished services. Kohi was a visionary who saw in the Special Police Establishment the potential of growing into the national investigative agency. He nurtured the organisation during his long stint as Inspector General and as Director and laid the solid foundation on which the organisation grew over the decades to become what it is today.

CBI Takes Shape

As the CBI, over the years, established a reputation of being India's premier investigative agency with adequate resources to deal with complicated cases, demands were made on it to take up investigation of more cases of conventional crime such as murder, kidnapping, terrorism, etc. Apart from this, the Supreme court and even the various High Courts of the country also started entrusting such cases for investigation to the CBI on petitions filed by aggrieved parties.

Taking into account the fact that several cases falling under this category were being taken up for investigation by the CBI, it was found expedient to entrust such cases to the Branches having local jurisdiction.

It was therefore decided in 1987 to constitute two investigation divisions in the CBI, namely, Anti-Corruption Division and Special Crimes Division, the latter dealing with cases of conventional crime, besides economic offences. The CBI is a central subject under the Constitution of India, meaning that it reports to the Indian Government and not to the individual states.

Role and Functions

The CBI is the premier investigating police agency in India. It is an elite force playing a major role in preservation of values in public life and in ensuring the health of the national economy. It is also the nodal police agency in India which coordinates investigation on behalf of Interpol Member countries. The services of its investigating officers are sought for all major investigations in the country. CBI as an organisation is held in high esteem by the Supreme Court, the High Courts, the Parliament and the public. The CBI has to investigate major crimes in the country having interstate and international ramifications. It is also involved in collection of criminal intelligence pertaining to three of its main areas of operation, viz., Anti-Corruption, Economic Crimes and Special Crimes.

CBI investigations have a major impact on the political and economic life of the nation. The following broad categories of criminal cases are handled by the CBI:

- Anti Corruption Division: Cases of corruption and fraud committed by public servants of all Central Govt. Departments, Central Public Sector Undertakings and Central Financial Institutions.
- Economic Crimes Division: Deals with cases including bank frauds, financial frauds, Import Export & Foreign

Exchange violations, large-scale smuggling of narcotics, antiques, cultural property and smuggling of other contraband items etc.

- Special Crimes Division: Deals with cases such as cases of terrorism, bomb blasts, sensational homicides, kidnapping for ransom and crimes committed by the mafia/the underworld.

Structure of CBI

The CBI is headed by a Director, an IPS Officer of the rank of Director General of Police or Commissioner of Police (State). Director is selected based on the procedure laid down by CVC Act 2003 and has a tenure of 2 years.

The other important ranks in the CBI are Special Director, Additional Director, Joint Director, Deputy Inspector General of Police, Senior Superintendent of Police, Superintendent of Police, Additional Superintendent of Police, Deputy Superintendent of Police, Inspector, Sub-Inspector, Assistant Sub-Inspector, Head Constable, Senior Constable and Constable.

According to annual reports Staff of CBI is usually divided between Ministerial staff, Ex-cadre posts which are usually of technical nature, Executive Staff and EDP Staff. Hindi Bhasha staff belongs to the Department of official languages.

Ministerial Staff includes LDC, UDC, Crime Assistants etc. Executive Staff includes Constables, ASI, Sub-Inspectors, Inspectors etc. EDP Staff includes Data Entry Operators, Data Processing Assistants, Assistant Programmers, Programmers and SSA.

Jurisdiction Powers, Privileges and Liabilities

The legal powers of investigation of CBI are derived from the DSPE Act 1946. This Act confers concurrent and coextensive powers, duties, privileges and liabilities on the members of Delhi Special Police Establishment (CBI) with

Police Officers of the Union Territories. The Central Government may extend to any area, besides Union Territories, the powers and jurisdiction of members of the CBI for investigation subject to the consent of the Government of the concerned State.

While exercising such powers, members of the CBI of or above the rank of Sub Inspector shall be deemed to be officers incharge of Police Stations of respective jurisdictions. The CBI can investigate only such of the offences as are notified by the Central Government under the DSPE Act.

Jurisdiction of CBI vis-a-vis State Police

Law and Order is a State subject and the basic jurisdiction to investigate crime lies with State Police. Besides, due to limited resources, CBI would not be able to investigate crimes of all kind. CBI may investigate:

- Cases which are essentially against Central Govt. employees or concerning affairs of the Central Govt. and the employees of the Central Public Sector Undertakings and Public Sector Banks.
- Cases in which the financial interests of the Central Government are involved.
- Cases relating to the breaches of Central Laws with the enforcement of which the Government of India is mainly concerned.
- Big cases of fraud, cheating, embezzlement and the like relating to companies in which large funds are involved and similar other cases when committed by organised gangs or professional criminals having ramifications in several States.
- Cases having interstate and international ramifications and involving several official agencies where, from all angles, it is considered necessary that a single investigating agency should be incharge of the investigation.

Former directors (1961-present)

Name	*Period*	*Notes*
D.P. Kohli	1963–68	
F. V. Arul	1968–71	
D Sen	1971-77	
S N Mathur	1977	Acting
C V Narsimhan	1977	Acting
John Lobo	1977–79	
R D Singh	1979-80	
J S Bajwa	1980–85	
M G Katre	1985-89	
A P Mukherjee	1989–90	
R Sekhar	1990	Acting
Vijay Karan	1990–92	
S K Datta	1992–93	
K V R Rao	1993–96	
J Singh	1996–97	
R C Sharma	1997–98	
D R Karthikeyan	1998	Acting
T N Mishra	1998–99	
R K Raghavan	1999–2001	
P C Sharma	2001–2003	
U S Misra	2003–2005	
V S Tiwari	2005–2008	
W Ashwini Kumar	2008–2010	
Amar Pratap Singh	2010–Present	

Corruption in CBI

Because of its intensely political overtones, it has been exposed by its former bigwigs like Joginder Singh and BR Lall who were Director and Joint Director respectively, to be engaging in nepotism, mal-prosecution and outright corruption. In his book, Who Owns CBI, BR Lall, an honest and upright officer details the modus operandi of manipulating and derailing investigation This organisation has become synonymous with corruption as information obtained under the RTI Act has revealed. Even the Top Bosses are known for stooping to illegal fund diversions. RTI activist Krishnanand Tripathi has alleged harassment from CBI in order to save itself from exposure through RTI. CBI has now been exempted from RTI act.

Controversies

Normally, cases assigned to the CBI are sensitive and of national importance. It is a usual practice for the respective state police departments, to initially register any case coming under its jurisdiction, and if necessary, through mediation by the central government, the cases may be transferred to the CBI. The CBI handles many high profile cases, and is never far from controversy.

Bofors Scandal

In January 2006, it was found that CBI had quietly unfrozen bank accounts of Italian businessman Ottavio Quattrocchi, one of the prime accused in the Bofors scandal of 1986 which had tainted the Rajiv Gandhi government. The CBI was responsible for the inquiry into the Bofors Case. Associates of then prime minister Rajiv Gandhi were linked to alleged pay-offs made in the mid-1980s by the Swedish arms firm AB Bofors, with $40 million in kickbacks moved from Britain and Panama to secret Swiss banks.

The 410 howitzer field guns purchased in the $1,300 million arms sale were reported to be inferior to those offered by a French competitor.

The CBI, which unfroze Rs 21 crore in a London bank in accounts held by Bofors scam accused Quattrocchi and his wife Maria in 2006, has facilitated his travel across the globe by asking Interpol to take him off the "wanted" list on 29 Apr

2009. Following a communication from the CBI, Interpol withdrew the Red Corner Notice against Quattrocchi. The development, that came barely three weeks before the end of the Manmohan Singh government's tenure, brought the issue of the Bofors scandal back to centre stage. It is often suspected that ruling governments interfere with the work of the CBI, and the handling of the Bofors investigation by CBI under Congress governments has created a new synonym for CBI. After letting off the Bofors accused, Oppositions have never tired to call it the 'Congress Bureau of Investigation'.

ISRO Spy Ring Case

In 1994 two scientists with the Indian Space Research Organisation (ISRO) and two Indian businessmen were arrested for allegedly conspiring to sell space secrets to two Maldivian women, who were originally described by newspapers as agents of Pakistani intelligence, for money and sex.

The CBI investigation did not reveal the existence of a spy ring, and by early 1995 it was clear that the case was more a product of inexperience and over exuberation on the part of the police and Intelligence Bureau.It was a well planned scheme to remove the then DGP Ramon S by concocted links to Maldivian lady. The scheme was plotted by some officers of Kerala police, the media and Muslim League as DGP was made of sterner stuff.

Hawala Scandal

In 1991 an arrest linked to militants in Kashmir led to a raid on hawala brokers, revealing evidence of large-scale payments to national politicians. The prosecution that followed was partly prompted by a public interest petition, and yet the court cases of the Hawala scandal eventually all collapsed without convictions. The CBI's role was again criticised. In concluding the Vineet Narain case, the Supreme Court of India directed that the Central Vigilance Commission should be given a supervisory role over the CBI.

Priyadarshini Mattoo Murder Case

The CBI has been under a cloud owing to its handling of the Priyadarshini Mattoo case, in which Santosh Kumar Singh, the alleged murderer of a 22-year old law student was acquitted for what the case judge called "deliberate inaction" by the investigating team. The accused was the son of a high ranking officer in the Indian Police Service, due to which the case had been shifted from the regular police force to the CBI. However, the 1999 judgment commented on how "the influence of the father of the accused has been there".

Embarrassed by the judgment, the-then CBI Director, R K Raghavan, requested two Special Directors, P C Sharma and G H Achari, to study the judgement. Subsequently the CBI appealed the verdict in Delhi High court in 2000, after which the High Court issued a bailable warrant against the accused. The case was again prominent in 2006 after much media coverage and public bashing (this was mainly due to a similar acquittal in another high profile case, though not handled by the CBI). The CBI filed an application for early hearing in July 2006. The High Court subsequently found Santosh Kumar Singh guilty of rape and murder and awarded a death sentence for the same in October 2006.

Nithari Killings

The CBI was given the responsibility of investigating the murders of dozens of children in the Nithari village near Noida, UP. This was after the local police was found to be incompetent and lethargic in their investigations. The serial killings were in the Indian and international media for weeks since decomposing bodies were found outside the house of the accused Moninder Singh Pandher.

Dawood Ibrahim Case

In August 2007, the CBI asked its Pakistani counterpart, the Federal Investigation Agency, for its comments on recent media reports about the detention of Dawood Ibrahim by authorities in Karachi.

Sister Abhaya Murder Case

Sister Abhaya murder case concerns a nun, who was found dead in a water well in Saint Pius X convent hostel in Kottayam, Kerala on 27 March 1992. Altogether there were five CBI inquiries into the murder case so far without any tangible results. The powerful Catholic Lobby had exerted their undue influence to subdue the case as a Priest and a nun were involved. Abhaya had caught them in a compromising position.

Sohrabuddin Case

CBI has been accused of acting for the ruling party Congress (UPA) to trap its opposition party mainly BJP. CBI, which is dealing with the Sohrabuddin case in Gujrat, questioned Geeta Johri an IPS officer, who claims the CBI is pressuring her to falsely implicate former Gujarat Minister Amit Shah in the Sohrabuddin fake encounter case, Rajkot Police Commissioner Geeta Johri has alleged in the Supreme Court.

Sant Singh Chatwal Case

Sant Singh Chatwal was an accused in the CBI's records for 14 years. CBI had filed two chargesheets naming him as accused; sent Letters Rogatory abroad; even sent a probe team to the US and put Chatwal and his wife behind bars from February 2 to February 5, 1997. On May 30, 2007 and August 10, 2008, former CBI Director Vijay Shankar and the agency's present Director Ashwani Kumar respectively signed orders saying there was no need to challenge the discharge of Sant Singh Chatwal and his co-accused. This was done in spite of advice of a string of investigators — including a Special Director and Joint Director — and it was decided not to appeal his discharge. This, in effect, closed the principal case of bank fraud in which Chatwal had been embroiled for over a decade. Along with four others, Chatwal was charged with being part of a "criminal conspiracy" to defraud the Bank of India's New York branch to the tune of US $8,992,815 (Rs 28.32 crore). In all, four chargesheets were filed by the CBI, with Chatwal named as accused in two. The trials in the other two cases are still in progress. RTI applicant Krishnanand Tripathi was denied access to public information concerning the closed cases. CIC later ordered the CBI to disclose the information. But CBI has recently been exempted from RTI act and it is unclear if this information will be disclosed. Sant Singh Chatwal has been awarded with Padma Bhushan despite these cases.

Malankara Varghese Murder Case

The Malankara Varghese murder case concerns the death of T.M.Varghese also known as Malankara Varghese,a member of Malankara Orthodox Church's managing committee and a timber merchant in 5 December 2002. On 9 May 2010 charged Father Varghese Thekkekara,a priest and manager of the Angamali diocese in the rival Jacobite Syrian Christian Church (a part of the Syriac Orthodox Church) with conspiracy in the murder of Malankara Varghese and named him as the prime accused. Till date,the prime accused has not been arrested, CBI is highly being criticized for this by Kerala High Court and Media.

Bhopal Gas Tragedy

The public perceived that the CBI was very ineffective in trying the Bhopal gas tragedy case, the former CBI director has now confessed that he asked to remain soft on extraditing the Union Carbide CEO Warren Anderson, and dropped charges, including culpable homicide, against those accused in this case, who received two year sentences.

Convictions

CBI has a high conviction rate.

Year	*Conviction Rate*
2008	66.2%
2007	67.7%

CBI Academy

CBI Academy at Ghaziabad, Uttar Pradesh, India, started functioning in 1996. The Academy is situated towards east of Delhi, in Ghaziabad district of Uttar Pradesh at a distance of around 40 km from New Delhi Railway Station and about 65 km from Indira Gandhi International Airport, Delhi. It is spread over of 26.5 acres (107,000 m^2) of lush green fields and plantations with a covered area consisting of the Administrative, Academic, Hostel and Residential Blocks. Prior to that a small Training Centre was functional at Lok Nayak Bhawan, New Delhi only for conducting short term in-service courses. CBI then, was dependent on State Police Training Institutions and NPA, Hyderabad for training basic courses of Dy.SsP, SIs and constables.

The Academy now caters to the training needs of all ranks of CBI. Training facilities for certain specialised courses are also made available to the officials of State Police, *Central Police Organisations* (CPO), *Vigilance organisations of public sector undertakings*, banks and government departments and Indian Armed Forces.

4

Research and Analysis Wing

The Research and Analysis Wing (R&AW or RAW) is India's external intelligence agency. It was formed in September 1968 after the poor performance of the Intelligence Bureau (which handled both internal and external intelligence) in the Sino-Indian war of 1962 and the India-Pakistani war of 1965 convinced the then government of India that a specialized, independent agency was required for competent external intelligence gathering. The primary function of the R&AW is collection of external intelligence, counter-terrorism and covert operations. In addition, it is responsible for obtaining and analysing information about foreign governments, corporations, and persons, in order to advise Indian policymakers.

The R&AW has its headquarters in New Delhi, and the current director of the organization is Sanjeev Tripathi, a 1973 Uttar Pradesh batch IPS officer who later shifted to the R&AW Allied Service (RAS) cadre.

History

Prior to inception of Research and Analysis Wing, overseas intelligence collection was primarily the responsibility of the Intelligence Bureau (IB), which was created by the British. In 1933, sensing the political turmoil in the world which eventually led to the Second World War, the Intelligence Bureau's responsibilities were increased to include the collection of intelligence along India's borders. In 1947, after independence, Sanjeevi Pillai took over as the first Indian Director of IB. Having been depleted of trained manpower by the exit of the British, Pillai tried to run the bureau on MI5 lines. In 1949, Pillai organized a small foreign intelligence operation, but the Indian debacle in the Sino-Indian war of 1962 showed it to be ineffective. Foreign intelligence failure during the Sino-Indian war (October 20-November 21, 1962) led then Prime Minister Jawaharlal Nehru to order a dedicated foreign intelligence agency to be established. After the Indo-Pakistani war of 1965, Indian Chief of Army Staff General Jayanta Nath Chaudhury also called for more intelligence-gathering.

Around the end of 1966 the concept of a separate foreign intelligence agency began to take concrete shape. In 1968, after Indira Gandhi had taken over as Prime Minister, it was decided that a full-fledged second security service was needed. R. N. Kao, then a deputy director of the Intelligence Bureau, submitted a blueprint for the new agency. Kao was appointed as the chief of India's first foreign intelligence agency, the Research and Analysis Wing. The R&AW was given the responsibility for strategic external intelligence, human as well as technical, plus concurrent responsibility with the Directorate-General of Military Intelligence for tactical trans-border military intelligence up to a certain depth across the LOC and the international border.

R&AW started as a wing of the main Intelligence Bureau with 250 employees and an annual budget of ₹2 crore (US$446,000)). In the early seventies, its annual budget had risen to 30 crore (US$6.7 million) while its personnel numbered several thousand. In 1971, Kao had persuaded the Government to set up the Aviation Research Centre (ARC). The ARC's job was aerial reconnaissance. It replaced the Indian Air Force's old reconnaissance aircraft and by the mid-70s, R&AW, through the ARC, had high quality aerial pictures of the installations along the Chinese and Pakistani borders. Presently, the budget of R&AW is speculated to be as high as US$150 million to as low as US$31 million. Slowly other child agencies like The Radio Research Center and Electronics & Tech. Services were added to R&AW in 70s and 90s. In 1990s the Special Frontier Force became the paramilitary wing of R&AW, providing the requisite muscle for covert military operations. In 2004 Government of India added yet another intelligence agency called the National Technical Facilities Organisation (NTFO), also known as National Technical Research Organisation (NTRO), believed to be functioning under R&AW, although it remains autonomous to some degree. While the exact nature of the operations conducted by NTRO is classified, it is believed that it deals with research on imagery and communications using various platforms.

Organization

R&AW has been organized on the lines of the CIA. The Director of R&AW is designated "Secretary (Research)" in the Cabinet Secretariat. Most of the previous Directors have been experts on either Pakistan or China. They also have the benefit of training in either the USA or the UK, and more recently in Israel. The "Secretary (R)", although is under direct command of Prime Minister, reports on an administrative basis to the Cabinet Secretary, who reports to the Prime Minister (PM). However, on a daily basis the "Secretary (R)" reports to the National Security Advisor. Reporting to the "Secretary (R)" are:

- An Additional Director responsible for the Office of Special Operations and intelligence collected from different countries processed by large number of Joint Secretaries, who are the functional heads of various specified desks with different regional divisions/areas/ countries: Area one-Pakistan; Area two-China and Southeast Asia; Area three-the Middle East and Africa; and Area four-other countries. Two Special Joint Secretaries, reporting to the Additional Director, head the Electronics and Technical Department which is the nodal agency for ETS, NTFO and the RRC.

- The Director General of Security having two important sections the Aviation Research Centre headed by one Special Director and the Special Services Bureau controlled by two Special Secretaries.

The internal structure of the R&AW is a matter of speculation, but brief overviews of the same are present in the public domain. Attached to the Headquarters of R&AW at Lodhi Road, New Delhi are different regional headquarters, which have direct links to overseas stations and are headed by a controlling officer who keeps records of different projects assigned to field officers who are posted abroad.

Intelligence is usually collected from a variety of sources by field officers and deputy field officers; it is either preprocessed by a senior field officer or by a desk officer. The desk officer then passes the information to the Joint Secretary and then on to the Additional Secretary and from there it is disseminated to the concerned end user.

R&AW personnel are called "Research Officers" instead of the traditional "agents". There is a sizable number of female officers in R&AW even at the operational level. In recent years, R&AW has shifted its primary focus from Pakistan to China and have started operating a separate desk for this purpose.

Secretaries

Most of the Directors of Research and Analysis Wing have been Indian Police Service (IPS) officers. RN Kao and Sankaran Nair belonged to the Imperial Police (IP), of the British colonial days which was renamed as the Indian Police Service after Indian Independence in 1947. N.F.Suntook had served in the Indian Navy, then in the Indian Police Service and in the Indian Frontier Administration Service. Vikram Sood was from the Indian Postal Service and was later permanently absorbed in the RAS cadre. A.S. Dulat was an Indian Police Service officer deputed from the Intelligence Bureau, while K.C. Verma is an ex-Intelligence Bureau officer. All the

Directors have been experts on China or Pakistan except for Ashok Chaturvedi, who is an expert on Nepal. Sanjeev Tripathi is the current Director of R&AW from the RAS cadre.

Designations

Recruitment

Initially, R&AW relied primarily on trained intelligence officers who were recruited directly. These belonged to the external wing of the Intelligence Bureau. In times of great expansion, many candidates were taken from the military, police and other services. Later, R&AW began directly recruiting graduates from universities. Today, R&AW has its own service cadre, the R&AW Allied Service (RAS) to absorb talent. Recruitment is mostly by deputation from the Armed Forces or Civil Service Officers. The Civil and Defense Service Officers permanently resign their cadre and join the RAS. However, according to recent reports, officers can return to their parent cadre after serving a specific period in the agency if they wish to. Most of the Directors have been officers from the IPS. R&AW also employs a number of linguists and other experts in various fields. Recruitment in R&AW is taken in the name of NATI (National Aptitude Test in Intelligence) followed by personality and psychological test and interviews. Delhi-based security think tank Institute for Defence Studies and Analyses noted in one of its reports that R&AW suffered from the 'tail-end syndrome' where the 'bottom of the entrance lists' of those appearing for the UPSC examinations were offered jobs.

Basic Training

Basic training commences with 'pep talks' to boost the morale of the new recruit. This is a ten-day phase in which the inductee is familiarized with the real world of intelligence and espionage, as opposed to the spies of fiction. Common usages, technical jargon and classification of information are taught. Case studies of other agencies like CIA, KGB, Chinese Secret Agency and ISI are presented for study. The inductee is also taught that intelligence organisations do not identify who is friend and who is foe, the country's foreign policy does. Basic classroom training to R&AW officers are imparted at R&AW's Training Institute in Gurgaon. A multi-disciplinary school of economic intelligence is also being set up in in Mumbai to train intelligence officers in investigating economic crimes like money laundering for terror purposes etc.

Advanced Training

After completing 'Basic Training' the recruit is now attached to a Field Intelligence Bureau (FIB). His/her training here lasts for 1–2 years. He/she is given firsthand experience of what it was to be out in the figurative cold, conducting clandestine operations. During night exercises under realistic conditions, he/she is taught infiltration and exfiltration. He/she is instructed to avoid capture and, if caught, how to face interrogation. He/she learns the art of reconnoiter, making contacts, and, the numerous skills of operating an intelligence mission.

At the end of the field training, the new recruit is brought back to the school for final polishing. Before his deployment in the field, he is given exhaustive training in the art of self-defense, an introduction to martial arts and the use of technical espionage devices. He/she is also drilled in various administrative disciplines so that he could take his place in the foreign missions without arousing suspicion. He/she is now ready to operate under the cover of an Embassy to gather information, set up his own network of informers, moles or operatives as the task may require. Field training is provided in the Indian Military Academy Headquarters at Dehradun. The training model has been criticised as being 'archaic and too police-centric' and not incorporating 'modern technological advances in methods of communication' etc.

Functions

The Secretary (R&AW) reported to the Vohra Committee that R&AW offices abroad have limited strength and are largely geared to the collection of military, economic, scientific and political intelligence.

R&AW monitors the activities of certain organisations abroad only insofar as they relate to their involvement with narco terrorist elements and smuggling arms, ammunition, explosives, etc. into India. It does not monitor the activities of criminal elements abroad, which are mainly confined to normal smuggling without any links to terrorist elements. The present strength of the Agency's offices abroad would not permit it to enlarge its field of activities. If, however, there is evidence to suggest that these organisations have links with Intelligence agencies of other countries, and that they are being used or are likely to be used by such countries for destabilising India's economy, it would become R&AW's responsibility to monitor their activities.

The primary mission of R&AW includes aggressive intelligence collection via espionage, psychological warfare, subversion and sabotage. R&AW maintains active collaboration with other secret services in various countries. Its contacts with FSB of Russia, KHAD, the Afghan agency, Israel's Mossad, the CIA and MI6 have been well-known, a common interest being Pakistan's nuclear programme. R&AW has been active in obtaining information and operating through third countries like Afghanistan, the United Kingdom, Hong Kong, Myanmar and Singapore.

R&AW obtains information critical to Indian strategic interests, both by overt and covert means. The data is then classified and filed with the assistance of the computer networks. International business houses, information technology sector and media centers can easily absorb R&AW operatives and provide freedom of movement. A task force report prepared by a New Delhi based security think tank highlighted that R&AW operatives have inadequate non-official cover for overseas operations which 'limits access to spot real targets' and causes issues on handling 'high-value assets'.

Espionage Techniques

Major Operations

- ELINT operations in Himalayas: After China tested its first nuclear weapons on October 16, 1964, at Lop Nur, Xinjiang, India and the USA shared a common fear about the nuclear capabilities of China. Owing to the extreme remoteness of Chinese testing grounds and strict secrecy surrounding the Chinese nuclear programme, it was almost impossible to carry out any HUMINT operation. So, the CIA in the late 1960s decided to launch an ELINT operation along with R&AW and ARC to track China's nuclear tests and monitor its missile launches. The operation, in the garb of a mountaineering expedition to Nanda Devi involved celebrated Indian climber M S Kohli who along with operatives of Special Frontier Force and the CIA-most notably Jim Rhyne, a veteran STOL pilot-was to place a permanent ELINT device, a transceiver powered by a plutonium battery, that could detect and report data on future nuclear tests carried out by China. The monitoring device was near successfully implanted on Nanda Devi, when an avalanche forced a hasty withdrawal. Later, a subsequent mountain operation to retrieve or replant the device was aborted when it was found that the device was lost. Recent reports indicate that radiation traces from this device have been discovered in sediment below the mountain. However, the actual data is not conclusive.
- Creation of Bangladesh and aftermath: In the early 1970s the army of Pakistan prosecuted a bloody military crackdown in response to the Bangladesh independence movement. Nearly 10 million refugees fled to India. R&AW was instrumental in formation of Bangladeshi guerilla organisation Mukti Bahini and responsible for supplying information, providing training and heavy

ammunition to this organization. It is also alleged that R&AW planned and executed the hijack of Indian Airlines Fokker Friendship aircraft Ganga as false flag operation to ban overflight by Pakistani aircrafts and disrupt Pakistani troop movement in East Pakistan. The war ended in successful creation of Bangladesh. However within months of independence of Bangladesh Mujibur Rahman was assassinated at his residence. R&AW operatives claim that they had advance information about Mujib-ur-Rahman's assassination but Sheikh Mujib tragically ignored R&AW's inputs. He was killed along with 40 members of his family. R&AW thus failed to prevent the assassination which led to the loss of a charismatic leader who had a soft corner for India after all they had done for his country's independence. However, R&AW has successfully thwarted plans of assassinating Sheikh Hasina Wazed, daughter of Mujibur Rahman, by Islamist extremists and the ISI.

- Operation Smiling Buddha: Operation Smiling Buddha was the name given to India's nuclear programme. The task to keep it under tight wraps for security was given to R&AW. This was the first time that R&AW was involved in a project inside India. On 18 May 1974, India detonated a 15-kiloton plutonium device at Pokhran and became a member of the nuclear club.
- Amalgamation of Sikkim: In 1947 Sikkim became a protectorate under India, which controlled its external affairs, defence, diplomacy and communications. It is alleged that in 1972 R&AW was authorized to install a pro-Indian democratic government there. After widespread rioting and demonstration against the King of Sikkim in 1975 a referendum was held in which 97.5% of the electorate (in a nation where 59% of the population could vote) voted to join the Indian Union. On 16 May 1975, Sikkim officially became the 22nd

state of the Indian Union, and the monarchy was abolished.

- Kahuta's Blueprint: Kahuta is the site of the Khan Research Laboratories (KRL), Pakistan's main nuclear weapons laboratory as well as an emerging center for long-range missile development. The primary Pakistani fissile-material production facility is located at Kahuta, employing gas centrifuge enrichment technology to produce Highly Enriched Uranium (HEU). R&AW first confirmed Pakistan's nuclear programs by analysing the hair samples snatched from the floor of barber shops near KRL; which showed that Pakistan had developed the ability to enrich uranium to weapons-grade quality. R&AW agents knew of Kahuta Research Laboratories from at least early 1978, when the then Indian Prime Minister, Morarji Desai, stopped R&AW's operations on Pakistan's covert nuclear weapons program. In an indiscreet moment in a telephone conversation one day, Morarji Desai informed the then Pakistan President, Zia-ul-Haq, that India was aware of Pakistan's nuclear weapons program. According to later reports, acting on this "tip-off", Pakistani Intelligence eliminated R&AW's sources on Kahuta, leaving India in the dark about Pakistan's nuclear weapons program from then on.
- Operation Meghdoot: R&AW received information from the London company which had supplied Arctic-weather gear for Indian troops from Northern Ladakh region some paramilitary forces that Pakistan too had bought similar Arctic-weather gear. This information was shared with Indian Army which soon launched Operation Meghdoot to take control of Siachen Glacier with around 300 acclimatized troops were airlifted to Siachen before Pakistan could launch any operation resulting in Indian head start and eventual Indian domination of all major peaks in Siachen.

- Kanishka Bombing case: On 23 June 1985 Air India's Flight 182 was blown up near Ireland and 329 innocent lives were lost. On the same day, another explosion took place at Tokyo's Narita airport's transit baggage building where baggage was being transferred from Cathay Pacific Flight No CP 003 to Air India Flight 301 which was scheduled for Bangkok. Both aircraft were loaded with explosives from Canadian airports. Flight 301 got saved because of a delay in its departure. This was considered as a major setback to R&AW for failing to gather enough intelligence about the Khalistani terrorists.
- Special Operations: In the mid-1980s, R&AW set up two covert groups, *Counterintelligence Team-X(CIT-X)* and *Counterintelligence Team-J(CIT-J)*, the first directed at Pakistan and the second at Khalistani groups. Rabinder Singh, the R&AW double agent who defected to the United States in 2004, helped run CIT-J in its early years. Both these covert groups used the services of cross-border traffickers to ferry weapons and funds across the border, much as their ISI counterparts were doing. According to former R&AW official and noted security analyst B. Raman, the Indian counter-campaign yielded results. "The role of our cover action capability in putting an end to the ISI's interference in Punjab", he wrote in 2002, "by making such interference prohibitively costly is little known and understood." These covert operations were discontinued during the tenure of IK Gujral and were never restarted. As per B Raman the former R&AW cabinet secretary, such covert operations were successful in keeping a check on ISI and were "responsible for ending the Khalistani insurgency". He also notes that a lack of such covert capabilities, since they were closed down in 1997, has left the country even more vulnerable than before and says that developing covert capabilities is the need of the hour.

- Operation Cactus: In November 1988, the People's Liberation Organisation of Tamil Eelam (PLOTE), composed of about 200 Tamil secessionist rebels, invaded Maldives. At the request of the president of Maldives, Maumoon Abdul Gayoom, the Indian Armed Forces, with assistance from R&AW, launched a military campaign to throw the mercenaries out of Maldives. On the night of November 3, 1988, the Indian Air Force airlifted the 6th parachute battalion of the Parachute Regiment from Agra and flew them over 2,000 km to Maldives. The Indian paratroopers landed at Hulule and restored the Government rule at Malé within hours. The operation, labelled *Operation Cactus*, also involved the Indian Navy. Swift operation by the military and precise intelligence by R&AW quelled the insurgency.
- Sri Lanka: R&AW started training the LTTE to keep a check on Sri Lanka, which had helped Pakistan in the Indo-Pak War by allowing Pakistani ships to refuel at Sri Lankan ports. However, the LTTE created a lot of problems and complications and the then Prime Minister of India Rajiv Gandhi was forced to send the Indian Peace Keeping Force (IPKF) in 1987 to restore normalcy in the region. The disastrous mission of the IPKF was blamed by many on the lack of coordination between the IPKF and R&AW. Its most disastrous manifestation was the Heliborne assault on LTTE HQ in the Jaffna University campus in the opening stages of Operation Pawan. The site was chosen without any consultation with the R&AW. The dropping paratroopers became easy targets for the LTTE. A number of soldiers were killed. The assassination of Rajiv Gandhi is also blamed as a fallout of the failed R&AW operation in Sri Lanka.
- Anti-Apartheid Movement: R&AW trained the intelligence officers of many independent African countries and assisted the anti-apartheid struggles in

South Africa and Namibia. Retired R&AW officers were deputed to work in training institutes of intelligence agencies of some African states.

- Operation Chanakya: This was the R&AW operation in the Kashmir region to infiltrate various ISI-backed Kashmiri separatist groups and restore peace in the Kashmir valley. R&AW operatives infiltrated the area, collected military intelligence, and provided evidence about ISI's involvement in training and funding Kashmiri separatist groups. R&AW was successful not only in unearthing the links between the ISI and the separatist groups, but also in infiltrating and neutralizing the militancy in the Kashmir valley. R&AW is also credited for creating a split in the Hizb-ul-Mujahideen. Operation Chanakya also marked the creation of pro-Indian groups in Kashmir like the Ikhwan-ul-Muslimeen, Muslim Mujahideen etc. These counter-insurgencies consist of ex-militants and relatives of those slain in the conflict. Ikhwan-ul-Muslimeen leader Kokka Parrey was himself assassinated by separatists.
- Help to the Northern Alliance: After the rise of Pakistan backed Taliban in Afghanistan, India decided to side with the Northern Alliance and the Soviet Union By 1996, R&AW had built a 25 bed military hospital at the Farkhor Air Base. This airport was used by the Aviation Research Centre, the reconnaissance arm of R&AW, to repair and operate the Northern Alliance's aerial support. This relationship was further cemented in the 2001 Afgan war. India supplied the Northern Alliance high altitude warfare equipment worth around US$8–10 million. R&AW was the first intelligence agency to determine the extent of the Kunduz airlift.
- Kargil War: R&AW was heavily criticized in 1999, following the Pakistani incursions at Kargil. Critics

accused R&AW of failing to provide intelligence that could have prevented the ensuing ten-week conflict that brought India and Pakistan to the brink of a full-scale war. While the Army has been critical of the information they received, R&AW has pointed the finger at the politicians, claiming they had provided all the necessary information. However, R&AW was successful in intercepting a telephonic conversation between Pervez Musharraf, the then Pakistan Army Chief who was in Beijing and his chief of staff Lt. Gen. Mohammed Aziz in Islamabad. This tape was later published by India to prove Pakistani involvement in the Kargil incursion.

- Operation Leech: Surrounded by Arakans and dense forest, Myanmar had always been a worrisome point for Indian intelligence. As the major player in the area, India has sought to promote democracy and install friendly governments in the region. To these ends, R&AW cultivated Burmese rebel groups and pro-democracy coalitions, especially the Kachin Independence Army (KIA). India allowed the KIA to carry a limited trade in jade and precious stones using Indian territory and even supplied them weapons. It is further alleged that KIA chief Maran Brang Seng met the R&AW chief in Delhi twice. However, when the KIA became the main source of training and weapons for all northeastern rebel groups, R&AW initiated an operation, code named *Operation Leech*, to assassinate the leaders of the Burmese rebels as an example to other groups. Six top rebel leaders, including military wing chief of National Unity Party of Arakans (NUPA), Khaing Raza, were shot dead and 34 Arakanese guerrillas were arrested and charged with gunrunning.
- War on Terror: Although R&AW's contribution to the War on Terror is highly classified, the organization gained some attention in the Western media after

claims that it was assisting the United States by providing intelligence on Osama Bin Laden and the Taliban's whereabouts. Maps and photographs of terrorist training camps in Afghanistan and Pakistan along with other evidence implicating Osama bin Laden in terrorist attacks were given to US intelligence officials. R&AW's role in the War on Terror may increase as US intelligence has indicated that it sees R&AW as a more reliable ally than Pakistani intelligence. It has further come to light that a timely tip-off by R&AW helped foil a third assassination plot against Pakistan's former President, General Pervez Musharraf.

- 2008 Mumbai attacks: About 2–6 months before 26/11 Mumbai attacks R&AW had intercepted several telephone calls through SIGINT which pointed at impending attacks on Mumbai Hotels by Pakistan based terrorists, however there was a coordination failure and no follow up action was taken. Few hours before the attacks, a R&AW technician monitoring satellite transmissions picked up conversations between attackers and handlers, as the attackers were sailing toward Mumbai. The technician flagged the conversations as being suspicious and passed them on to his superiors. R&AW believed that they were worrying and immediately alerted the office of the National Security Advisor. However the intelligence was ignored. Later, just after the terrorists had attacked Mumbai, R&AW technicians started monitoring the six phones used by the terrorists and recorded conversations between the terrorists and their handlers. On January 15, 2010, in a successful snatch operation R&AW agents nabbed Sheikh Abdul Khwaja, one of the handlers of the 26/11 attacks, chief of HuJI India operations and a most wanted terror suspect in India, from Colombo, Sri Lanka and brought him over to Hyderabad, India for formal arrest.

Controversies

From its inception R&AW has been criticised for being an agency not answerable to the people of India (R&AW reports to Prime Minister only). Fears arose that it could turn into the KGB of India. Such fears were kept at bay by the R&AW's able leadership (although detractors of R&AW and especially the Janata Party have accused the agency of letting itself be used for terrorising and intimidating opposition during emergencies). The main controversy which has plagued R&AW in recent years is over bureaucratization of the system with allegations about favoritism in promotions, corruption, ego clashes, no financial accountability, inter-departmental rivalry etc. R&AW also suffers from ethnic imbalances in the officer level. Noted security analyst and former Additional Secretary B.Raman has criticised the agency for its asymmetric growth; "while being strong in its capability for covert action it is weak in its capability for intelligence collection, analysis and assessment. Strong in low and medium-grade intelligence, weak in high-grade intelligence. Strong in technical intelligence, weak in human intelligence. Strong in collation, weak in analysis. Strong in investigation, weak in prevention. Strong in crisis management, weak in crisis prevention."

- In the February 8, 2010 edition *Outlook Magazine* reported on former R&AW Chief, Ashok Chaturvedi, utilizing Government of India funds to take his wife along on international trips. After retirement, Chaturvedi had a diplomatic passport issued for himself and his wife. Per *Outlook Magazine*: "Only grade 'A' ambassadors—usually IFS officers posted in key countries like the UK and US—are allowed to hold diplomatic passports after retirement. The majority, who do not fit that bill, hold passports issued to ordinary citizens. In fact, all former R&AW chiefs Outlook spoke to confirmed they had surrendered their diplomatic passports the day they retired. And their spouses weren't entitled to diplomatic passports even while they were in service."

- In September 2007, R&AW was involved in a controversy due to a high profile CBI raid at the residence of Major General (retired) V K Singh, a retired Joint Secretary of R&AW who has recently written a book on R&AW where it was alleged that political interference and corruption in the intelligence agency has made it vulnerable to defections. One of the instances of corruption mentioned in the book was the preference given by R&AW departments towards purchasing intelligence from the 'Rohde and Schwarz' company. A reason for such corruption as explained by the author is that "*...R&AW was not answerable to any outside agency-the control of the Prime Minister's Office was perfunctionary, at best-many officers thought that they were not only above the law but a law unto themselves.*" A case under the Official Secrets Act has also been filed against V K Singh.
- On August 19, 2008 the R&AW Director (Language) who was also head of the R&AW Training Institute in Gurgaon from 2005 tried to commit suicide in front of Prime Minister's Office, alleging inaction and wrong findings to a sexual harassment complaint filed against a Joint Secretary, who was on deputation to R&AW. She was discharged from duty on the ground that she was mentally unfit and that her identity was disclosed. She was later separately charged with criminal trespass, human trafficking and for her repeated attempts to commit suicide. The Central Administrative Tribunal (CAT) ordered R&AW to reinstate her however R&AW filed an appeal against the CAT order which is pending before Delhi High Court. On January 20, 2011 she was sent for psychological evaluation and medical detention by a Delhi High Court judge when she tried to strip herself in the court protesting over the slow pace of her trial. The psychological evaluation report stated that 'she may be suffering a mental problem due to loss of job and her continuous run-ins

at the courts, but she was certainly not suffering from any permanent or grave mental disorder.'

- A senior technical officer was arrested by CBI on graft charges, on February 4, 2009. The scientist, a Director level employee, worked in the division that granted export licenses to companies dealing in "sensitive" items, including defence-related equipment. He was accused of demanding and accepting a bribe of Rs.1 lakh from a Chennai based manufacturer for obtaining an export license.
- In September 2009, seven Additional Secretaries from the RAS cadre had gone on protest leave after A. B. Mathur, an IPS officer, superseded them to the post of Special Secretary. Over the years the tussle between the RAS cadre and officers on deputation from IPS cadre has caused friction in the working of the agency.

Defections and Spy Scandals

- In 2004, there was spy scandal involving the CIA. Rabinder Singh, Joint secretary and heading R&AW's South East Asia department, defected to America on June 5, 2004. R&AW had already become suspicious about his movements and he was under surveillance and his telephones were also tapped. He was confronted by Counter Intelligence officials on 19 April 2004. Despite all precautions, Rabinder Singh managed to defect with 'sensitive files' he had allegedly removed from R&AW's headquarters in south New Delhi. This embarrassing fiasco and national security failure were attributed to weak surveillance, shoddy investigation and lack of coördination between the Counter-Intelligence and Security (CIS), IB and R&AW. According to unconfirmed reports, Singh has surfaced in Virginia, USA. Recently in an affidavit submitted to the court, R&AW deposed that Singh has been traced to New Jersey.

- In 2007, there was a spy scandal involving Bangladesh. A Bangladeshi DGFI agent concealed his nationality, and was known by the name of Diwan Chand Mallik. He was known to have some important documents which were damaging for national security. He joined in 1999 and used to live in East Delhi. A case of cheating and forgery was filed at the Lodhi Colony police station on the basis of a complaint by a senior R&AW official.

In Popular Culture

Unlike the more widely known intelligence services, R&AW gets little attention from the populace, which seems unaware of the existence of such an organisation or even India's internal intelligence agency, the Intelligence Bureau. However, efforts have been made to explain the activities of R&AW in various movies. However, these films are directed to the more serious film-goer. Unlike Hollywood, which has portrayed FBI, CIA, MI6 etc. in various films, Bollywood has been shy to explore the area of espionage, especially R&AW on the silver screen. Excessive secrecy surrounding activities and rare declassification of information are blamed as the main reason behind this.

However there are films from Bollywood which refers to *agents*, *espionage*, *terrorism* etc. but till recently none of them openly mentioned R&AW. One of the earliest Indian films portraying espionage was *Prem Pujari* starring Dev Anand in 1970. In 1973, just after the war with Pakistan came *Hindustan Ki Kasam* (Starring Raaj Kumar, Priya Rajvansh). However, films like *The Hero: Love Story of a Spy* (Starring Sunny Deol, Preity Zinta and Priyanka Chopra), *Aankhen* (1968, Ramanand Sagar Production, Starring Dharmendra, Mala Sinha), *Such a Long Journey* (1998, UK Canada Co-production, Directed by Sturla Gunnarsson, starring Naseeruddin Shah), *16 December* (Starring Milind Soman, Sushant Singh, Dipanita Sharma), *Hindustan Ki Kasam* (1999, starring Ajay Devgan in double role, Amitabh Bachchan),

Asambhav (2004), starring Arjun Rampal as Army Captain and Jammel Khan essaying the role of a fictional R&AW agent Atul Bhatnagar etc. have openly mentioned R&AW and its allied units. Popular Hindi movie *Veer-Zaara* has mentioned the intelligence agency R&AW, when the lead character Veer (portrayed by Shahrukh Khan) was accused by Pakistani police of being an undercover spy for R&AW. In *Mission Istanbul*, model actress Shweta Bhardwaj played the role of Lisa Lobo, a R&AW agent in Istanbul, who helps journalist Vikas Sagar, played by Zayed Khan, in foiling the anti-India terrorist attempts by a terror group. In *Maan Gaye Mughal-e-Azam* Rahul Bose plays a R&AW officer (Arjun Rastogi) who attempts to thwart explosives delivery in the city. In *Chamku* R&AW is shown as undertaking a covert program much in the lines of the *Bourne series* to build up an assassination team.

Apart from Bollywood, the other film industries of India have also cashed in on the patriotic appeal of espionage. Telugu movie star Krishna's film titled *Goodachari No. 1* explores the life of an undercover agent working to thwart ISI activities in India. Cine star Bala Krishna's latest film in the direction of Swarna Subba Rao, titled *Vijayendra Varma* is based on a real life story of a R&AW agent, where he donned the role of the R&AW officer in the film. The Tamil movie *Ottran* casts Arjun Sarja as a R&AW officer. A 1990s Malayalam film *Highway* portrays Suresh Gopi as a R&AW agent investigating a bomb blast. Kamal Hasan in a film titled *Dasavathaaram* and later a dubbed Hindi version titled *Dashavatar* essayed the role of a Telugu (in original film)/ Bengali(in Hindi version) R&AW operative.

The thriving entertainment channels in India have also started to tap into the theme of Intelligence agencies. *Time Bomb 9/11*, a series aired on Zee TV, features Rajeev Khandelwal in the role of a R&AW field officer who attempts to defuse a nuclear bomb set in India, as well as saving the life of the Indian Prime Minister. Zee Bangla also featured a serial named *Mohona* where the chief protagonist is a

R&AW officer. In Anthony Horowitz's book *Crocodile Tears*, reluctant teen spy Alex Rider is assisted multiple times by R&AW agent Rahim.

RESEARCH AND ANALYSIS WING : INDIA'S FOREIGN INTELLIGENCE AGENCY

The Research and Analysis Wing [RAW] is India's foreign intelligence agency. RAW has become an effective instrument of Indian national power, and has assumed a significant role in carrying out India's domestic and foreign policies. RAW has engaged in espionage against Pakistan and other neighboring countries. It has enjoyed the backing of successive Indian governments in these efforts. Working directly under the Prime Minister, the structure and operations of the Research & Analysis Wing are kept secret from Parliament.

Founded in 1968, RAW focused largely on Pakistan. Its formation was initially motivated by reports of Pakistan supplying weapons to Sikh militants, and providing shelter and training to guerrillas in Pakistan. Numerous missions were assigned to RAW upon its creation. These included monitoring political and military developments in neighboring countries that affects Indian national security. Consequently, considerable attention is paid by RAW to Pakistan and China, countries that are traditional rivals of India.

RAW has evolved from its origins as a part of the Intelligence Bureau to develop into India's predominant intelligence organization. In 1968, RAW had 250 agents and a budget of Rs. 2 crore. This has expanded to a 2000 total of an estimated eight to ten thousand agents and a budget that experts place at Rs. 1500 crore, alternately estimated at $145 million. Pakistan has accused the Research and Analysis Wing of sponsoring sabotage in Punjab, where RAW is alleged to have supported the Seraiki movement, providing financial support to promote its activities in Pakistan and organizing an International Seraiki Conference in Delhi in November-December 1993. RAW has an extensive network of agents and anti-government elements within Pakistan, including dissident elements from various sectarian and ethnic groups of Sindh and Punjab. Published reports in Pakistan allege that as many as 35,000 RAW agents entered Pakistan between 1983-93, with 12,000 working in Sindh, 10,000 in Punjab, 8,000 in North West Frontier Province and 5000 in Balochistan.

RAW has a long history of activity in Bangladesh, supporting both secular forces and the area's Hindu minority. The involvement of RAW in East Pakistan is said to date from the 1960s, when RAW supported Mujibur Rahman, leading up to his general election victory in 1970. RAW also provided training and arms to the Bangladeshi freedom fighters known as Mukti Bahini. RAW's aid was instrumental in Bangladesh's gaining independence from Pakistan in 1971.

During the course of its investigation the Jain Commission received testimony on the official Indian support to the various Sri Lankan Tamil armed groups in Tamil Nadu. From 1981, RAW and the Intelligence Bureau established a network of as many as 30 training bases for these groups in India. Centers were also established at the high-security military installation of Chakrata, near Dehra Dun, and in the Ramakrishna Puram area of New Delhi. This clandestine support to the Liberation Tigers of Tamil Eelam (LTTE), some of whom were on the payroll of RAW, was later suspended. Starting in late 1986 the Research and Analysis Wing focused surveillance on the LTTE which was expanding ties with Tamil Nadu separatist groups. Rajiv Gandhi sought to establish good relations with the LTTE, even after the Indian Peace Keeping Force [IPKF] experience in Sri Lanka. But the Indian intelligence community failed to accurately assess the character of the LTTE and its orientation India and its political leaders. The LTTE assassination of Rajiv Gandhi was apparently motivated by fears of a possible re-induction of the Indian Peace Keeping Force (IPKF) in Sri Lanka and a crackdown on the LTTE network in Tamil Nadu.

RAW was heavily criticized in 1999, following the Pakistani incursions at Kargil. Critics accused RAW of failing to provide intelligence that could have prevented the ensuing ten-week conflict that brought India and Pakistan to the brink of full-scale war. While the army has been critical of the lack of information they received, RAW has pointed the finger at the politicians, claiming they had provided all the necessary information. Most Indian officials believe that in order to prevent another such occurrence, communication needs to be increased between the intelligence agencies, which would require structural reform. Most recently, RAW has gained attention for providing the US with intelligence on Al-Qaeda and Taliban targets for the war on terrorism in Afghanistan. Maps and photographs of terrorist training camps in Afghanistan and Pakistan, along with other evidence implicating Osama bin Laden in terrorist attacks, were given to US intelligence officials.

The objectives of RAW include: To monitor the political and military developments in adjoining countries, which have direct bearing on India's national security and in the formulation of its foreign policy. To seek the control and limitation of the supply of military hardware to Pakistan, mostly from European countries, the USA and China.

The chief of the RAW is designated Secretary (Research) in the Cabinet Secretariat, which is part of the Prime Minister's Office (PMO). Most of the position's occupants have been experts on either Pakistan or China. The head of the Research & Analysis Wing (RAW), the external intelligence agency, enjoys greater autonomy of functioning than their counterparts in the UK and US and has the same privileged direct access to the Prime Minister as their UK counterparts. The control of the Cabinet Secretary over the RAW is limited to administrative and financial matters, with very little say in operational and policy matters.

They also have the benefit of training in either US or the UK, and more recently in Israel. The Secretary (R) reports on an administrative basis to the Cabinet Secretary, who reports to the Prime Minister (PM). However, on a daily basis the Secretary (R) reports to the National Security Advisor. Reporting to the Secretary (R) are: Two Special Secretaries and one Special Director of the ARC, the Aviation Research Centre; Four Additional Secretaries, responsible for different geographical regions; A large number (above 40) Joint Secretaries, who are the functional heads of various desks.

The structure of the RAW is a matter of speculation, but brief overviews of the same are present in the public domain. Attached to the HQ of RAW at Lodhi Road, New Delhi are different regional headquarters, which have direct links to overseas stations and are headed by a controlling officer who keeps records of different projects assigned to field officers who are posted abroad. Intelligence is usually collected from a variety of sources by field officers and deputy field officers; it is either pre-processed (vetted) by a senior field officer or by a desk officer. The desk officer then passes the information to the Joint Secretary and then on to the Additional Secretary and from there it is disseminated to the concerned end user. The Director RAW is a member of the JIC Steering Committee and is authorized to brief the Prime Minister should the need arise.

Some officers of the RAW are members of a specialized service, the Research and Analysis Service (RAS), but several officers also serve on deputation from other services. The RAW has sub-organizations like the Aviation Research Center (ARC), the Radio Research Center (RRC) or the Electronics and Technical Service (ETS), which have considerable capacity for technical intelligence gathering. Another important branch under the operational control of the RAW is the Directorate General of Security (DGS). This agency has oversight over organizations like the Special Frontier Force (SFF), the Special Services Bureau (SSB) etc... Liaison with the military is maintained through the Military Intelligence Advisory Group and the Military Advisor to the Director RAW.

Though the RAW is primarily intended for collecting intelligence beyond India's national borders, it has over time come to have a strong presence in all fields of intelligence gathering. The RAW was brought into internal security issues during the Sikkim situation, it played a role in the events of the emergency of 1977-79, it was asked to operate in Punjab to counter-balance the presence of the ISI (and so also in Kashmir), and the RAW has provided the security for the India's nuclear program. Right from its formation in 18 September, 1968, R N Kao, the founding father of RAW, picked up the best men from within government and from outside for RAW. A combination of military, academicians, bureaucrats and policemen was a fine start for RAW which modelled itself on the lines of CIA.

RAW: INDIA'S EXTERNAL INTELLIGENCE AGENCY

India's external intelligence agency, the Research and Analysis Wing (RAW), has long faced allegations of meddling in its neighbors' affairs. Founded in 1968, primarily to counter China's influence, over time it has shifted its focus to India's other traditional rival, Pakistan. RAW and Pakistan's spy agency, the Inter-Services Intelligence (ISI), have been engaged in covert operations against one other for over three decades. The ongoing dispute in Kashmir continues to fuel these clashes, but experts say Afghanistan may be emerging as the new battleground. Islamabad sees India's growing diplomatic initiatives in Afghanistan as a cover for RAW agents working to destabilize Pakistan. It accuses RAW of training and arming separatists in Pakistan's Balochistan Province along the Afghan border. RAW denies these charges, and in turn, accuses the ISI of the July 2008 bombing of the Indian embassy in Kabul.

The History of RAW

Until 1968, the Intelligence Bureau (IB), which is responsible for India's internal intelligence, also handled external intelligence. But after India's miserable performance in a 1962 border war with China, the need for a separate external intelligence agency was clear. During that conflict, "our intelligence failed to detect Chinese build up for the attack," writes Maj. Gen. VK Singh, a retired army officer who did a stint in RAW, in his 2007 book, India's External Intelligence: Secrets of Research and Analysis Wing.

As a result, India established a dedicated external intelligence agency, the Research and Analysis Wing (RAW). Founded mainly to focus on China and Pakistan, over the last forty years the organization has expanded its mandate and is credited with greatly increasing India's influence abroad. Experts say RAW's powers and its role in India's foreign policy have varied under different prime ministers. Successes that RAW claims it contributed to include:

- the creation of Bangladesh in 1971;
- India's growing influence in Afghanistan;
- Sikkim's accession to India in the northeast in 1975;
- the security of India's nuclear program;
- the success of African liberation movements during the Cold War.

The first head of RAW, Rameshwar Nath Kao, who headed the IB's external intelligence division, led the agency until he retired in 1977. Many experts, including officers who worked with him, credit him with RAW's initial successes: India's triumph in the 1971 war with Pakistan, and India's covert assistance to the African National Congress's anti-apartheid struggle in South Africa. "To a large extent, it was Kao who raised RAW to the level of India's premier intelligence agency, with agents in virtually every major embassy and high commission," writes Singh. But the organization has been criticized for its lack of coordination with domestic intelligence and security agencies, weak analytical capabilities, and complete lack of transparency.

The Structure and Function of RAW

Not much is known regarding the structure of RAW, say experts. The organization started with 250 people and about

$400,000. It has since expanded to several thousand personnel, but there is no clear estimate of its staffing or budget, as both remain secret. However, an estimate by the U.S.-based Federation of American Scientists suggests that in 2000, RAW had about eight to ten thousand agents and a budget that experts place at $145 million. Unlike the United States' Central Intelligence Agency (CIA) or Britain's MI6, RAW reports directly to the prime minister instead of the Ministry of Defense. The chief of RAW is designated secretary (research) in the Cabinet Secretariat, which is part of the prime minister's office. Some officers of RAW are members of a specialized service, the Research and Analysis Service, but several officers also serve on deputation from other services such as the Indian Police Service.

RAW had two priorities after its formation, writes B. Raman, a former RAW official, in the 2007 book,The Kaoboys of R&AW: Down Memory Lane. The organization worked to strengthen its capability for intelligence gathering on Pakistan and China and for covert action in East Pakistan (now Bangladesh). Some experts say that RAW's efforts in East Pakistan, which was created from the partition of the Indian state of Bengal and completely separated from the rest of Pakistan, was aimed at fomenting independence sentiment. Over time, RAW's objectives have broadened to include:

- Monitoring the political and military developments in adjoining countries, which have direct bearing on India's national security and in the formulation of its foreign policy.
- Seeking the control and limitation of the supply of military hardware to Pakistan, mostly from European countries, the United States, and China.

Experts disagree on the amount of influence RAW asserts on India's foreign policy. Sumit Ganguly, a professor of political science at Indiana University, says the agency has no influence on foreign policy. However, Dipankar Banerjee, a retired army official and current director of the Institute of Peace and

Conflict Studies, a New Delhi-based think tank, says the head of RAW has direct access to the head of state, to whom he provides input and analysis. From the early days, RAW had a secret liaison relationship with the Mossad, Israel's external intelligence agency. The main purpose was to benefit from Israel's knowledge of West Asia and North Africa, and to learn from its counterterrorism techniques, say experts.

RAW's Role in Bangladesh, Myanmar, and Sri Lanka

RAW played a significant role in the formation of Bangladesh along with the Indian army and other Indian security and intelligence agencies. Besides providing intelligence to policymakers and the army, RAW trained and armed Mukti Bahini, a group of East Pakistanis fighting for the separate state of Bangladesh. Analysts say that RAW also facilitated the northeastern state of Sikkim's accession to India in 1975, and provided military assistance to groups hostile to the pro-China regime in Myanmar, such as the Kachin Independence Army.

But it was the support for the Tamil separatist group, Liberation Tigers of Tamil Eelam (LTTE) in Sri Lanka, that brought RAW much criticism from human rights organizations. RAW helped to train and arm the LTTE in the 1970s, but after the group's terrorist activities grew in the 1980s-including its alliances with separatist groups in the southern Indian state of Tamil Nadu-RAW withdrew this support. In 1987, New Delhi made a pact with the Sri Lankan government to send peacekeeping troops to the island and Indian forces ended up fighting the group RAW had armed. In 1991, Rajiv Gandhi, prime minister of India at the time of the peacekeeping force deployment, was assassinated by an LTTE suicide bomber.

Covert Action in Afghanistan, Pakistan

Since its inception in 1968, RAW has had a close liaison relationship with KHAD, the Afghan intelligence agency, due to the intelligence it has provided RAW on Pakistan. This relationship was further strengthened in the early 1980s when the foundation was laid for a trilateral cooperation involving the RAW, KHAD, and the Soviet KGB. Raman says RAW valued KHAD's cooperation for monitoring the activities of Sikh militants in Pakistan's tribal areas. Sikhs in the Indian state of Punjab were demanding an independent state of Khalistan. According to Raman, Pakistan's ISI set up clandestine camps for training and arming Khalistani recruits in Pakistan's Punjab Province and North West Frontier Province. During this time, the ISI received large sums from Saudi Arabia and the CIA for arming the Afghan mujahadeen against Soviet troops in Afghanistan. "The ISI diverted part of these funds and arms and ammunition to the Khalistani terrorists," alleges Raman.

In retaliation, in the mid-1980s, RAW set up two covert groups of its own, Counter Intelligence Team-X (CIT-X) and Counter Intelligence Team-J (CIT-J), the first targeting Pakistan in general and the second directed at Khalistani groups. The two groups were responsible for carrying out terrorist operations inside Pakistan (*Newsline*), writes Pakistani military expert Ayesha Siddiqa. Indian journalist and associate editor of Frontline magazine, Praveen Swami, writes that a "low-grade but steady campaign of bombings in major Pakistani cities, notably Karachi and Lahore" was carried out. This forced the head of ISI to meet his counterpart in RAW and agree on the rules of engagement as far as Punjab was concerned, writes Siddiqa. The negotiation was brokered by then-Jordanian Crown Prince Hassan bin-Talal, whose wife, Princess Sarvath, is of Pakistani origin. "It was agreed that Pakistan would not carry out activities in the Punjab as long as RAW refrained from creating mayhem and violence inside Pakistan," Siddiqa writes.

In the past, Pakistan also accused RAW of supporting Sindhi nationalists demanding a separate state, as well as Seraikis calling for a partition of Pakistan's Punjab to create a separate Seraiki state. India denies these charges. However, experts point out that India has supported insurgents in

Pakistan's Balochistan, as well as anti-Pakistan forces in Afghanistan. But some experts say India no longer does this. As this Backgrounder explains, Pakistan is suspicious of India's influence in Afghanistan, which it views as a threat to its own interests in the region. Experts say although it is very likely that India has active intelligence gathering in Afghanistan, it is difficult to say whether it is also involved in covert operations.

Relations with the CIA

The CIA assisted in the creation of RAW, says South Asia expert Stephen P. Cohen of the Brookings Institution. However, India's intelligence relations with the CIA started even before the existence of RAW, note experts. After India's war with China in 1962, CIA instructors trained Establishment 22, a "covert organisation raised from among Tibetan refugees in India, to execute deep-penetration terror operations in China," writes Swami. But the CIA's operations with the ISI to fight the Soviets in Afghanistan in the 1980s made RAW very wary.

However, it did not stop RAW from seeking the CIA's assistance in counterterrorism training. Raman writes: "One had one more bizarre example of how international intelligence cooperation works." The CIA trained the officers of the ISI in the use of terrorism against an adversary, and at the same time, he writes, it trained RAW and IB officers "in some of the techniques of countering that terrorism." India's intelligence agencies also feel the lack of an equal relationship with the CIA, say experts. Swami says RAW's grievance is that there is little information they get on Pakistan from the United States; however, Washington expects New Delhi to provide it with intelligence on Afghanistan.

In 1997, Prime Minister I.K. Gujral shut down both the CITs aimed at Pakistan on moral grounds. Before Gujral, Prime Minister P.V. Narasimha Rao had ended RAW's eastern operations in the early 1990s, as part of his efforts to build bridges with China and Myanmar, say analysts.

Successive RAW leaders attempted to gain fresh authorization for deterrent covert operations, but without success, says Swami. Siddiqa writes: "The Indian government probably realized that encouraging covert warfare would not only destabilize bilateral relations but was also dangerous for the peace and stability of the entire region."

Weaknesses in RAW

The intrusion of Pakistan-backed armed forces into the Indian state of Jammu and Kashmir (GlobalSecurity) in 1999 prompted questions about RAW's efficacy. Some analysts saw the conflict as an intelligence failure. However, RAW officials argued they had provided the intelligence but political leadership had failed to act upon it. The Indian government constituted a committee to look into the reasons for the failure and recommend remedial measures. The report of the Kargil review committee was then examined by a group of ministers, established in 2000. The group recommended a formal written charter and pointed out lack of coordination and communication within various intelligence agencies.

Following the review, a new organization was set up-the National Technical Research Organization (NTRO)-modeled on the U.S. National Security Agency-which would be the repository of the nation's technical intelligence-spy satellites, unmanned aerial vehicles (UAVs), and spy planes. The government also decided to create a Defense Intelligence Agency (DIA), whose head would be the adviser to the Chief of Staffs Committee and the defense minister. The DIA was empowered to conduct transborder operations.

However, the shakeup of the intelligence apparatus has not removed the problems that persisted, especially relating to the overlap of agency activities, say experts. Earlier, RAW was the only organization permitted to conduct espionage operations abroad. Now both the IB and DIA have also been given the authority to conduct such operations, writes Singh. There have also been occasional media reports of penetration inside RAW by other agencies, in particular the CIA. Swami writes that RAW is exceptional amongst major spy agencies in maintaining no permanent distinction (*Hindu*) between covert operatives who execute secret tasks, and personnel who must liaise with services such as the CIA or public bodies, such as analysts and area specialists. "As a result, personnel with sensitive operational information are exposed to potentially compromising contacts," he writes.

INDIAN INTELLIGENCE: THE FIDDLING HAS TO STOP...

The evolution of the Indian intelligence community since 1947 has been on the basis of periodic reviews of our enquiries into perceived intelligence failures. After the Sino-Indian war of 1962, a review of the performance of the IB led to the creation of the Directorate-General of Security (DGS). After the Indo-Pakistan war of 1965 and the Mizo revolt of 1966, a review of the performance of the IB led to the decision to divest the IB of the responsibility for the collection of external intelligence and to create the Research & Analysis Wing (R&AW) by bifurcating the IB for this purpose. The DGS, which was previously under the charge of the Director, Intelligence Bureau (DIB), was transferred to the charge of Secretary (R), as the head of the R&AW is known.

A crisis-driven review is retrospective in nature. It looks into the past—what went wrong, why, and how can its recurrence be prevented? A need-driven review is prospective in nature. A review of the performance of the intelligence community before and during the 1999 Kargil conflict by a Special Task Force, headed by Shri G.C.Saxena, former head of the R&AW, led to the creation of the Defence Intelligence Agency as a nodal point for the analysis of all military intelligence, whether collected by the civilian or military intelligence agencies. The idea was that it would work under the supervision of the proposed Chief of the Defence Staff. Since the re-commendation by another Task Force for the creation of this post has not yet been implemented, one understands that the DIA now functions under the Chief of the Integrated Defence Staff.

The review by the Task Force headed by Shri Saxena also led to the creation of the National Technical Research Organisation (NTRO), to focus on the collection of technical intelligence (TECHINT). The Task Force was of the view that the NTRO should handle all future investments in manpower and equipment and future collection efforts and that the existing capabilities of the IB, the R&AW, the DGS and the military intelligence agencies should not be affected, since their existing capabilities played an important role in counter-terrorism. The Task Force was also of the view that the new agency should focus on cyber intelligence and cyber counter-intelligence for which at that time (in 2000), there was no significant capability in the existing intelligence agencies.

One understands that this recommendation was modified during implementation. Instead of letting the R&AW and the DGS maintain their existing capabilities, there was a bifurcation of these capabilities in order to transfer some of them to the NTRO. Instead of undertaking a crash programme for the development of a capability for cyber intelligence and cyber counter-intelligence, it started performing some of the tasks, which were already being performed by the R&AW and the DGS. The obvious result: an emaciated DGS and a weakening of our capabilities for the collection of TECHINT regarding China and terrorism. Instead of creating capabilities, which did not exist before 2000, there was a highly disputed partition of the existing intelligence assets.

In the past, the highest priority was to the collection of intelligence about State actors, particularly about State adversaries. Now, enhanced priority is given to the collection of intelligence about non-State adversaries such as terrorist organizations.

These were crisis-driven reviews undertaken after perceived intelligence failures in order to identify deficiencies and act to remove them. Since 1947, India has never had a need-driven review of our intelligence assets and capabilities. A crisis-driven review is retrospective in nature. It looks into the past—what went wrong, why, and how can its recurrence be prevented? A need-driven review is prospective in nature. It looks into the likely needs of the future and creates assets and capabilities to be able to meet those needs as and when they arise.

In other countries such as the US, one has crisis-driven reviews as well as need-driven reviews. A need-driven review is undertaken every time a new President or Prime Minister takes office. Unless one has a clear idea of the likely future intelligence needs in the short, medium and long-terms, one cannot build up human and other resources, which would be in a position to meet those needs. It is high time we have a need-based review of our intelligence assets and capabilities and make such reviews a regular feature whenever a new Prime Minister takes over. Reviews of performance and capabilities should not wait for disasters and crises before they are undertaken.

Intelligence priorities have undergone considerable changes during the last decade. In the past, the highest priority was to the collection of intelligence about State actors, particularly about State adversaries. Now, enhanced priority is given to the collection of intelligence about non-State adversaries such as terrorist organizations, trans-national crime mafias, narcotics smugglers, money-launderers etc. Intelligence agencies all over the world have been facing difficulty in upgrading their capabilities for the collection of intelligence about non-State adversaries.

The ability to collect intelligence—whether about a State or a non-State adversary—depends on one's ability to penetrate. It is easier to penetrate a State than a non-State actor. The conventional tradecraft and techniques of intelligence collection, which served us well for penetrating a State actor, are not adequate for the penetration of a non-State actor. The state of our intelligence agencies and the way they have evolved over the years have not paid attention to the requirements of this transition. As the non-State actors become more and more unconventional in their reflexes and responses, the intelligence agencies responsible for monitoring and countering them cannot continue to be conventional in their reflexes and responses.

The IB has evolved into a hotch-potch agency handling collection of intelligence relating to law and order and internal security, performance of physical security and immigration control tasks, counter-intelligence and networking with the police and intelligence set-ups of different States. We have to set up a new agency focusing on the collection of intelligence about non-State actors through human and technical penetration.

The R&AW too has evolved into a hotch-potch agency handling collection of external intelligence relating to State as well as non-State adversaries and networking with foreign intelligence agencies. At a time when terrorism has become global in dimension and reach, the R&AW's counter-terrorism capabilities are hardly global. At a time when the global terrorists are fast mastering the use of the Internet, mobile telephones and other scientific gadgets, the R&AW is yet to acquire a similar mastery of net-centric counter-terrorism and the use of advances in science and technology in counter-terrorism.

The dangers of conventional wars with State adversaries have not disappeared. The Indian State is better prepared and better endowed today than it was in the past to counter State adversaries, but its ability to counter non-State adversaries and their unconventional wars is inadequate as seen from the spread of ideological terrorism across the tribal belt in Central India and the unextinguished prairie fire of jihadi terrorism across India as a whole. We have had successes in our fight against pan-Islamic jihadi terrorism with trans-national linkages, but the successes have not yet been significant enough to dent their strength and motivation.

The threats to our internal security from non-State actors will keep us preoccupied in the short and medium terms. These threats have acquired new dimensions in the form of threats to maritime trade and coastal establishments, energy security and critical infrastructure and terrorism involving the likely use of weapons of mass destruction material. If the intelligence agencies have to play their due role in effectively preventing these threats from materializing, they have to develop new tradecrafts and new techniques for the penetration of non-State actors through human and technical moles for the collection of intelligence. This is a specialized and full-time task which neither the IB nor the R&AW, as they are constituted today, would be able to perform adequately.

We have to set up a new agency focusing on the collection of intelligence about non-State actors through human and technical penetration. It should have the powers to operate everywhere–inside India or in the neighbouring countries or elsewhere–from where threats to our internal security from non-State actors could arise. It has to have a mix of civilian and military experts, and scientific and technical personnel. Since collection of cyber intelligence to facilitate net-centric counter-terrorism would be one of its essential tasks, it should also tap the private IT sector for assistance and co-operation.

So long as our disputes and differences with Pakistan and China remain, we have to maintain a strong intelligence capability–human as well as technical–with regard to likely threats from them. How should be maintain and further develop the existing capabilities with regard to State adversaries, while creating new capabilities with regard to non-State actors? That should be the question before our national security managers. The R&AW and the military intelligence Directorates-General would continue to be the driving force for this purpose. The time has come to have a second look at the present policy of the R&AW claiming a monopoly in the field of external intelligence and discouraging any enhanced role for the military-intelligence Directorates-

General in this regard. The days of the intelligence Empire have to go. The intelligence empire has to be replaced by the intelligence community working jointly in the national interest.

Our capability with regard to Pakistan is good, but not good enough as one saw in 1999. Our capability with regard to China is better than it was in 1962, but is not as good as China's capability with regard to India. In promoting a policy of renewed friendship and détente with India, China has not downsized the India-centric capabilities, which it had built up in the days of its confrontation with India. On the contrary, it has continued to strengthen them. India, on the other hand, has allowed the good vibrations with regard to the improving relations with China to induce once again a feeling of complacency and somnolence. Nothing illustrates this more dramatically than the way we have allowed, since 2000, a gradual attrition of the China-dedicated capabilities of the DGS. Counter-intelligence continues to be a weak point in our intelligence set-up. The regularity with which penetrations take place in sensitive departments and intelligence agencies is a disturbing testimony to this. A review and revamping of our counter-intelligence capabilities is an urgent need of the hour. In India, there is hardly any understanding outside the intelligence community of the way the intelligence agencies ought to function and the way they actually function. The intelligence agencies prefer it that way.

Concepts regarding intelligence management have been changing rapidly across the world just as concepts regarding national security management, defence management, economic management and business management have been changing. These concepts relate to factors such as open vs secret intelligence, operations vs analysis, secrecy in operational matters vs transparency in administrative matters, accountability to the parliament and the public vs safeguarding the needs of operational secrecy.

Unfortunately, the winds of change sweeping across the intelligence communities of other countries have left us untouched so far. Indian intelligence agencies continue to lead the life of a frog in the well. Many questions, which should have been posed years ago, still remain to be posed: Should it be made clear to the intelligence agencies and their officers that their performance would be judged by the quantum and value of the secret intelligence provided by them and that they need not report open information? Should the annual audit reports of the accounts of the intelligence agencies by the officers of the Comptroller and Auditor-General of India with their objections and actions taken thereon be made available to the Estimates and Public Accounts Committees of the Parliament? Should there be a dedicated intelligence oversight committee of the parliament to look into aspects such as the quality of the human resources in our intelligence community, the methods of their recruitment and training, promotion policies, the value of the produce from the consumers' point of view and its cost effectiveness? How can we meet the need for a constant weeding-out of unsuitable officers ? We should show the courage and readiness to pose these questions and find answers suited to our needs instead of aping the rest of the world.

In India, there is hardly any understanding outside the intelligence community of the way the intelligence agencies ought to function and the way they actually function. The intelligence agencies prefer it that way. The agencies try to create an impression as if intelligence is a highly esoteric profession, which non-professionals would not be able to understand. They should, therefore, keep out of it. This attitude has to change.

What our policy-makers have been doing till now is not revamping our intelligence capabilities, but fiddling with them. The fiddling has to stop and genuine revamping has to start.

SYNOPSIS OF RESEARCH AND ANALYSIS WING

The Research and Analysis Wing (R&AW) is India's primary external intelligence agency. It was formed in September 1968, after it became apparent that the newly independent Republic of India lacked a credible external intelligence gathering agency after after the Indo-China War of 1962 and the Indo-Pakistani War of 1965. Its primary function is the collection of external intelligence, counter-terrorism, sabotage, counter-sabotage and covert external operations; in addition, it is responsible for obtaining and analysing information about foreign governments, corporations and individuals, in order to assess and advise Indian foreign policymakers. Until the creation of RAW, the Intelligence Bureau [IB] handled both internal and external intelligence.

Formation & History

Following an intelligence failure during the 1965 Sino-Indian Border War, then Prime Minister Jawaharlal Nehru order a dedicated foreign intelligence agency to be established, which became the Research and Analysis Wing. Prior to its inception, intelligence collection was primarily the responsibility of the Intelligence Bureau, an incorporated vestige of the Colonial Raj. In 1933, sensing the political turmoil which eventually led to the Second World War, the Intelligence Bureau's responsibilities were increased to include the collection of border intelligence along Unified India. In 1947, after independence, Sanjeevi Pillaii took over as the first Indian Director of the IB. Having been depleted of trained manpower by the exit of the British, Pillaii attempted to run the bureau on MI5 lines. Following the Indo-Pakistani War of 1965, in which the Army was alerted to cross-border infiltration by civilian intelligence, the Indian Chief of Army Staff General Jayantha Nath Chaudhury called for a more cohesive intelligence-gathering.

Around the end of 1966, the concept of a separate foreign intelligence agency began to assume concrete shape. In 1968, after Indira Gandhi had taken over, it was decided that a full-fledged second security service was required. R. N. Kao, then deputy director of the Intelligence Bureau, submitted a blueprint for the new agency and was appointed as the Chief of India's first foreign intelligence agency. The R&AW was given the responsibility of strategic external intelligence, human as also technical, as well as concurrent responsibility together with the Directorate-General of Military Intelligence for tactical trans-border military intelligence up to a certain depth across the LOC and the international border.

The RAW was started as a wing of the main Intelligence Bureau with roughly 250 employees and an annual budget of Rs 2 crore (approximately $450,000) four decades ago. In the early seventies, its annual budget had risen to Rs. 30 crores while its personnel numbered several thousand. The Joint Intelligence Committee (JIC), under the Cabinet Secretariat, is responsible for co-ordinating and analysing intelligence activities between the RAW, the Intelligence Bureau and the Defense Intelligence Agency (DIA). In practice, however, the effectiveness of the JIC has been varied. With the establishment of the National Security Council in 1999, the role of the JIC has been merged with the NSC. The RAW's legal status is unusual, in that it is not an "Agency", but a "Wing" of the Cabinet Secretariat. Hence, R&AW is not answerable to the Parliament of India on any issue, which keeps it out of reach of the *Right to Information Act*.

In 1971, R.N. Kao, director-founder of the RAW, had persuaded the Government to set up the Aviation Research Centre (ARC). The ARC's mandate was aerial reconnaissance and replaced the Indian Air Force's former reconnaissance aircraft and by the mid-70s. R&AW, through the ARC, had high quality aerial pictures of the installations along the Chinese and Pakistani borders. In 2008-09, the Governmen of India was rumoured to have added another intelligence agency dedicated to collection of technical intelligence. The National Technical Facilities Organisation (NTFO), also known as National Technical Research Organisation (NTRO), is believed to be functioning under R&AW, although it remains autonomous to some measure. It is believed to be dealing with technological espionage, and research on imagery and communications using various platforms.

Objectives

The objectives of the R&AW at present are:

- To monitor political and military developments in adjacent countries, including China and Pakistan, which have a direct or indirect bearing upon India's national security and upon the formulation of its foreign policy; Technical and Technological espionage under the auspices of the National Technical Facilities Organisation (NTFO).

- To make the control and limitation of the supply of military hardware to Pakistan, mostly from European countries, the USA and China, a priority.
- To gather intelligence on leadership, capabilities and organization of various insurgency groups operating in adjacent states that pose a national security or integrity threat, and to thwart these using covert operations, assassinations, sabotage, indirect political coercion and exo-agent and interagent collusion where possible.
- To further geopolitical goals, encourage a strategic balance and evince a deterrence of external collusion with domestic insurgency groups by establishing working relationships with secessionist agencies abroad.
- To provide security for India's nuclear program.

Organization

The structure of the RAW is a matter of speculation, but brief overviews of the same are present in the public domain. Attached to the HQ of RAW at Lodhi Road, New Delhi are different regional headquarters, which have direct links to overseas stations and are headed by a controlling officer who keeps records of different projects assigned to field officers who are posted abroad. Intelligence is usually collected from a variety of sources by field officers and deputy field officers; it is either pre-processed (vetted) by a senior field officer or by a desk officer. The desk officer then passes the information to the Joint Secretary and then on to the Additional Secretary and from there it is disseminated to the concerned end user. The Director RAW is a member of the JIC Steering Committee and is authorized to brief the Prime Minister should the need arise.

The chief of the RAW is designated Secretary (Research) in the Cabinet Secretariat, which is part of the Prime Minister's Office (PMO). Most of the position's occupants have been experts on either Pakistan or China. The head of the Research & Analysis Wing (RAW), the external intelligence agency, enjoys greater autonomy of functioning than their counterparts in the UK and US and has the same privileged direct access to the Prime Minister as their UK counterparts. The control of the Cabinet Secretary over the RAW is limited to administrative and financial matters, with very little say in operational and policy matters. They also have the benefit of training in either US or the UK, and more recently in Israel. The Secretary (R) reports on an administrative basis to the Cabinet Secretary, who reports to the Prime Minister (PM). However, on a daily basis the Secretary (R) reports to the National Security Advisor.

An Additional Director is responsible for the Office of Special Operations and intelligence collected from different countries processed by large number of Joint Secretaries. Reporting to the Secretary (R) are: Two Special Secretaries and one Special Director of the ARC, the Aviation Research Centre; Four Additional Secretaries, responsible for different geographical regions; A large number (above 40) Joint Secretaries, who are the functional heads of various desks. Another important branch under the operational control of the RAW is the Directorate General of Security (DGS). This agency has oversight over organizations like the Special Frontier Force (SFF), the Special Services Bureau (SSB) &c. Liaison with the military is maintained through the Military Intelligence Advisory Group and the Military Advisor to the Director RAW.

Recruitment

Initially, the R&AW relied primarily on trained intelligence officers who were recruited directly. These belonged to the external wing of the Intelligence Bureau. In times of great expansion, many candidates were taken from the military, police and other services. Later, the agency began directly recruiting graduates from universities. Today, R&AW has its own service cadre, the Research and Analysis Service (RAS) to absorb talent. Recruitment is mostly by deputation from the Armed Forces or Civil Service Officers. The Civil and Defense Service Officers permanently resign their cadre and join the Research and Analysis Service (RAS). However, according to recent reports, officers can return to their parent cadre after serving a specific period in the agency if they wish to. Some officers of the RAW are members of a specialized service, the Research and Analysis Service (RAS), but several officers also serve on deputation from other services. The RAW has sub-organizations like the Aviation Research Center (ARC), the Radio Research Center (RRC) or the Electronics and Technical Service (ETS), which have considerable capacity for technical intelligence gathering.

Operations

Numerous missions were assigned to RAW upon its creation. These included monitoring political and military developments in neighboring countries that affects Indian national security. Consequently, considerable attention is paid by RAW to Pakistan and China, countries that are traditional rivals of India. RAW has evolved from its origins as a part of the Intelligence Bureau to develop into India's predominant intelligence organization.

Pakistan has 'accused' the Research and Analysis Wing of sponsoring sabotage in Punjab, where RAW is alleged to have supported the Seraiki movement, providing financial support to promote its activities in Pakistan and organizing an International Seraiki Conference in Delhi in November-December 1993. RAW has an extensive network of agents and anti-government elements within Pakistan, including dissident elements from various sectarian and ethnic groups of Sindh and Punjab. Published reports in Pakistan allege that as many as 35,000 RAW agents entered Pakistan between 1983-93, with 12,000 working in Sindh, 10,000 in Punjab, 8,000 in North West Frontier Province and 5000 in Balochistan. The RAW also provided training and arms to the Bangladeshi freedom fighters known as the 'Mukti Bahini' in the Indo-Pak War of 1971. The RAW's aid was instrumental in the creation and liberation of Bangladesh in 1971.

During the course of its investigation the Jain Commission received testimony on the official Indian support to the various Sri Lankan Tamil armed groups in Tamil Nadu. From 1981, RAW and the Intelligence Bureau established a network of as many as 30 training bases for these groups in India. Centers were also established at the high-security military installation of Chakrata, near Dehra Dun, and in the Ramakrishna Puram area of New Delhi. This clandestine support to the Liberation Tigers of Tamil Eelam (LTTE), some of whom were on the payroll of RAW, was later suspended.

Starting in late 1986 the Research and Analysis Wing focused surveillance on the LTTE which was expanding ties with Tamil Nadu separatist groups. Rajiv Gandhi sought to establish good relations with the LTTE, even after the Indian Peace Keeping Force [IPKF] experience in Sri Lanka. But the Indian intelligence community failed to accurately assess the character of the LTTE and its orientation towards India and its political leaders. The LTTE assassination of Rajiv Gandhi was apparently motivated by fears of a possible re-induction of the Indian Peace Keeping Force (IPKF) in Sri Lanka and a crackdown on the LTTE network in Tamil Nadu. The RAW was heavily criticized in 1999, following the Pakistani incursions at Kargil. Critics accused RAW of failing to provide intelligence that could have prevented the ensuing ten-week conflict that brought India and Pakistan to the brink of full-scale war. While the army has been critical of the lack of information they received, RAW has pointed the finger at the politicians, claiming they had provided all the necessary information. Most Indian officials believe that in order to prevent another such occurrence, communication needs to be increased between the intelligence agencies, which would require structural reform.

Amalgamation of Sikkim: Bordered by Tibet, Nepal, Bhutan and West Bengal in the Eastern Himalayas, Sikkim was ruled by a Maharaja. The Indian Government had recognized the title of Chogyal (Dharma Raja) for the Maharaja of Sikkim. In 1972, the RAW was authorized to install a pro-Indian democratic government there, concomitant of which, in less than three years, Sikkim became the 22nd State of the Indian Union, on April 26, 1975.

Operation Kaktus: In November 1988, the People's Liberation Organisation of Tamil Eelam (PLOTE), composed of about 200 Tamil secessionist rebels, invaded Maldives. At the request of the president of Maldives, Maumoon Abdul, the Indian Armed Forces, with assistance from R&AW, launched a military campaign to throw the mercenaries out of Maldives. On the night of November 3, 1988, the Indian Air Force airlifted the 6th parachute battalion of the Parachute Regiment from Agra and flew them over 2,000 km to Maldives. The Indian paratroopers landed at Hulule and restored the Government rule at Malýÿ within hours. The operation, labelled Operation Kakus, also involved the Indian Navy. Swift operation by the military and precise intelligence by RAW quelled the insurgency.

Operation 'Chanakya': This was the R&AW operation in the Kashmir region to infiltrate various ISI-backed Kashmiri separatist groups and restore peace in the Kashmir valley. R&AW operatives infiltrated the area, collected military intelligence, and provided evidence about ISI's involvement in training and funding Kashmiri separatist groups. The R&AW was successful at: i) unearthing the links between the ISI and the separatist groups; and ii) in infiltrating and neutralizing the militancy in the Kashmir valley. The RAW is also credited for creating a split in the Hizb-ul-Mujahideen. Operation 'Chanakya' also marked the creation of pro-Indian groups in Kashmir like the Ikhwan-ul-Muslimeen, Muslim Mujahideen etc. These counter-insurgencies consist of ex-militants and relatives of those slain in the conflict. Ikhwan-ul-Muslimeen leader Kokka Parrey was later himself assassinated by separatists.

The Northern Alliance in Afghanistan: After the rise of Pakistan and American-backed Taliban in Afghanistan during the Soviet war, India decided to side with the Northern Alliance and the Soviet Union. By 1996, the R&AW had built a military hospital at the Farkhor Air Base and used the airport to repair and operate the Northern Alliance's aerial support. The relationship was further cemented in the 2001 Afgan war. India supplied the Northern Alliance high altitude warfare equipment worth around $810 million, and the R&AW was also able to determine the extent of the Kunduz airlift.

Operation Leech: Surrounded by the Arakans and dense forest, Burma/Myanmar had always been a worrisome point for Indian intelligence. As the major player in the area, India sought to promote democracy and install friendly puppet governments in the region. To these ends, it is alleged that the RAW cultivated Burmese rebel groups and pro-democracy coalitions, in particular the Kachin Independence Army (KIA). India allowed the KIA to carry limited trade in jade and precious stones using Indian territory as a conduit and later supplied them weapons. It is further alleged that the KIA chief Maran Brang Seng met RAW officials in Delhi twice. However, after it became apparent that the KIA became the main source of training and weapons for northeastern rebel groups, the RAW initiated a campaing of assassination of KIA leaders that included six top leaders, including the military wing chief of National Unity Party of the Arakans (NUPA), Khaing Raza, and the arrest and termination of several other Arakanese guerillas.

Special Operations in Punjab: In the mid 1980's, the R&AW set up two covert groups, Counterintelligence Team-X(CIT-X) and Counterintelligence Team-J(CIT-J), the first directed at Pakistan and the second at Khalistani groups. Rabinder Singh, an R&AW double agent who defected to the United States in 2004, helped run CIT-J in its early years. Both these covert groups used the services of cross-border traffickers to ferry weapons and funds across the border, much as their ISI counterparts were doing. According to former R&AW official and noted security analyst B. Raman, the Indian counter-campaign yielded results. "The role of our cover action capability in putting an end to the ISI's interference in Punjab", he wrote in 2002, "by making such interference prohibitively costly is little known and understood." The 'War on Terror': Although RAW's contribution to the War on Terror is highly classified, the organization gained some attention in the Western media after claims that it was assisting the United States by providing intelligence on Al-Qaeda and Taliban targets for the war on terrorism in Afghanistan. Maps and photographs of terrorist training camps in Afghanistan and Pakistan, along with other evidence implicating Osama bin Laden in terrorist attacks, were given to US intelligence officials. R&AW's role in the War on Terror may increase as US intelligence has indicated that it sees R&AW as a more reliable ally than Pakistani intelligence. It has further come to light that a timely tip-off by R&AW helped foil a third assassination plot against Pakistan's former President, General Pervez Musharraf.

Controversies

The main controversies which have plagued the R&AW in recent years are over bureaucratization of the system, favoritism in promotions, ego clashes and inter-departmental rivalry. R&AW also suffers from ethnic and representative imbalances in the officer level. In 2006, Indian magazine Outlook reported that although India has a Muslim minority numbering around 160 million, not a single high level muslim officer existed in R&AW. Noted security analyst and former Additional Secretary B.Raman has criticised the agency for its asymmetric growth and has sought to summarize its abilities in the following: "while being strong in its capability for covert action it is weak in its capability for intelligence collection, analysis and assessment. Strong in low and medium-grade intelligence, relatively weak in high-grade intelligence. Strong in technical intelligence, weak in human intelligence. Strong in collation, weak in analysis. Strong in investigation, weak in prevention. Strong in crisis management, weak in crisis prevention."

In September 2007, R&AW was involved in a controversy due to a high profile Central Bureau of Investigation Task

Force raid at the residence of Major General (retired) V K Singh, a retired Joint Secretary of R&AW who has recently written a book on R&AW where it was alleged that political interference and corruption in the intelligence agency has made it vulnerable to defections. A case under the Official Secrets Act has also been filed against V K Singh. Another controversy erupted for the agency when a senior technical officer was arrested by the CBI on graft charges, on February 4, 2009. The scientist, a Director level employee, worked in the division that granted export licenses to companies dealing in sensitive items, including defence-related equipment. He was accused of demanding and accepting a bribe of Rs.1 lakh from a Chennai based manufacturer for obtaining an export license.

In June 2004, the spy scandal involving former Joint Secretary and head of R&AW's South East Asia department Rabinder Singh's defection to the United States seriously tarnished the image of the organization as an effective agency. The RAW had already become suspicious about his movements and he was put under physical and telephone surveillance following the mistrust. He was confronted by Counter Intelligence officials on 19 April 2004, Despite all precautions, Rabinder Singh managed to defect with 'sensitive files' he had allegedly removed from R&AW's headquarters in south New Delhi. The embarrassing fiasco and major national security failure was attributed to weak surveillance, shoddy investigation and lack of coordination between the Counter-Intelligence and Security (CIS), the IB and the R&AW. Recently in an affidavit submitted to the court, R&AW deposed that Singh has been traced to and put under surveillance in New Jersey.

In 2007, a spy scandal involving a Bangladeshi DGFI agent and known by the name of Diwan Chand Mallik was brought to light when he was known to have known posessed some important documents damaging to national security. A case of forgery was filed at the Lodhi Colony police station against the individual on the basis of a complaint by a senior R&AW official, however he was failed to be taken into custody.

R.A.W.: AN INSTRUMENT OF INDIAN IMPERIALISM

India's intelligence agency Research and Analysis Wing (R.A.W.), created in 1968, has assumed a significant status in the formulation of the country's domestic and foreign policies, particularly the latter. Working directly under the prime minister, it has over the years become an effective instrument of India's national power. In consonance with Kautilya's precepts, R.A.W.'s espionage doctrine is based on the principle of waging a continuous series of battles of intrigues and secret wars. (Kautilya, or more popularly, Chanakya, was an ancient Indian political theorist.)

Since its creation, R.A.W. has been a vital, though unobtrusive, actor in the Indian policy-making apparatus. But it is the massive international dimensions of R.A.W. operations that merit a closer examination. To the credit of this organization, it has in a very short span of time mastered the art of spy warfare. Credit must go to Indira Gandhi who in the late 1970's gave it a changed and much more dynamic role. To suit her much publicized Indira Doctrine (India Doctrine), Gandhi specifically asked R.A.W. to create a powerful organ within the organization that could undertake covert operations in neighboring countries. It is this capability that makes R.A.W. a more fearsome agency than the superior K.G.B., C.I.A., M.I.6, B.N.D., or Mossad.

Its internal role is confined only to monitoring events that have a bearing on the external threat. R.A.W.'s boss works directly under the prime minister. An Additional secretary to the government of India, under the director of R.A.W., is responsible for the Office of Special Operations, intelligence collected from different countries, internal security (under the director general of security), the electronic/technical section, and general administration. The additional secretary as well as the director general of security is also under the director of R.A.W. The director of security has two important sections: the Aviation Research Center and the Special Services Bureau. The joint director has specified desks with different regional divisions/areas (countries): area one, Pakistan; area two, China and Southeast Asia; area three, the Middle East and Africa; and area four, other countries. The Aviation Research Center (A.R.C.) is responsible for interception, monitoring and jamming of a target country's communication systems. It has the most sophisticated electronic equipment and also a substantial number of aircraft equipped with state-of-the-art eavesdropping devices. A.R.C. was strengthened in mid-1987 by the addition of three new aircraft, all Gulf Stream-3s. These aircraft can reportedly fly at an altitude of 52,000 feet and have an operating range of 5,000 kilometers. A.R.C. also controls a number of radar stations located close to India's borders. Its aircraft also carry out oblique reconnaissance, along the border with Bangladesh, China, Nepal, and Pakistan.

Having been given virtual carte blanche to conduct destabilization operations in neighboring countries inimical to India, R.A.W. seriously undertook restructuring of its organization accordingly. R.A.W. was given a list of seven countries—Bangladesh, Sri Lanka, Nepal, Sikkim, Bhutan, Pakistan, and Maldives—that India considered its principal regional protagonists. It very soon systematically and brilliantly crafted covert operations in all these countries to coerce, destabilize, and subvert them in consonance with the foreign policy objectives of the Indian government.

R.A.W.'s operations against the regional countries were conducted with great professional skill and expertise. Central to the operations was the establishment of a huge network inside the target countries.

It used and targeted political dissent, ethnic divisions, economic backwardness, and criminal elements within these states to foment subversion, terrorism, and sabotage. Having thus created conducive environments, R.A.W. stage-managed future events in these countries in such a way that military intervention appears a natural concomitant of the events. In most cases, R.A.W.'s hand remained hidden, but more often than not target countries soon began unearthing this "hidden hand." A brief expose of R.A.W.'s operations in neighboring countries, "Open Secrets: India's Intelligence Unveiled " by M. K. Dhar (Manas Publications, New Delhi, 2005), revealed the full expanse of its regional ambitions to suit the India Doctrine.

Bangladesh

Indian intelligence agencies were involved in erstwhile East Pakistan, now Bangladesh, beginning in the early 1960's. Its operatives were in touch with Sheikh Mujib for quite some time. Sheikh Mujib went to Agartala in 1965. The famous Agartala case was unearthed in 1967. In fact, the main purpose of raising R.A.W. in 1968 was to organize covert operations in Bangladesh. As early as 1968, R.A.W. was given a green light to begin mobilizing all its resources for the impending surgical intervention in erstwhile East Pakistan. When in July 1971 General Manekshaw told Prime Minister Indira Gandhi that the army would not be ready until December to intervene in Bangladesh, she quickly turned to R.A.W. for help. R.A.W. was ready. Its officers used Bengali refugees to set up the guerilla force Mukti Bahini. Using this outfit as a cover, the Indian military sneaked deep into Bangladesh. The story of Mukti Bahini and R.A.W.'s role in its creation and training is now well known. R.A.W. never concealed its Bangladesh operations.

The creation of Bangladesh was masterminded by R.A.W. in complicity with the K.G.B. under the covert clauses of the Indo-Soviet Treaty of Friendship and Cooperation (adopted as the 25-Year Indo-Bangladesh Treaty of Friendship and Cooperation in 1972).

R.A.W. retained a keen interest in Bangladesh even after its independence. Subramaniam Swamy, Janata Dal member of Parliament, a close associate of Morarji Desai, said that Rameswar Nath Kao, former chief of R.A.W., and Shankaran Nair were upset about Sheikh Mujib's assassination and chalked a plot to kill Gen. Ziaur Rahman. However, when Desai came to power in 1977 he was indignant at R.A.W.'s role in Bangladesh and ordered operations in Bangladesh to be called off; but by then R.A.W. had already gone too far. General Zia continued in power for quite some time but was assassinated after Indira Gandhi returned to power, though she denied involvement in his assassination (*Weekly Sunday*, Calcutta, Sept. 18, 1988).

R.A.W. was involved in training of Chakma tribes and Shanti Bahini, who carried out subversive activities in Bangladesh. It also unleashed a well-organized plan of psychological warfare, created polarization among the armed forces, propagated false allegations of the use of Bangladesh territory by Pakistan's Inter-Services Intelligence agency, created dissension among the political parties and religious sects, controlled the media, denied the use of river waters, and propped up a host of disputes in order to keep Bangladesh under constant political and socio-economic pressure.

Sikkim and Bhutan

Sikkim was the easiest and most docile prey for R.A.W. Indira Gandhi annexed the Kingdom of Sikkim in the mid-1970's. The deposed King Chogyal Tenzig Wangehuck was closely followed by R.A.W.'s agents until his death in 1992.

Bhutan, like Nepal and Sikkim, is a land-locked country totally dependent on India. R.A.W. developed links with members of the royal family as well as top bureaucrats to implements its policies. It cultivated agents from among Nepalese settlers and put itself in a position to create difficulties for the government of Bhutan. In fact, the king of Bhutan has been reduced to the position of merely acquiescing to New Delhi's decisions and goes by its dictates in the international arena.

Sri Lanka

Post-independence Sri Lanka, despite having a multi-sectoral population, was a peaceful country until 1971 and was following an independent foreign policy. During the 1971 Indo-Pakistan war, despite heavy pressure from India, Sri Lanka allowed Pakistan's civil and military aircraft and ships to stage through its air and seaports with unhindered refueling facilities. It had also permitted Israel to establish a nominal intelligence presence and permitted the installation of a high-powered transmitter by Voice of America, which was resented by India. It was because of these "irritants" that Indira Gandhi planned to bring Sri Lanka into the fold of the so-called Indira Doctrine (India Doctrine). Kao was told by Gandhi to repeat their Bangladesh success. R.A.W. went looking for militants it could train to destabilize the regime. Camps were set up in Tamil Nadu and old R.A.W. guerrilla trainers were dug out of retirement. R.A.W. began arming the Tamil Tigers and training them at centers such as Gunda and Gorakhpur. As a sequel to this ploy, Sri Lanka was forced into the Indian power web when the Indo-Sri Lanka Accord of 1987 was singed and the Indian Peacekeeping Force landed in Sri Lanka.

The Ministry of External Affairs was upset at R.A.W.'s role in Sri Lanka as they felt that R.A.W. was continuing negotiations with Tamil Tiger leader Parabhakaran in contravention to the Indian government's foreign policy. According to R. Swaminathan, (former special secretary of R.A.W.) it was this outfit that was used as the intermediary between Rajib Gandhi and Tamil leader Parabhakaran. Former Indian high commissioner in Sri Lanka J. N. Dixit even accused R.A.W. of having given 10 million rupees to the L.T.T.E. (Liberation Tigers of Tamil Eelam). At a later stage, R.A.W. built up the E.P.R.L.F. (Eelam People's Revolutionary Liberation Front) and E.N.D.L.F. (Eelam National Democratic Liberation Front) to fight against the L.T.T.E., which made the situation in Sri Lanka highly volatile and uncertain later on.

Maldives

Under a well-orchestrated R.A.W. plan, on Nov. 30, 1988, a 300-to 400-strong well-trained force of mercenaries armed with automatic weapons, initially said to be of unknown origin, infiltrated in boats and stormed the capital of Maldives. They resorted to indiscriminate shooting and took high-level government officials hostage. At the Presidential Palace, the small contingent of loyal national guards offered stiff resistance, which enabled President Maumoon Abdul Gayoom to move to a safe place where he issued urgent appeals for help from India, Pakistan, Sri Lanka, Britain, and the United States.

Indian Prime Minister Rajiv Gandhi reacted promptly and about 1,600 combat troops belonging to the 50th Independent Para-Brigade in conjunction with Indian naval units landed at Male, the capital of Maldives, under the code name Operation Cactus. A number of Indian air force transport aircraft, escorted by fighters, were used for landing personnel, heavy equipment, and supplies. Within hours of landing, Indian troops flushed out the attackers from the streets and hideouts. Some of them surrendered to Indian troops, and many were captured by Indian naval units while trying to escape with their hostages in a Maldivian ship, Progress Light. Most of the 30 hostages, including Ahmed Majtaba, Maldives' minister of transport, were released. The Indian government announced the success of Operation Cactus and complimented the armed forces for a good job done.

The Indian defense minister, while addressing air force personnel at Bangalore, claimed that the country's prestige had been raised because of the peace-keeping role played by Indian forces in Maldives. The international community in general and South Asian states in particular, however, viewed with suspicion the over-all concept and motives of the operation. The Western media described it as a display by India of its newly acquired military muscle and its growing role as a regional police force. Although the apparent identification of two Maldivian nationals among the mercenaries, at face value, link it with previous such attempts, other converging factors indicative of external involvement could hardly be ignored. That the mercenaries sailed from Manar and Kankasanturai in Sri Lanka, which were in complete control of the Indian Peacekeeping Force, and the timing and speed of India's intervention proved its involvement beyond any doubt.

Nepal

Since the partition of the subcontinent, India has openly meddled in Nepal's internal affairs by contriving internal strife and conflicts through R.A.W. to destabilize the successive legitimate governments and prop up puppet regimes that would be more amenable to Indian machinations. Armed insurrections were sponsored and abetted by R.A.W. and later requests for military assistance to control these conflicts were managed through pro-India leaders. India has been aiding and inciting the Nepalese dissidents to collaborate with the Nepali Congress. For this they were supplied arms whenever the king or the Nepalese government appeared to be drifting away from India's dictates and impinging on India's hegemonic designs in the region. In fact, under the garb of the so-called democratization measures, the Maoists were actively encouraged to collect arms and resort to open rebellion against the legitimate Nepalese governments. The contrived rebellions provided India an opportunity to intervene militarily in Nepal, ostensibly to control the insurrections, which were masterminded by R.A.W. itself. It was an active replay of the Indian performance in Sri Lanka and Maldives a few years earlier. R.A.W. is particularly aiding the people of Indian origin and has been providing them with arms and ammunition. R.A.W. has also infiltrated the ethnic Nepali refugees who have been extradited by Bhutan and taken refuge in eastern Nepal. R.A.W. can exploit its links with these refugees whenever either country goes against Indian interests. Besides, the Nepalese economy is totally controlled by Indian moneylenders, financiers, and business mafia.

Afghanistan

Since December 1979, throughout the Afghan War, the K.G.B., K.H.A.D. (W.A.D.) (a former Afghan intelligence outfit), and R.A.W. stepped up their efforts to concentrate on influencing and covertly exploiting the tribes on both sides of the Pakistan-Afghanistan border. There was intimate coordination between the three intelligence agencies not only in Afghanistan but also in Pakistan, where destabilization was sought through a subversion and sabotage plan related to Afghan refugees and mujahideen in the tribal belt and inside Pakistan. They jointly organized spotting and recruitment of hostile tribesmen and trained them in guerrilla warfare, infiltration, subversion, sabotage, and the establishment of saboteur forces/terrorist organizations in the pro-Afghan tribes of Pakistan in order to carry out bombings in Afghan refugee camps in the Northwest Frontier province (NWFP) and Baluchistan to threaten and pressure them to return to Afghanistan. They also carried out bomb blasts in populated areas deep inside Pakistan to create panic and hatred in the minds of locals against Afghan refugee mujahideen to pressure Pakistan to change its policies on Afghanistan.

Pakistan

Pakistan's size, strength, and potential have always overawed India. It has always considered Pakistan to be the main opponent to its expansionist doctrine. India's animosity toward Pakistan is psychologically and ideologically deep-rooted and unassailable. India's 1965 and 1971 wars with Pakistan over Kashmir, which resulted in the dismemberment of Pakistan and the creation of Bangladesh, are just two examples.

R.A.W. considers Sindh province to be Pakistan's soft underbelly. It has made it the prime target for sabotage and subversion. R.A.W. has enrolled an extensive network of agents and antigovernment elements and is convinced that with a little push restless Sindh will revolt. Taking full advantage of the agitation in Sindh in 1983, and the periodic ethnic riots, which have continued to today, R.A.W. has deeply penetrated Sindh and cultivated dissidents and secessionists, thereby creating hard-liners unlikely to allow peace to return to Sindh. R.A.W. is also similarly involved in Baluchistan.

R.A.W. is also being blamed for confusing the ground situation is Kashmir so as to keep the world's attention away from the gross human rights violations in Indian-occupied Kashmir. Pakistan's Inter-Services Intelligence agency (I.S.I.), being almost 20 years older than R.A.W. and having acquired a much higher standard of efficiency in its functioning, has become the prime target of R.A.W.'s designs. The I.S.I. is considered to be a stumbling block in R.A.W.'s operations and has been made a target of massive misinformation and propaganda campaigns. The tirade against I.S.I. continues unabated. The idea is to keep I.S.I. on the defensive by alleging that it has had a hand in supporting the Kashmiri mujahideen and the Sikhs in Punjab. R.A.W.'s fixation on I.S.I. has taken the shape of I.S.I.-phobia, as in India everyone traces the origin of all happenings and shortcomings to the I.S.I. Whenever and wherever there is a kidnapping, a bank robbery, a financial scandal, a bomb blast, or what have you, the I.S.I. is deemed to have had a hand in it.

In summary, R.A.W. over the years has admirably fulfilled its tasks of destabilizing target states through the unbridled export of terrorism. The Indira Doctrine spelt out a difficult and onerous role for R.A.W. It goes to its credit that it has accomplished its assigned objectives due to the endemic weakness in the state apparatus of these nations and the failures of their leaders.

5

The Intelligence Bureau: India's Premier Intelligence Agency

To understand the evolution of the Indian Intelligence Bureau, the oldest surviving intelligence agency of the world, it is necessary to peep into the process of evolution it passed through. The Imperial British government felt the need for organising a strong military and civil intelligence outfit soon after its victory over the rebellious Indian forces in 1857. The victory had reposed multifaceted responsibility on the burgeoning British Crown and its ever-expanding empire in India. It had to effectively suppress the Muslim and Hindu rulers to consolidate and expand its territories; ensure law and order in the directly controlled and administered territories; maintain vigil on the territories ruled by native princes and to gather intelligence about friendly and hostile preparations of regimes in China, Afghanistan and the expanding empire of Russia. Defeat of the Mughal power had also brought about cascading political turmoil in other parts of the Muslim world in the Middle East, Africa and Southeast Asia.

There is a popular belief amongst the intelligence community that the Intelligence Bureau was conceived and set up as the "Central Special Branch' by an order of the Secretary of State for India in London, on December 23, 1887. Some authors surmised that the first intelligence outfit in

India was started in 1885 when Major General Sir Charles Metcalfe MacGregor was appointed Quartermaster General and head of the Intelligence Department of the Indian Army.

It was yet claimed that the Intelligence Bureau should trace its origins to the 'Anti-Thuggee and Dacoity Department' since its inception in 1835. This claim made by certain quarters in the intelligence fraternity is also not accurate.

The British Thuggee concerns dated back to 1828, due largely to the efforts of Lord William Bentinck, Governor General of India, who had started an extensive campaign involving profiling, intelligence gathering, and executions of the Thuggee groups. The campaign was heavily based on informants recruited from captured thugs who were offered protection on the condition that they told everything they knew. By the 1870's, the Thuggee cult was extinct, but the concept of 'criminal tribes' and 'criminal castes' is still in the mindset of India.

A police organisation known as the "Thuggee and Dacoity Department" was established within the Government of India, with Colonel William Sleeman as superintendent of the department in 1835. The Department remained in existence until 1904 when it was replaced by the Central Criminal Intelligence Department. It would, therefore, be seen that the Intelligence Bureau had only partially inherited its origins to the "Thuggee and Dacoity Department" and to the 'Central Special Branch' established in London in December 1887. The MI unit started in 1885 had evolved into a separate Military Intelligence outfit.

While on the question of the Thuggees it should be stated that even Ziauddin Barni's History of Firoz Shah (written about 1356) had mentioned about the Thuggee problem and creation of a special force in Delhi that had rounded up over 200 Thuggeees and were banished to the political kalapani of Lakhnauti (Laxmanabati-Gaur) in modern Bengal. The Emperor had not christened his special force as a Thuggee Department, nonetheless, he used more or less the same tactics as the British did centuries later. In fact, very minor strand of Indian Intelligence fraternity was born in the womb of the "Thuggee Department". It was given criminal investigation, military utility and political mandates from day one, soon after the the British Crown set to the mission of consolidating and expamnding ite Empire in India and territories around the first Colony in world history that showered manna on the entire western world. Intelligence was one of the arms used by the British to run their writs in India and other parts of global colonies. In this venture Indian intelligence and army helped the British more than the original sons of the Albion.

The need for the creation of this Central Special Branch was realised for procuring early and authentic information by the Central Government regarding the political, economic and social conditions of the people in British India. It was also to monitor the growth and development of popular feeling on issues concerned with security and keeping a watchful control over the inter-provincial activities and movements of criminals and the conditions that predisposed to crime. The tasks assigned to the Central Special Branch were to coordinate the working of the Special Branches of the provincial governments in British India, created under the same order of the Secretary of State, and to guide the new units set up directly under its own charge in the various princely states.

The new organisation started functioning as a wing of 'Anti-Thuggi and Dacoity Department', which had attained notable success and renown since its inception in 1835 as an all India outfit to contain the incipient terrorism of that period and subsequently took over its infrastructure. Since then, the nomenclature of the organisation underwent several changes.

As a result of the recommendation of the Police Commission of 1902-03, the Central Special Branch was remodeled and rechristened as the 'Central Criminal Intelligence Department', which was made responsible for all matters pertaining to national security in addition to its role in prevention of inter-provincial crime, and was designated as the nodal agency of the Government of India.

The word 'Criminal' was dropped from the name of the organisation by 1918 as its burgeoning security tasks started to far overshadow its criminal responsibilities. The present name, the Intelligence Bureau, came to be adopted by the organisation in the year 1920.

ROLE AND FUNCTIONS; AND THE INTELLIGENCE BUREAU IN RECENT HISTORY

With the advent of the provincial governments run by Indian politicians in 1935, the Government of India decided that the Intelligence Bureau should have its own apparatus and arrangements for the collection of strategic intelligence in the provinces, to augment the information supplied by the Provincial CIDs and Special Branches. Field units of the IB were thus organised in 1935, initially at six centres in the country, each under a Central Intelligence Officer, and subsequently elsewhere. The growth of national security problems and their increasing complexities led to the concept of setting up of Subsidiary Intelligence Bureaus in the field, under the charge of Deputy Directors, in the fifties, to organize more scientific and systematic intelligence gathering. The analytical and directional setup at the Bureau's headquarters at Delhi also gradually grew, with newer and newer challenges and sources of threat to national security being identified over the years.

From its inception in the year 1887, the organization has constantly striven to pursue the goal of maintaining the unity and integrity of the country, to thwart the machinations of subversive elements, and defeat the forces of disruption and de-stabilisation. In the years prior to Independence, a good deal of the IB's effort was devoted to tackling problems of securing the boundaries of the country, preserving the basic essential services against disruption, and dealing with sustained militancy from organized groups. It was in this period that much of the formal shape was given to law enforcement on a countrywide scale and the IB played a significant role throughout this process.

As the specter of Communism began to haunt Europe and other parts of the world after 1921, the attention of the Intelligence Bureau was also diverted to meeting this imminent threat to the reigning forces in the country. Utilization of the professional operators and agents of the IB against USSR designs in the Central Asian Countries and Afghanistan would require a separate volume to account for. It was after 1947 that the IB really came into its own as the intelligence arm of new India. It had inherited the imperial traditions and expected to imbibe the democratic aspirations of modern India. Half of the bifurcated IB went to Pakistan as the Pakistan Intelligence Bureau with Mohammad Ali as the chief.

The Indian part of the Intelligence Bureau was taken over by T.G. Saanjeevi Pillai. Besides the inherent strength of the organisation, the calibers of its first two Directors in the post Independence period-Shri Pillai and his successor, the legendary 'Father of Intelligence' in modem India; Shri B. N. Mullik-largely enabled the IB to measure up to these new and unprecedented challenges. Between them these two pioneers laid the foundations of a vibrant intelligence organization giving a new dimension and dynamism to the newer thrust areas of its tasks and responsibilities. The IB was thus able to address itself to the complex security needs of a modern, democratic and forward looking nation, successfully withstanding the vicissitudes of the system and time. The groundwork laid by them has enabled a string of their dedicated successors to build up the IB into a sophisticated intelligence apparatus in the succeeding decades. Some of the stalwarts who built up the IB brick by brick are: M. M. L. Hooja, R. K. Kapoor, H. A. Baraari, M. K. Narayanan, R. P. Joshi and V. G. Vaidya etc.

Today, the Intelligence Bureau has to deal with a myriad of challenges such as terrorism and insurgency on the one hand, and espionage and subliminal attempts to undermine the democratic fabric of the country by external agencies, on the other. The organisation carries out forward and counterintelligence operations against any incursion from hostile neighbouring countries or any of their client states. It maintains a watchful vigil through penny-packet posts on the Sino-Indian, Indo-Pak and Indo-Burma land borders, and also keeps track of developments and movements on the eastern and western sea borders of the country in the field or counter-intelligence, the IB has to deal with a greater number of hostile intelligence agencies than its counterparts in most other countries. There are no East-West or North-South divides in the area of spying and espionage, and while the nation sleeps, the operatives of the IB have to remain vigilant as a substantial part of espionage activity takes place in the hours of darkness. As for its successes in this sphere, despite the liberal traditions of the country and other handicaps the organisation's record of busting spy rings and capture of espionage agents has indeed been gratifying.

The responsibility of collection of foreign intelligence was given to the IB during the Second World War period. However, the organisation made tremendous strides within a few years and by the mid-1950s concrete intelligence about Pakistan's intentions and capabilities for instance, had achieved a sophisticated dimension. With India developing into a major nation-State, strategic intelligence collection outside the country was handed over to a new organisation carved out from the IB, as a whole-time responsibility, in September 1968. It is known as Research and Analysis Wing of the cabinet secretariat.

In the sphere of combating insurgency, notwithstanding the initial lack of sufficient experience, the IB had been able to devise, by the late 1950s and more so from the mid-1960s, a counter-insurgency doctrine of its own. It is substantially different from the conventional wisdom based on the Malaysian or Vietnamese experience and has enabled the IB to play a significant role in containing insurgent movements in several parts of the country. In the arena of counterterrorism, another relatively new field of action, the IB again displayed quick adaptability. Despite major handicaps including its rather thin organisational spread on the ground, the Bureau has striven hard to make its contribution in the nation's war against the most serious threat to ita peace and stability.

The security functions of the IB are perhaps one of the less publicized areas of its tasks. Personnel and document security are today among the most important responsibilities of a security agency in any modern nation-state. In this sphere of its tasks, the security checks and vetting procedures of the Bureau and the countermeasures evolved by it have been acknowledged by several foreign agencies as amongst the best in the world, excepting perhaps those possible in a totalitarian or authoritarian society. Security of key industries and vital installations is also an important charge of the IB. The Central Industrial Security Force (CISF) was born out of the industrial security wing of the IB. Besides its responsibilities relating to conceptualisation of threats and devising of counter measures to protect these national assets against sabotage and other disruptive attempts, the Bureau has a built-in provision for an early warning system whenever portents of serious industrial unrest are present.

Similarly the border security duties of the IB, especially along Pakistan border were taken over by the newly created Border Security Force. The Indo-Tibet Border Police and the Special Services Bureau also owe their birth out of IB's existing wings concerning these areas of national security. The IB is, therefore, naturally described as the mother of all intelligence and security agencies of India.

In the sphere of VIP security, the IB is responsible not only for the perception and conceptualisation of all threats to important personages including the Prime Minister, President and other Indian dignitaries as well as other internationally protected personalities, but also for drawing up the 'Blue Books' and other guidelines for ensuring their security. Later a specialist VIP security agency, the Special Protection Group was created to cater to security needs of listed VIPs.

In its role as the premier intelligence-cum-security agency of the country, the IB has to service the various Ministries and Departments of the union Government with timely intelligence inputs and advice on all aspects of national security. Ever since their inception in 1935 the IB's field units have sought to play a somewhat similar role vis-a-vis the state governments. However, IB's cooperation with state intelligence units mainly concerned security matters and activities of the main political parties like the Indian national Congress, Communist Party of India, Muslim League, and Hindu Mahasabha etc. After independence when Congress governments ruled everywhere exchanges between the IB and state intelligence units appeared to be smooth. However, with the advent of non-Congress government in various states such cooperation has remained limited to national security concerns and for other matters the central and state intelligence units functioned (and are still functioning) independently. Even in internal security areas degree of cooperation depends on the contours of the state governments (such as communal parties, sectarian parties etc). Over the period, threat of jihad and violent activities by jihadi tanzeems based in Pakistan and Bangladesh have paved the ways for better liaison between the state and central intelligence units. This will be emphasized later.

Such efforts, aimed at an interchange of information to effectively meet any grave threat to public peace and internal security, take place at several levels-regular interactions with Chief Ministers and Governors, maintaining regular liaisons with the Chief and Home Secretaries, and direct involvement with the DG Police and State Intelligence and police officials.

On its part, the IB has also been receiving qualified cooperation and support in the performance of its national security tasks, from various state governments. Differences in political ideology and attitude towards various segments of the population often modulate the degree of cooperation. The help provided by the State police and intelligence outfits to the IB constitutes a very vital link in the national security chain.

ORGANIZATION, STRUCTURE, SUCCESSES AND FAILURES

The Intelligence Bureau is a pyramidal organisation. The Director, IB is supported at his headquarters by Special Directors, Additional Directors, Joint Directors, Deputy Directors and Assistant Directors. The cascading ranks flow down to Deputy Central Intelligence Officer, Assistant Central Intelligence Officer (Gr. 1 and 2). Basically the structural formation follows the police formations with the Security Assistant (constable) at the lowest ladder. The staffing pattern is divided into two broad divisions: Intelligence Generation cadre and Technical cadre.

In the central core the structural layout is divided on functional, territorial and operational basis. For example a particular Additional Director/Special Director can be responsible for supervising certain geographical areas and subject-desks. Desks cover the entire gamut of national life, right from political parties to student unions, trade unions, NGOs, to communal and other disruptive activities. The numerous desks are clubbed under common denominative hierarchical lines applied to interrelated subjects. Subjects like ethnic insurgency and religious strife are dealt with by subject desk as well as Operations Desks. The details are so innumerable that it would confuse a common reader. Suffice it to say that all spheres of human activities inside and in the neighbourhood of the country are allocated to the charter of duties of the Intelligence Bureau.

It must be added that newer dimensions of coverage are added from time to time keeping in view the windows of threat to national security. For example in recent times the unpleasant task of monitoring of VHF, HF communications (mobile phones etc), Internet communications and Website activities have been added to the domain of coverage. These are done to keep vigil on the forces which use these electronic communication methodologies to carry out subversive activities. The sky is not the limit as far as growing charters of duties of the IB are redefined from time to time.

In the States IB units are designated as Subsidiary Intelligence Bureau. These units are headed mostly by a zonal Additional Director with Joint Directors, Deputy Directors and Assistant Directors manning different states. It is the age of top heavy administrative work philosophy. The work earlier done by a Joint Assistant Director is now being done by a Joint Director or Deputy Director. Pyramidal upgradation of ranks has put the IB hierarchy at par with the State police and other administrative services of the Union and the States.

However, it is difficult to asses if such upgradation has added better cutting edges to the grassroots level functionaries, who remain responsible for producing the uncut diamonds of intelligence inputs. The Intelligence Bureau gathers intelligence on given subjects and from allocated target areas through applications of Tradecraft. Tradecrafts are both general and technical. The General Intelligence generation depends on intensive training of the grassroots level operators in the technology of intelligence generation-mainly through Human Intelligence (HumInt), which uses human agents for collection of intelligence. The Tradecraft matters are highly complicated and are harder nuts to crack.

Tradecraft also include Technical Intelligence(TechInt).It is a vast universe of intelligence tools, which include Signal Intelligence (SigInt), Electronic Intelligence (ElecInt), Photo Intelligence, Satellite Intelligence, Remote Sensing Intelligence etc. Specially trained officers are grilled over fires over years to shapeup good TechInt officers. In short TechInt is an important accessory to HumInt; in some cases TechInt can superceded the authenticity of HumInt.

Internal intelligence generation, as stated earlier encompass all conceivable state, political, group and organised activities of the nation. Coverage of communal conflagration and simmering discontents are covered with as much alacrity as possible.

While intelligence generation is an important aspect of the IB, it is also responsible for denying intelligence to the intelligence agencies of other countries which are constantly engaged in stealing intelligence from India and in carrying out sabotage and subversion. This is in the domain of Counter-intelligence. Specially designed Tradecrafts are used in Counterintelligence works of the IB. This is as vast a field as intelligence generation is. The IB is solely responsible for Counterintelligence on Indian soil, though the RAW has taken over limited CI works in Indian domain to protect its own assets and operations.

The other important aspect in which the IB specialises is the field of counterinsurgency, counterterrorism and counter-sabotage and subversion related operations. This vast area include ethnic problems like the Naga insurgency, separatist movements of ULFA and the not so old terror regime let loose by the a group of misdirected and misguided Sikhs. Intelligence operations in Kashmir combine intelligence generation, counterintelligence, and counterinsurgency and counter-terrorism operations. Besides Kashmir, such combination of operations is often demanded of the IB in other insurgency prone areas in the north-east.

Another major area of operation is border intelligence. With vast borders with China, Myanmar, Bangladesh and Pakistan, India has been very vulnerable. It is not known to countrymen that young IB officers have to compulsorily spend several years on inaccessible and dangerous border posts to gather border intelligence. These officers are grilled over ice in the IB's in-house mountaineering institute. As well, three IB officers had earned the rare distinction of climbing the Everest Peak.

The other important task that is the spin off of worldwide militant Islamic resurgence and Jihad sponsored by inimical forces in Pakistan and (to a lesser extent) Bangladesh has posed a challenged to the intrinsic efficiency of the IB. This new dimension of national security has brought with it several complications which require a separate volume to narrate.

However, the IB has risen up to the new challenges and has started encompassing the roots, branches and twigs of such movements. It must be understood that Jihadist movements on Indian soil are spin offs of Jihad movements in Afghanistan, Pakistan and Bangladesh. Problems with roots in neighbouring countries are tougher to tackle. If one asks me to give a rating to the IB as an old operative I should give it Three Stars; not bad for the handicaps with which the agency has to work.

It is often alleged that IB generally fails in catering advance information about jihadist operations, schemes and operations. It must be remembered that in most cases the operations are conceived by the ISI of Pakistan and in some cases groups draw direct inspiration from Al Qaeda.

Once the operations are conceived and targets are selected the ISI and the DGFI confer franchise to the jihadi tanjeems like the Lashkar-e-Tayeba, Harkat-ul-Jiahd-al Islami along with resources and often with assistance of 'sleeper cells' in the target areas of the targeted operations. The 'sleeper cells' might belong to foreign intelligence agencies and the tanzeems.

Therefore, it has been difficult for the IB to generate intelligence from neighbouring countries. Moreover, jihadis belong to Muslim, predominantly Sunni Muslim communities and owing allegiance to Wahhabi and Salafi ideologies. Plainly speaking the IB has had very limited access to the Muslim community and despite best efforts has not been able to attract sufficient Muslim candidates to the cutting edge level of the Intelligence Bureau. Despite all these handicaps the IB has been vastly successful in infiltrating jihadi 'sleeper cells.' The faceless operators of the IB are now faced with serious internal security challenges. Some of these challenges are rooted in the history of the country, which it inherited from the British rulers. India was divided on the basis of religion. Independent India was reorganized on the basis of language. However, India's ethnic geographic maps were not researched and redrawn with imagination and political vision.

The Naga insurgency was a spin off of British legacy and ethnic and Christian exclusivism introduced by the British. Very little attention was paid to the tribal aspirations of the Mizo, Bodo-Kachari, Tripuri, Khasi-Garo and Meitei-non-Naga tribes of Manipur. The ambience of insurgency erupted due to such political shortsightedness, which was expeditiously exploited by Pakistan and China and assorted rebellious Burmese tribes. It can be said to the credit of the IB that its faceless officers rendered exemplary services to the nation in these ethnic-resurgent areas.

Again in the Northeast Assam was pushed to the path of insurgency/terrorism due to failure of the consecutive state and central governments to prevent the milling waves of illegal immigration of Pakistani/Bangladeshi Muslim population to Assam (West Bengal included). Added factors were severe economic imbalance, economic and administrative neglect and general unconcern of the people of the Hindi heartland and Southern peninsula about the people of the Northeast. Still, the IB has given good account of its presence in Assam despite several built in deficiencies.

Other areas of national fault lines that threw serious challenges to the IB are Punjab terrorism and the present phase of Maoist movement in the north-eastern states. Punjab problem was a self-inflicted injury, caused by unholy political competition by the Congress and the Akali Dal. Pakistan took advantage of the disastrous approaches adopted by political forces and the governments and supported the terrorists for nearly ten years. It must be added to the credit of the IB that its functionaries gave excellent coverage and helped both in the peace-making process and operational intelligences.

The present phases of Maoist movements, though treated as a police problem, are basically and intrinsically connected to lack of practical and equitable land reforms, rural job generation, promotion of rural-home-based traditional industries, failure to transmit the urban developmental benefits to the rural areas and political malfeasance.

Centuries of exploitation by the British and post-independence neglect and unimaginative economic programming and implementation have created an economic void, social imbalance and lack of basic state infrastructures. The IB has no other option but to work within the given system and socio-economic-political ambience. Under these tough circumstances the IB has not been successful in generating expected level of intelligence. There are several reasons for these limitations.

It is often alleged that IB is misused for political purposes. All ruling parties misuse the IB for political intelligence, for mere political survival or for stymieing political opposition. Political horse trading is an integral part of our fledgling democracy.

Institutions like IB are also used for these purposes. Such misuses take place because agencies like IB, R&AW, CBI etc are not regulated by any Act of the Parliament. These important tools of governance are not accountable to anyone except their controlling ministries, the Home and the Prime Minister.

Agencies like the CIA, FBI and MI5 are regulated by Acts of the highest lawmaking bodies. Despite that the CIA and the MI6 were misused by the USA and UK for waging war on Iraq. However Watchdog bodies of the Congress, Senate and the Parliament had exposed the misdeeds of the governments of the USA and UK and rectifiable measures were adopted. It is high time for India to make these agencies accountable and provide them with protective armours of the Law. Democracy without Accountability is worse than military dictatorship.

The intelligence Bureau does not work in isolation. The Director Intelligence Bureau is regarded as the topmost police officer of the country. The IB maintains regular liaisons with the state police intelligence branches and internal intelligence units of the Para Military Forces and the three wings of the Military Intelligence. It has regular interaction with the RAW on matters of national security aspects.

The level and degree of cooperation between the state police intelligence and the IB waxes and wanes with the political contour of the governments. Certain states ruled by certain ideological parties, caste based parties and regional parties do not always cooperate to the fullest extent, wherever their turfs of special interests are concerned. However, since 1993 continuous efforts are being made to bring about perfect coordination and smooth exchange of intelligence.

The annual conference of DGPs/IGPs and CPOs attempt to iron out areas of differences and bring about smoother coordination. A multi-agency coordination body has been established to ensure smooth exchange of intelligence and operational coordination. The National Security Council also coordinates all efforts to develop healthier bridges between the IB and the state police intelligence units and other central intelligence agencies. In that sense, the IB has become an important focal point of the internal security parameters of the country.

Following terrorist strikes the media and general public often lay allegations of intelligence failure. The word 'failure' is limited to a particular incident. It must be remembered that *jihadi tanjeems* from neighboring countries have set up networks inside India. It is not possible for IB alone, without parallel inputs from the RAW and the state police intelligence units locate, identify and neutralize jihadi terrorist modules set up in India. Inputs about planning and execution schemes originating from Pakistan and Bangladesh are expected from the RAW. There is a fairly large coverage gap on this front. Moreover, it must be understood that in terrorist warfare intelligence agencies remain ahead of the terrorist outfits in nearly half of these cases. In the rest of these cases the terrorists succeed in evading timely detection. An average of fifty percent success is rated very high in guerrilla and urban terror warfare.

The IB suffers from several drawbacks: lack of ground spread, manpower and often hesitant support from the political establishment of the country. Lack of political will, for whatever reasons it might be, is at the root of weakness of our intelligence mechanism. That said, the Intelligence Bureau is doing a fine job within the limitations of the system and resource constraints.

The same criteria are applicable to the state police intelligence agencies also. Some painful and hesitant steps have been initiated for some sorts of police reforms. Hopefully some reforms measures for state intelligence branches would be considered.

It is high time that the government of India considers initiating Acts of Parliament for the agencies like IB, RAW and CBI, carry out internal reforms, provide better sinews of operations and make these institutions accountable to the people's forum. Finally these agencies should also be freed from political interference.

INTELLIGENCE BUREAU (INDIA)

The Intelligence Bureau is India's internal intelligence agency and reputedly the world's oldest intelligence agency. It was recast as the Central Intelligence Bureau in 1947 under the Ministry of Home Affairs. The reason for the perception may be due to the fact that, in 1885, Major General Sir Charles MacGregor was appointed Quartermaster General and head of the Intelligence Department for the British Indian Army at Simla. The objective then was to monitor Russian troop deployments in Afghanistan, fearing a Russian invasion of British India through the North-West during the late 19th century. In 1909, the Indian Political Intelligence Office was established in England in response to the development of Indian anarchist activities, which came to be called the Indian Political Intelligence (IPI) from 1921. This was a state-run surveillance and monitoring agency. The IPI was run jointly by the India Office and the Government of India and reported jointly to the Secretary of the Public and Judicial Department of the India Office, and the Director of Intelligence Bureau (DIB) in India, and maintained close contact with Scotland Yard and MI5. Recently, the private American Intelligence agency STRATFOR has listed the Indian Intelligence Bureau as one of the world's 5 Best Intelligence agencies.

Responsibilities

Shrouded in secrecy, the IB is used to garner intelligence from within India and also execute counter-intelligence and counter-terrorism tasks. The Intelligence Bureau comprises employees from law enforcement agencies, mostly from the Indian Police Service and the military.

In addition to domestic intelligence responsibilities, the IB is particularly tasked with intelligence collection in border areas, following the 1951 recommendations of the Himmatsinhji Committee (also known as the North and North-East Border Committee), a task entrusted to military intelligence organizations prior to independence in 1947.

All spheres of human activity within India and in the neighborhood are allocated to the charter of duties of the Intelligence Bureau. The IB was also tasked with other external intelligence responsibilities as of 1951 till 1968, when the Research and Analysis Wing was formed. The current chief of the organization is Rajiv Mathur.

Activities

Understanding of the arcane workings of the IB is largely speculative. One known task of the IB is to clear licenses to amateur radio enthusiasts. The IB also passes on intelligence between other Indian Intelligence agencies and the Police.

The IB also grants the necessary security clearances to Indian diplomats and judges before they take the oath. On rare occasions, IB officers interact with the media during a crisis situation. The IB is also rumored to intercept and open around 6,000 letters daily.It also has a email spying system similar to FBI's Carnivore System.

The Intelligence Bureau is also authorized to conduct wiretapping without a warrant. This clause is mostly misused by ruling governments to spy on their political opponents, sometimes indicting them on false criminal charges. The IB also has numerous authors who write letters to various newspapers and magazines to support the government's perspective. According to recent reports, the Government is trying to bring in a restriction on wiretapping without a warrant.

Workings

The `Class I' (gazette) officers carry out coordination and higher-level management the IB. These officers are (again in increasing order of seniority) Asst. Director, the Joint Deputy Director, the Deputy Director, Joint Director, Additional Director, Special Director or Special Secretary and finally the Director. The SIB's are headed by officers of the rank of Joint Director or above but smaller SIB's are also sometimes headed by Deputy Directors. The SIB's have their units at district head quarters headed by Deputy Central Intelligence Officers or DCIO's.

The IB maintains a large number of field units and headquarters (which are under the control of Joint or Deputy Directors). It is through these offices and the intricate process of deputation that a very `organic' linkage between the state police agencies and the IB is maintained. In addition to these, at the national level the IB has several units (in some cases Subsidiary Intelligence Bureaus) to keep track of issues like terrorism, counter-intelligence, VIP security, threat assessment and sensitive areas (i.e. Jammu and Kashmir and such).

Operations and Lapses

The Intelligence Bureau reportedly has a lot of successes to its credit, but operations conducted by the IB are rarely declassified. Due to the extreme secrecy surrounding the agency, there is little concrete information available about it or its activities. The IB was initially India's internal and external intelligence agency. Due to lapses on the part of the Intelligence Bureau to predict the Sino-Indian War of 1962, and later on, intelligence failure in the India-Pakistan War in 1965, it was bifurcated in 1968 and entrusted with the task of internal intelligence only. The external intelligence branch was handed to the newly created Research and Analysis Wing.

The IB has had mixed success in counter-terrorism. It was reported in 2008 that the IB had been successful in bursting some terror modules. It alerted the police before the Hyderabad blasts and gave repeated warnings of a possible attack on Mumbai through the sea before the November 2008 Mumbai attacks. On the whole, however, the IB came in for some sharp criticism by the media after the relentless wave of terror attacks in 2008. Most experts agree that the rot that has set in is very deep, and that only a comprehensive reform in all aspects can equip the IB to face the rapidly growing terror threat. Heavy politics, under-funding and a huge shortage of professional field agents are the chief problems facing the agency. The overall strength of the agency is believed to be around 25,000, with only 3500-odd field agents operating in the entire country. Of these, many are engaged in political intelligence. Out of the remaining, hardly 500 keep an eye on terror activity-in a country of a billion-plus people.

LIST OF INDIAN INTELLIGENCE AGENCIES

India has a number of intelligence agencies of which the best known are the Research and Analysis Wing, India's external intelligence agency and the Intelligence Bureau, the internal intelligence agency.

1. Research and Analysis Wing
2. Intelligence Bureau
3. Defense Intelligence Agency (DIA)
4. Joint Cipher Bureau
5. All India Radio Monitoring Service
6. Joint Intelligence Committee
7. Signals Intelligence Directorate
8. Aviation Research Centre
9. Directorate of Air Intelligence
10. Directorate of Navy Intelligence.

6

A History of Intelligence Failure

It is now widely accepted that both American and British intelligence failed in assessment of presence of weapons of mass destruction in Iraq during 2002-03. It is also agreed that some of that faulty intelligence was fed by interested parties. This intelligence failure was subjected to investigation both in US and UK and has led to various reforms. Recently, the office of the Historian, Bureau of Public Affairs, United States Department of State, released documents relating to US foreign relations in the period 1969-76. Volume XI of those documents relate to the South Asia crisis, 1971. According to the summary, "New evidence suggested to Nixon and Kissinger that rather than being restrained by Moscow, India was contemplating expanded military operations against West Pakistan."

An intelligence report of a briefing that Indira Gandhi gave in early December indicated that India enjoyed strong support from the Soviet Union which had promised to counter-balance any move China might make against India in support of Pakistan. With that much support Indira outlined her war aims: She would not accept a settlement until Bangladesh was liberated, "the Southern area of Azad Kashmir" was liberated and the Pakistani armoured and Air Force strength was destroyed to prevent any future challenge to India.

Nixon and Kissinger took this as proof that India planned not only to foster the independence of East Pakistan, but to use the opportunity to inflict a crushing military defeat on Pakistan, which would lead to the break-up of West Pakistan. Kissinger attributed to the Indira Gandhi government the goal of Balkanising West Pakistan. If the crisis resulted in the dismemberment of Pakistan, Kissinger worried that China might conclude that the US was "just too weak" to prevent the humiliation of an ally. He felt that the Chinese would then look to other options "to break their encirclement". He concluded that the situation represented "a big watershed". Various actions of Kissinger just as the Enterprise mission, his suggestion to China to apply military pressure on India and his direct pressure on the Soviet Union all followed the above assessment based on intelligence which at that time was claimed to have been obtained by a leakage at the Indian Cabinet level.

Seymour Hersh in his book on Kissinger, claimed that the source was Morarji Desai, who was not at all in the Cabinet and at that time had no friend in the Cabinet Committee on Political Affairs. In fact the intelligence on which Kissinger was acting in 1971 was perhaps of a worse quality than the one on which the US concluded that Iraq had WMD in 2002-03. In other words the CIA had a long history of such poor quality intelligence collection.

WHY DOES INDIAN INTELLIGENCE FAIL?

Each time there is a terrorist and jihadi strike in India, we blame the intelligence agencies of failing to anticipate and prevent the attack.

Why do we Fail?

We fail because the central Intelligence Bureau, the government's cutting edge internal security tool, is ill-prepared to combat aggressive operations of Pakistan's Inter Services Intelligence agency, Bangladesh's Directorate General of Forces Intelligence and Islamist *tanzeems*.

The Bureau has well-trained, motivated and dedicated

operators to gather intelligence and operate along areas of national fault lines. The IB operates through its Central Operations Units and Subsidiary Units in states. From the Northeast to Gujarat, Kashmir to Kanyakumari, it has a vast geographical area and extremely complex problems to grapple with. And with Bangladesh, Myanmar, Nepal and Pakistan factors thrown in, the Bureau finds it nose drowned under the flood of events that threaten the nation. The IB is simply not equipped to handle the enormous canvas, which is getting murkier by the day.

Among other things, it suffers from:

- Lack of trained manpower at the operative level;
- Inadequacy of modern training to combat acts of terrorism and insurgency;
- Lack of electronic and technical intelligence equipments for combating the vast and expanding fields of information and communication technology;
- Near inability to generate Human Assets in target areas where the indigenous and foreign jihadists establish nests, modules, cells and chains of secondary support system. The IB has not yet opted for certain 'unorthodox' tradecraft that can enable it to penetrate the target areas. It relies more on limited electronic and technical intelligence to cover trans-border movements, induction of arms, explosives and trained jihadists from Pakistan and Bangladesh;
- The IB has very little support from sister agencies like the R&AW about location, preparation and planning of the jihadist *tanzeems* in Pakistan, Bangladesh and other countries-the UK, USA, Indonesia, Thailand, Nepal and certain European destinations.
- Support system from other friendly countries are not threat and issue specific. India can urge the friendly nations to reorient their tools to cover the jihadist thrust in the subcontinent, as it has emerged as the

neuronal epicentre of East-Far East-West journey of jihadist impulses.

- The information and operations sharing mechanism between the Centre and the states is in rudimentary stage. It should be augmented under the auspices of the National Security Council. The Electronic, Technical and Image Intelligence data collation and monitoring system at the central and state levels require integration under the auspices of the NSC. The same facility should be able to integrate with the existing agencies that are engaged in handling suspected line, air and electronic cipher traffic and the www menace.
- The Intelligence Bureau require immediate geographic, operational and resources expansion. The Union government, as indicated by the prime minister, should pay immediate attention to these burning needs. This exercise should be completed within next five years after speedy determination of National Intelligence Estimate (revised periodically). Otherwise, the IB will continue to lag behind the cancer of jihadist thrust. The authorities should not forget that besides carrying out serial bombings the jihadists under the protective umbrella of the ISI, Bangladesh's DGFI and the Al Qaeda Inc are capable of importing and indigenously manufacturing of weapons of mass destruction. The CIA does not rule out the possibility of Al Qaeda Inc developing crude and dirty nuclear bombs.
- People have the right to know the threat quantum they face from inimical forces and should also be assured that the government, besides scanning the sensex graph and the GNP/GDP arithmetic is duty bound to protect lives and properties of the citizen. People are threatened by a new kind of war, which is known to the people of the Northeast, Punjab and Kashmir. But for the heartland and peninsular India,

it is a new experience. They have to live with it and compel their politicians to look beyond the ballot boxes and 'secular fences.' The state and central governments must prove that they are capable of governing. They should be able to protect or prepare to perish.

- The Intelligence Bureau is not equipped to monitor the web sites of the Islamist jihadist groups. They do not have superfast computers, nationwide networking and surveillance capability on the servers of the ISP providers. Only prolonged studies and research can decipher the coding pattern and transmission trademark of each terror group. These require regular logging and liasing with western agencies who have made forward strides, especially after the 9/11 Al Qaeda attack. Other nodal points in the government should embark upon the task of monitoring the virtual www world and share their inputs online with the central and state intelligence agencies.
- The IB is also required to develop a focused, dedicated and self-contained research and operations group to work at ground and desk levels to assess, anticipate, follow and pre-empt conspiracies and execution plans of the ISI, DGFI, Islamist *tanzeems* across the subcontinent.

The IB should be empowered to act and neutralise such enemies of the country, wherever possible, in concerted operations with the State agencies. The question of empowering the IB with limited 'retaliatory forward operations' capability should be seriously examined with a view to paying back the responsible *tanzeems* in their own coin.

We fail because the IB is not allowed by the government to expose its wares to the larger audience of any parliamentary watchdog body. The country is not entitled to know why they fail and why they cannot be made failproof. The agency is out of bounds for the RTI Act of 2005. It should at least be made accountable to Parliament, so that people can know how their money is being spent and how the political masters manipulate the agencies.

The people have a right to know. Failures cannot be covered up behind the veil of departmental security rules. We fail because our coastal policing and intelligence gathering mechanism is appallingly poor. Besides the Coast Guard, which normally patrol the deeper shallow waters and the Border Security Force, which covers certain eastern riverine borders with Bangladesh, the state governments do not take coastal policing seriously. The existing police forces are not adequate, trained and equipped to police the vast western coastal area from Kot Lakhpat to Wapi in Gujarat and Daman near Maharashtra to Bhatkal in Karnataka and beyond in Kerala.

Besides over a dozen major ports, the western coast has nearly 150 minor ports, over 200 landing sites and over 500 shallow landing creeks. The police and Customs presence in the major ports aside, there is skeletal or no Customs or police presence in minor ports and nothing at all in the landing sites and shallow creeks. The police departments have a few slow moving dhows and negligible fast boats without GPS technology. Pakistan and other jihadist forces can land any amount of arms and explosives through the vast unmanned western coastal area. India has no blueprint to tackle this menace.

A nation under attack still thinks 'people's resilience' is the only weapon to fight the jihadist forces. When shall we wake up to the needs for a special coastal policing and intelligence system? We fail because our disaster management mechanism is appallingly neglected. There exists a high sounding body in Delhi, fat at the top minus vital limbs. The state governments are not concerned about managing disasters beyond paying ex-gratia grants to the dead and injured. The Central Disaster Management outfit should be integrated with the state outfits and a unified command structure is required to be in position with adequate resources. Response time should be minimised to 10 minutes at proximate locations and not more than 20 minutes at difficult locations.

We fail because Pakistan, Bangladesh and other Islamist forces are rapidly salvaging the 'communal debris' left by the scars of Partition. Politicians are aiding these forces by mimicking the British 'divide and rule' policy. They are fuelling the ruffled sentiments that arise out of poverty, lack of education and opportunities. Our system has failed to address these crying needs.

The political class has failed to bridge the gaps left by Partition. They have widened the gaps through vote catching slogans and are doing precious little for them. The poor among the Muslims are as poor as the poor in any other community. They live, because they happen to be born. Nothing beyond!

We fail because we suspect each other. We fail because even the Hindus are fragmented. We fail because we do not behave as a united people. Our unity, our ability to rebuff dubious politicians and our resolve to rise above the ghost of history can act as sure deterrence against the war imposed on us. This is not a war by Muslims against Hindus. It is a war against India by the foreign-based jihadist forces headed by Pakistan, Bangladesh and International Islamist Inc. Every Indian is required to unitedly fight these enemies.

The foreign forces should not succeed in subverting our own people by taking advantage of lapses committed by the political caricatures. We must remember that Indian Muslims did not fight in Afghan jihad and Pakistan's Kashmir jihad. They are one of us and we shall triumph together.

A CASE OF INTELLIGENCE FAILURE?

THE performance of the intelligence and security agencies with regard to the terrorist strike at the Akshardham temple in Gandhinagar was one of the topics touched upon by Deputy Prime Minister and Home Minister L.K. Advani when he inaugurated the annual conference of Directors-General and

Inspectors-General of Police in New Delhi on September 29. "He complimented the security agencies for providing an early breakthrough in the case which clearly pointed to the attack being not merely an act of terrorism, but of cross-border terrorism... Pointing out that the oft-quoted charge of intelligence failure against the intelligence agencies had become too cliched, he said their sources were doing reasonably well. But the absence of specific intelligence input made it difficult for the government to take any action." (*The Hindu*, September 30, 2002)

This is not the first time that the Indian intelligence community has solved a terrorist crime within hours, identified those responsible for it and brought them to book. They had done so on innumerable occasions in the past. The most notable examples are the action against the Liberation Tigers of Tamil Eelam (LTTE) squad which assassinated Rajiv Gandhi in May 1991 and the success in solving the Mumbai blast case in March 1993. A common complaint against security agencies in countries confronted with the scourge of terrorism is that they are brilliant in investigating terrorist acts after they have been committed but they often fail to prevent such acts. U.S. agencies have been confronted with similar charges after the 9/11 terrorist attacks and are currently facing a Congressional investigation in connection with the matter.

It would be unfair to the agencies to say that they are not able to prevent acts of terrorism through timely intelligence. For every successful act of terrorism, there are at least half a dozen that are thwarted by the agencies either through timely intelligence or effective physical security. Details of many of these are often kept outside public knowledge in order to ensure that sources are not compromised and the *modus operandi* followed by the agencies is not revealed.

Despite this, it is natural that public opinion would judge the agencies not by their unannounced successes but by their well-known failures. There have been plenty of failures in

India. Such failures were either due to the lack of precise intelligence or the inadequacy of follow-up action when such intelligence was available. Among other incidents, the lack of accurate intelligence contributed to the assassination of Rajiv Gandhi by the LTTE in 1991, the Mumbai blasts in March 1993 and the Coimbatore blasts in February 1998. The abortive attempt to kill Rajiv Gandhi at Rajghat in 1987, the Purulia arms drop in December 1995 and the attack on Parliament House in New Delhi on December 13, 2001 are notable examples of security failures despite the availability of prior intelligence.

Indian intelligence analysts are excellent in their evaluation of likely terrorist threats. In 1989, long before the LTTE mounted its attack on Rajiv Gandhi, the agencies had assessed that there was a likely threat to his life from the terrorist outfit during his travels to the South. Similarly, after the widespread anti-Muslim disturbances in Gujarat earlier this year, many analysts including this writer, had warned of the possibility of a major act of retributive terrorism in Gujarat.

In an April 2002 article on punishment terrorism, published on the web site of the South Asian Analysis Group (SAAG), this writer had stated: "Past anger amongst Indian Muslims over the demolition of the Babri Masjid has been aggravated by the recent massacres in Ahmedabad. There had been massacres of the members of the minority communities (Sikhs and Muslims) during communal riots in the past too, but what, in the perception of the Muslims, distinguishes the recent happenings in Ahmedabad from those of the past is the total insensitivity of the local administration to the feelings of the Muslims and what they regard as its conscious inactivism and the absence of even a modicum of effort by the government towards [providing] a healing touch. There is, therefore, a strong possibility of a major act of retributive punishment terrorism in Gujarat in the coming months. It need not necessarily come from [Osama] bin Laden's outfit. There is a greater possibility that it would come from enraged sections of the local Muslims. An encore of Mumbai-March 1993 is on the cards." One is given to understand that similar warnings had been issued by our agencies, indicating the likely targets of retributive terrorism and underlining the security precautions to be taken. Most of the potential targets identified were reportedly associated with the Gujarat government, the Union government and sensitive sectors of the economy. The possibility of a terrorist strike in a temple against innocent members of the Hindu community who had nothing to do with the government was probably not foreseen.

Even if such a possibility had been anticipated, the security agencies would not have been able to prevent the attack unless they had precise intelligence as to when, where and how the terrorists would strike. The fact that the terrorists managed to carry out the assault on the temple would indicate that no such intelligence was available.

Accurate preventive intelligence comes from communication intercepts, moles planted in or recruited from inside terrorist organisations and members of the public. Communication intercepts would be available only if the terrorists use modern means of communications. Penetration of terrorist organisations is an extremely difficult task. It is easier to access the sensitive establishments of an adversary such as Pakistan than a terrorist organisation. It poses ethical problems which are not appreciated by public opinion. If an agency plants a mole in a terrorist organisation, its leadership would first ask him to carry out a killing or some other similar act to test his motivation. If the source comes back and asks his handling intelligence officer whether he should kill in order to establish his credibility in the terrorist outfit, the handling officer would be faced with a severe dilemma. He cannot authorise such acts in the hope that future terrorist attacks might be prevented.

There cannot be a regular flow of preventive intelligence without the cooperation of the community to which the terrorists belong. Is it reasonable to expect the agencies to get such information if political leaders continue to hurt the feelings of the minority community through words and action, rubbing salt into their wounds and causing further alienation? If no such assistance is forthcoming from the public, the political leadership is as much responsible as the agencies for the failure of intelligence in internal security matters.

In other countries, every instance of perceived intelligence failure is followed by an exhaustive inquiry to establish how the breakdown occurred so that corrective steps can be taken. There is currently a Congressional investigation into allegations of intelligence failure with reference to 9/11 and President Bush has indicated his intention to order a similar inquiry by an independent body.

Prior to 1999, there were hardly any steps taken to ascertain why an intelligence failure occurred during the Mizo revolt of 1966. The Kargil Review Committee (KRC) studied the 1999 intelligence failure that made the Pakistani intrusions possible. The Special Task Force on the revamping of the intelligence apparatus, which followed the KRC, went into the need for follow-up action recommended by the KRC. However, it did not specifically address the equally important question of perceived intelligence failures in terrorism-related matters. Unless and until we establish a tradition of setting up an inquiry into each instance of a major intelligence or security failure, we will never be able to identify our deficiencies and correct them. Every country gets the intelligence agencies it deserves. Very few Indian political leaders and Members of Parliament have genuine expertise in counter-terrorism related matters. Hardly any time is devoted in Parliament to an objective and professional discussion of the capabilities of our agencies in this matter.

INDIAN INTELLIGENCE GROPES IN THE DARK

That exchange sounded like a communication between the bombers, promising an intelligence-led breakthrough. But it proved to be a red herring-the newspaper vendors had only rejoiced because after the blasts they expected the sale of their evening papers to zoom.

Barring this one telephone call, there is nothing else that could provide intelligence with a clue to the explosions in Ahmedabad. Intelligence officials say perhaps this is because the bombers are no more speaking for long periods before and after the explosions.

After his arrest last year, Jalaluddin alias Babubhai-the "India operations commander" of the Bangladesh-based militant group Huji-revealed that he had instructed his jihadis (holy warriors) to "minimise telephone or internet communication" during operations.

No leads

"India's technical intelligence capability has developed with help from the US and local scientific knowhow, so we told our brothers to use personal couriers," a senior Intelligence Bureau (IB) official quoted Jalaluddin as saying. Since the serial blasts in the southern city of Hyderabad last August, India's intelligence has failed to pick up leads.

"That explains the complete dearth of intelligence on the groups responsible for this year's serial explosions in Jaipur, Bangalore and Ahmedabad. Our intelligence has become too dependent on technology," says BB Nandi, one of India's best known spymasters. "We are making the same mistakes that Western intelligence agencies made by pinning too much hope on technology. That's important, but there's no substitute for a good agent in the right place," Mr. Nandi says.

While Western intelligence agencies like the CIA and MI-6 are trying to augment human intelligence capabilities after a string of failures such as the 9/11 attacks in the US, Indian intelligence is not learning from their mistakes. Intelligence officials say that Pakistan and Bangladesh-based Islamic militant groups have increasingly made their Indian units autonomous-in recruitment, training, funding and operations-so that nothing can be traced back to the patron nations.

"The serial bombings in Jaipur, Bangalore and Ahmedabad prove that Pakistan's ISI has successfully Indianised the jihad by creating Indian equivalents of Lashkar-e-Toiba or Huji," says B Raman, another former spymaster specialising in Islamic militant groups.

"They still provide general direction, so you have a series of explosions in India immediately after the bombing of the Indian embassy in Kabul and the stepped up hostilities in Kashmir," he says. "But the surrogates are largely independent now in choosing targets or gathering explosives."

'Real Bane'

And why can't India's intelligence agencies penetrate these home-grown Islamic militant groups if they are run and led by Indian Muslims with roots in India? The Intelligence Bureau (IB), which is responsible for domestic and counter-intelligence, is supposed to co-ordinate the fight against militancy through its multi-agency co-ordination.

But the Research and Analysis Wing (RAW), which is responsible for external intelligence, has a major role in checking the foreign sources of militancy. "The real bane of Indian intelligence is that it is largely run by police officials, most of whom serve on deputation from states and are floating in and out of the IB and other federal intelligence wings. They lack both the commitment and the expertise," says retired IB official Ashok Debbarma.

Strangely, the lower echelons of IB and RAW are direct recruits, trained specifically for intelligence. But they lack the motivation because they can rarely rise to senior positions. "None of the world's best intelligence agencies are run by policemen. They are all run by career intelligence officers. It is only in India that the Indian Police Service (IPS) monopolises most senior intelligence positions," Mr. Debbarma said.

He said some police officials have done well in IB and RAW but most have failed in a fast changing world. "The best brains go to foreign service and administrative service and only those at the bottom of the heap are recruited into the police service," Mr. Debbarma says.

A Losing Battle

Interestingly, Gujarat Chief Minister Narendra Modi has demanded the creation of an Indian intelligence service that, he says, should recruit the best available talent and deploy them in positions that fit their special talent. "We should get the best brains for intelligence, but we only get rejects now," Mr. Modi said after the Ahmedabad explosions.

Many say Indian intelligence is losing its fight against Islamic militancy because the agencies do not recruit enough Muslims. "There are very few Muslims in Indian intelligence, only a few in the state police special branches and really a handful in the federal agencies. How can we plant agents amongst jihadis unless we have Muslim officers?" asks a former IB official who does not wish to be named.

The IB is also woefully short of officers-against a sanctioned strength of 250 officers, only 100 places have been filled up. "Most IPS officers use the IB as a transit point. They come here only when they don't get a good posting in their state cadre," says retired IB official Subir Dutta.

INDIA'S INTELLIGENCE SERVICES STRUGGLE WITH WAR ON TERRORISM

A diffuse but highly networked group of terrorists, driven by a dangerous cocktail of extremist ideology and a simmering sense of anguish and revenge, currently pose a serious threat to India's economic and social structure. The militants exploit gaping holes in India's counter-terrorism architecture and strategy as well as the nation's ambivalent policies toward religious minorities, particularly the 150-million strong but largely impoverished Muslim community.

What has complicated the Indian intelligence agencies' task since the flowering of al-Qaeda and a global jihadist movement after 9/11 is the alacrity with which various terrorist groups and their support structures have reworked their strategy and operational methods to effectively dodge a series of worldwide bans. The most dramatic change in the Indian context has been the realignment of terrorist forces, with prominent groups like the Lashkar-e-Tayyeba (LeT) and Jaish-e-Mohammad (JeM)—proscribed by the United States and other countries, including Pakistan—stepping back to allow Harkat-ul Jihad al-Islami (HuJI), an al-Qaeda ally with a pan-South Asian presence, to lead the terror campaign in India.

Other changes have been noticed in the structure and modus operandi of India's terrorist groups. The new recruits to the cause are local men: young, educated and without previous involvement in extremist activities. These men form the nucleus of groups throughout India who tap into the local criminal-hawala network of couriers and handlers to move money and explosives—often locally acquired—to carry out terrorist strikes. The group carrying out the operation typically disengages and disappears after striking, leaving hardly any trace of its existence. Since the simultaneous explosions in Delhi in 2005, investigating agencies frequently encounter red herrings left by the terrorists to confuse the investigation and allow greater time to disband and escape.

Changing Circumstances

Two critical aspects in the growth of Indian terrorism are the mounting evidence pointing to the involvement of the HuJI in terror attacks and the alliance of this group with the Students' Islamic Movement of India (SIMI), a banned network of young Muslim activists who openly claim Osama bin Laden as their idol (The Hindu, April 3, 2007). For a long time India's federal and state investigating agencies did not see the link as a serious development, continuing instead to rely on past experience by focusing on LeT and JeM activists.

One of the primary reasons for this poor assessment was the inability of the intelligence agencies and the whole cornucopia of coordinating agencies at state and federal levels to think beyond the entrenched "conventional wisdom" of analysing terrorist groups through ideological prisms, thereby completely missing the possibility that these groups might work together for a common goal. This has happened not only in India but even in Pakistan, where one such coalition of terror groups called Brigade 313 was involved in assassination attempts on President Pervez Musharraf (Newsline, August 2004; Asia Times, July 14, 2004). Equally restricting has been the reluctance, and even refusal, to share information among the intelligence and security agencies. Along with an inept information-sharing architecture at the national level, this reluctance has proved to be the most critical flaw in counter-terrorism intelligence operations (The Hindu, October 30, 2001). The problem came to the fore recently when police in the Karnataka state of southern India arrested one Riyazuddin Nasir on charges of vehicle theft. Nasir would have been let out on bail for these minor charges but for a single intelligence official in Delhi who decided to search the database for connections with terrorist activities. Nasir was found to be a HuJI operative and one of India's most wanted men (The Hindu, February 12).

Failure to Cooperate

It is not really difficult to see where the problem is—an intelligence structure which has yet to emerge from its debilitating colonial legacy and a complementary stranglehold of bureaucracy. The structure and operational philosophy of state police and intelligence units have not changed much since British days—they are mostly structured as agencies to protect law and order and spy on rivals rather than act as investigative and intelligence units. Criminal investigators are usually inserted into terrorism investigations only after an incident takes place. There are no independent anti-terror units carrying out both intelligence and investigations into terrorist groups at the state level.

At the top of the intelligence pyramid is the National Security Council Secretariat (NSCS), headed by an all-powerful, politically-appointed National Security Advisor (NSA), who often has much more than terrorism on his mind. Intelligence operations within the country are carried out by the Intelligence Bureau (IB) and its wide network of officers and men, all reporting to the Ministry of Home Affairs. The ministry is headed by a cabinet minister and one or two ministers of state—besides a secretary and other senior officials—who often get tempted, at least close to the elections, to utilize the IB for assessing the electoral chances of their party while spying on their rivals. EM Rammohan, a former member of the National Security Advisory Board, notes: "Instead of concentrating on security issues, they are busy chasing the Opposition so that the ruling party is kept in power. Is that the job of the IB?" (outlookindia.com, July 31, 2006).

External intelligence is the responsibility of the Research and Analysis Wing (RAW), working directly under the Cabinet Secretary but reporting to the NSA for all practical purposes. RAW keeps a sharp eye on the activities of terrorist groups with bases in foreign countries. According to former IB joint-director Maloy Krishna Dhar, RAW's reluctance to share information with IB is legendary. There have also been instances where personality clashes have deterred effective coordination between the NSA and RAW chiefs.

The second set of intelligence agencies are the military ones, led by the Directorate General of Military Intelligence (DGMI) with a network of field offices and forward posts in the border areas as well as representatives in diplomatic missions. Since the DGMI has been historically part of the Army, the Air Force and Navy have individual intelligence units collecting and collating information relevant to their operations and bases. The Defence Intelligence Agency (DIA), created in 2002 to correct this anomaly, is entrusted with the task of coordinating the whole spectrum of military intelligence but is presently short-staffed, poorly funded and burdened with an ambitious and expanding circle of objectives.

Paramilitary organizations like the Central Reserve Police Force and Border Security Force maintain their own intelligence units to support counter-insurgency operations in Kashmir and elsewhere. Their intelligence operations have often been stymied by the Army's reluctance to share intelligence tapped from its wide network of informers and sources. Other government agencies providing physical security, like the Special Protection Group, Central Industrial Security Force and National Security Guards, all maintain their own intelligence units.

At the bottom of the pyramid are the state police, whose intelligence networks remain the primary source of information and main agency for implementing action on the ground. The most critical element in this structure is the investigative branch of the local police forces. These go by various names, such as the Criminal Investigation Department, the Special Branch or the Crime Branch. There is no uniformity in responsibilities or operational duties. Typically these units carry out the investigation and prosecution of terrorist, hawala, arms and counterfeit cases, placing them in the unique position of being able to detect the emergence of terror networks or coalitions.

Unfortunately they remain the weakest link in the intelligence chain as these units carry the burden of acting as colonial-style law enforcement agencies and not as modern units capable of organizing preventive measures based on intelligence collection. These forces are commonly afflicted with poor morale and problems related to accountability, pay and training. Even in metropolitan centers like Delhi and Mumbai, the police-criminal nexus and pervasive corruption have rendered effective intelligence from federal agencies worthless. There was clear intelligence available about terrorist attacks in Mumbai at least a month before the July 2006 commuter train blasts. This intelligence was not followed up on, nor were preventive measures put in place at railway stations. A week after the Mumbai blasts, Prime Minister

Manmohan Singh was quoted by the media as saying that "past responses have been inadequate in dealing with these problems which are of a different intensity, magnitude, scale and scope" (The Tribune [Chandigarh, Punjab], July 21, 2006).

Reforming the Intelligence Structure

Of the several steps taken in recent years to overcome these outstanding difficulties, two held great promise. One was the creation of the National Technical Research Organization (NTRO), with a focus on collecting technical intelligence (TECHINT), cyber intelligence and cyber counter-intelligence. Beginning with RAW's Aviation Research Centre (ARC) assets, NTRO is rapidly expanding and strengthening its intelligence capabilities to fulfill this mandate. On the other hand, the NTRO mandate adds one more agency to the mix, as the IB, RAW and the Army's Signals Directorate will continue to maintain autonomous TECHINT units.

The second step was the establishment of a Multi-Agency Centre (MAC) and a Joint Task Force on Intelligence within IB as a hub of India's counter-terrorism effort. The mission objective was to run an umbrella organization comprising state-level units called SMACs and the development of a national counter-terrorism database supported by state-level police-intelligence Joint Task Forces and inter-state Intelligence Support Teams (The Hindu, February 12). Conceived after the pattern of the CIA's Counter-Terrorism Center, the MAC was to be responsible for the joint analysis of intelligence flowing from different quarters and coordinating relevant follow-up actions.

Five years after MAC was approved, it is today composed of a skeletal staff and five SMACs, using a database hosted on a bare-bones computer system designed in-house, with no real-time links to state police forces or other intelligence agencies. There is no sign of the development of the comprehensive database on terrorists on which the entire counter-terrorism information grid was to be built. Senior intelligence officials have pointed out that the interrogation reports of 16,000 Islamist terrorists caught between 1991 and 2005 could prove to be a goldmine of actionable intelligence (The Hindu, February 6). These inadequacies can be overcome by beefing up the present staff strength and widening the recruitment base to include the qualified technical personnel needed to develop, integrate and man the information grid. But progress is delayed due to unseemly bureaucratic wrangling over funding for an additional 140 positions at MAC. Added to this problem is the Indian Army's refusal to depute officials to the agency, citing disciplinary and administrative problems (The Hindu, February 12).

Difficulties like these and the tepid response of the state governments to a 2007 Supreme Court directive ordering improvements in the functioning of police and intelligence agencies continue to bedevil India's attempts to fashion an effective counter-terrorism strategy. Meanwhile terrorist groups continue to display a marked advantage in adapting to newer technologies and modes of operation, allowing them to function more quickly and quietly than the Indian intelligence community.

THE SHE-MOLE'S CASE: MAKING AN ASS OF OURSELVES

1991: Liviu Radu, a Romanian diplomat posted in New Delhi, was kidnapped by some Khalistani terrorists. He was got released as a result of an operation mounted by the Intelligence Bureau (IB) and the Research & Analysis Wing (R&AW). A Western intelligence agency co-operated in the operation. A senior officer of the Ministry of External Affairs (MEA) told the media about the identity of the Western agency. It was prominently carried by some sections of the media. The Western country concerned through its Embassy in New Delhi strongly protested against the failure of the MEA officer to protect the identity of its agency.

1993: After the serial blasts in Mumbai in March 1993, the Federal Bureau of Investigation (FBI) of the US secretly sent a team of its explosive experts to Mumbai to help the investigators of the Mumbai Police. They were put up in a Mumbai hotel under a non-official cover. The leader of the team was surprised to receive a phone call from a journalist of the British Broadcasting Corporation (BBC) then posted in New Delhi, who was aware of their FBI identity. Enquiries revealed that a senior officer of the Mumbai Police had told the journalist about their FBI identity and revealed to him the name of the hotel where they were staying. There was a strong protest from the FBI over the indiscretion of the Mumbai Police officer.

2010: Madhuri Gupta, a Second Secretary working in the Press and Information wing of the Indian High Commission in Islamabad, was arrested on a charge of working for the Pakistani intelligence. While reporting on her arrest and interrogation, sections of the media named another officer of the High Commission and claimed that he was from the Indian intelligence. According to a report carried by a national daily, this was mentioned to the journalists by an officer of the MEA.

It is important to protect the identity of serving intelligence officers posted abroad for three reasons. Firstly, the exposure of his identity will make it impossible for him to perform his intelligence tasks in future. Secondly, it could pose a serious threat to his life from terrorists. And, thirdly, it could create operational problems.

In the 1970s, the revelation of the identity of a serving officer of the Central Intelligence Agency (CIA) posted in Europe led to his assassination by some terrorists. The Congress passed a law making it a criminal offence for anyone to reveal the identity of a serving intelligence officer. Since then,American officials and media take care not to reveal the identity of a serving intelligence officer even if they come to know of it. Dick Cheney, the Vice-President under George Bush, came under severe criticism for asking one of his aides to brief a journalist about the identity of a serving woman officer of the CIA. Cheney's aide had to face an enquiry for carrying out the request of Cheney, which amounted to a crime.

In other countries too, officials as well as the media take great care to protect the identity of serving intelligence officers posted in foreign countries. In Israel, as in the US, it is a crime to reveal the identity of a serving intelligence officer. In India, we have neither laws nor traditions to protect the identities of serving intelligence officers posted abroad. During the last five years, Indian media has exposed the identities of at least a dozen serving external intelligence officers posted abroad, thereby damaging their utility as intelligence officers and exposing them to likely physical threats from terrorists.

This is highly unwise on the part of the journalists, but how can we blame them when they are tipped off by other officers of the Government, who do not realise the importance of protecting the cover and security of intelligence officers serving abroad. There could be strong opposition from the Indian media to the Government enacting a law similar to the US law to protect the identity of intelligence officers serving abroad, but it should at least ensure that such leakages and disclosures do not take place from the officials of the Government.

The case of Madhuri Gupta has been handled in an unprofessional manner, with almost a leak an hour. If some of these leaks are to be believed, she must be the greatest intelligence agent ever produced in the history of espionage from a diplomatic mission comparable to the legendary Cicero, a Nazi agent in the British Embassy in Ankara. If our news channels are to be believed, what all she has done: Exposed the identities of Indian agents in Pakistan; exposed the identities of Indian agents in other countries; gave to the Pakistani intelligence copies of classified documents including what is described as the classified minutes of the Prime Minister's office on India's relations with Pakistan etc etc. If he was alive, Cicero's handling officer would have envied her handling officer in the Pakistani intelligence. There are at least a dozen journalists claiming exclusive access to the results of the interrogation and yet reporting the same unbelievable stories in almost the same language. These dozen journalists are also claiming exclusive access to the interrogation reports. Some of them have even been giving what they claim are quotes from the interrogation reports. I known how interrogation reports are recorded. They are not recorded the way they are shown on some of our TV channels.

Who is Madhuri Gupta? What is her background? She is an Urdu translator posted in Islamabad to monitor the Urdu media. The Press and Information wing in which she was working deals only with open information and handles the Pakistani media. It is not a wing of the mission having access to classified documents. It is the cut and paste from the media wing. And yet our media has been reporting that classified reports passed through her hands. She was not even the head of the wing. She was one of its staff.

It is not getting whether to laugh or cry when one saw an anchor criticising Pakistan for not co-operating with India in the investigation of the case. What does he expect Pakistan to do? Admit that she was their agent and tell us the details of what she did for the Pakistani intelligence? The world will be laughing at the kind of reporting that has been going on on our TV channels. Normally, the print media used to be more responsible in reporting. Senior sub-editors used to exercise some check over the exuberance of the reporters and carefully vet their stories before accepting them. Now, even print media journalists are competing with their TV colleagues in being more and more sensational. What is important is not whether one is correct and believable, but whether one's story is sufficiently sensational. The more sensational, the better.

Truth, reliability, balance and restraint in reporting have been the victims of the "breaking news" culture in our TV media. Madhuri Gupta's case is a serious breach of our national security.Even if she had not revealed any classified information to the Pakistani intelligence, the very fact that the Pakistani intelligence succeeded in recruiting her speaks poorly of our counter-intelligence controls. The case deserves to be investigated and analysed in a serious manner on the basis of established facts. Instead, it has been converted into a slapstick serial which will go on until another equally attention-catching serial replaces it.

The Government and our officers who have been talking to the media do not realise the importance of keeping the Pakistani intelligence guessing as to what she has been telling her interrogators. Intelligence agencies worth their salt keep their adversary guessing when they identify and arrest one of its agents. When the KGB, the Soviet intelligence agency, shot down and arrested Francis Gary Powers, the U-2 pilot of the CIA, for quite some time they did not reveal that they had caught him alive. They made an ass of the CIA and then President Dwight Eisenhower by keeping them guessing as to what happened to Powers.

Inatead of making an ass of the Pakistani intelligence by keeping it guessing as to what happened to Madhuri Gupta, our intelligence agencies, the MHA and the MEA are making an ass of themselves by vying with one another in leaking out to the media all sorts of stories after revealing prematurely information about her arrest.

7

Intelligence Reform

A discourse is on in the country on the need for intelligence reforms and its future contours. Think-tanks are busy on the subject. The Vice President spoke about it publicly during a talk at the RAW Hqrs in January last year. An MP is proposing to introduce a private bill in the Lok Sabha on the subject in the near future. There can be no disagreement anywhere that the quality of intelligence mechanisms and their products need urgently to be upgraded. History establishes that intelligence can be a game changer. As challenges in a rapidly changing geostrategic environment around India keep mounting, the inevitability of having to make difficult choices must be recognized.

The intelligence organisations should be made totally autonomous with regards to operations and internal administration. These organisations have to function unconventionally... The magnitude of the tasks ahead can be best illustrated by a small analogy. We have an aeroplane, engineered decades earlier, to fly at a height of 5000 feet. Now aeroplanes are needed to fly at 20000 feet and more. No amount of technological tinkering with this plane will enable it to reach the requisite heights. An invention of an entirely new machine alone can be the answer. The intelligence organisations of today largely resemble the aeroplane in this example. To fulfill the requirements of a modern day intelligence set-up fundamental changes are called for.

Two major factors stand in obstruction. One is the reigning political and bureaucratic culture. The other is the structure of the intelligence. Both must alter radically if intelligence has to keep its tryst with destiny. Culture is a phenomenon which takes decades and centuries to evolve and change. It took the French many years after reformation and renaissance in Europe to develop the culture of composite nationalism and agree among themselves to the frontiers of the French nation which today remain the same as established two hundred years ago. France became the first country to become a nation from several states of French people. Therefore to expect that the political and bureaucratic culture will change in the country within a reasonable time will remain a futile dream.

The Foreign Secretary and the Indian Ambassador at Kabul before returning, advised the R&AW to get their team also back to Delhi. But, this team stayed on and kept the Indian flag flying over the Embassy while the MEA staff went home.

However what is within the realm of possibility is to change the structure of intelligence. The CIA provides a good model and its achievements in the field of intelligence are quite inspiring, though it has had its share of failures. Quite often the failures were the result of lack of co-ordination and improper assessments, not production of intelligence. Without a shot being fired and foreign troops invading, the Soviet Union disintegrated largely because of uncompromising psy-war and other operations of the CIA. In Afghanistan the Talibans were ousted by use of US air power, operating from ships, Diego Garcia and other bases including those in USA, and just 3000 or so number of people from the CIA and special operation groups. No military boots from the West stepped into Afghanistan till after the Taliban had been ousted.

Indian intelligence needs to be established on the same basis, insulating it from political and bureaucratic controls except where policy and objectives are concerned. The intelligence organisations should be made totally autonomous with regards to operations and internal administration. These organisations have to function unconventionally the nature of which the politicians and bureaucrats fail to understand, creating hurdles.

The foundations of the organisations rest on the recruitment and training of the correct individual. They must have total freedom to recruit from wherever they deem necessary on terms which will attract the best talent in the country from the universities, industry, media, specialists in engineering etc. There will always be a huge requirement of R&D within and the cutting edge can be achieved by recruiting the very best. This is how the CIA functions. Internal mechanisms can be developed to root out nepotism and cronyism in recruitment. Apart from the freedom to hire they should also have the liberty to fire. Such a system has produced for the CIA the best band of operational officers in the world. ...all flow of intelligence products should be directed towards another single authority, the National Intelligence Coordinator (NIC) who will prepare the national intelligence estimates, analysis and assessments and besides, identify the intelligence gaps to different agencies.

The recruits will be members of the in-house services. No outside service including IPS should be allowed to dominate though there may be a revolving door policy to admit anyone from anywhere found suitable.

The creation of an elite cadre within the organisations cannot be over emphasized. Mr. BN Mullick, the second DIB in the country after independence, had created an earmarking scheme in the IB which became operational in 1954, earmarking 4 or 5 top candidates selected by UPSC for IPS. They worked in the IB for their entire career after initial training. With further rigorous training within the IB, they became an elite core, extremely efficient, committed, and excelling both in operations and analysis. They employed caution but were not risk averse. All the DIBs subsequently have come from this corps. Several years later the scheme was wound up due to bureaucratic pressure, opposing continuous stay of such IPS officers in Delhi and other posts of IB when they could not have a similar privilege of spending their entire career outside their state cadres. The last DIB from the EMS retired last year. The political controllers of the day could not prevent the demise of this scheme. It is a telling commentary on their vision, understanding and management of intelligence.

Talking of commitment an anecdote will speak volumes. In 1988 when Afghanistan had become an extremely dangerous place during President Najibullah's regime the diplomats of the western countries including the US had been withdrawn en bloc. The Indian Government also recalled their staff with the diplomats to Delhi. The Foreign Secretary and the Indian Ambassador at Kabul before returning, advised the R&AW to get their team also back to Delhi. But, this team stayed on and kept the Indian flag flying over the Embassy while the MEA staff went home. The structures of the organisations have to be founded in law to ensure autonomy and insulation from non professionals. The law should provide for an Ombudsman as well as parliamentary committees that can evaluate performance with respect to objectives of the prescribed charters but all operational matters should remain outside their jurisdiction. There should, thus, be no executive control save as provided under the parliamentary laws.

Accepting autonomy for these organisations will remain a touchy question with the political and bureaucratic classes in the country. Police reforms remain to be carried out in the country despite Supreme Court judgments and prodding since the State Governments do not wish to loose their control over such a powerful instrument as the Police. The CBI also remains similarly shackled. Therefore, despite the growing awareness that intelligence reforms are the need of the day, meaningful progress in this field will remain unpredictable.

The reforms, as and when the discourse reaches the stage of finality, should also focus on the role of the National

Security Adviser (NSA) about which there is much confusion today. Is he an intelligence czar or the master co-coordinator or the principal analyst for the Cabinet Committee of Security (CCS), the highest policy making body in the country? Some enlightened and knowledgeable people hold the view that he can be dispensed with. Besides, if he is to remain constantly traveling to foreign parts, one will start wondering whether he can do justice to all the three roles combined. Ideally, he should be the recipient of finalized assessments on the basis of which he places before the CCS a range of considered scenarios for policy options.

On the other hand, all flow of intelligence products should be directed towards another single authority, the National Intelligence Coordinator (NIC) who will prepare the national intelligence estimates, analysis and assessments and besides, identify the intelligence gaps to different agencies. He will also be responsible for ensuring coordinated field actions, especially during fast moving developments.

The authority for executive control to bring about coordination thus rests at his level. Operational responsibility will be the business of the agencies. In a democracy like India with multi faceted challenges of its external and internal realities, graduating from a regional power to a world status, from a soft power to hard power, retaining two separate institutions, NSA and NIC, would be advisable, the latter feeding the former on assessments. The former will have a much wider canvass to take care of with foreign policy increasingly getting entwined with economic and defense real politick calculations. The latter will provide the material and the evidence to formulate and tighten the nuts and bolts of policy.

INDIAN INTELLIGENCE REFORMS

More than 50 years after gaining independence from the British, Indian Intelligence continues to operate within the same framework left by the British. The system was created to deal with problems and requirements of a different age. Since then we have moved into a new era where the national security architecture of the world keeps changing in a kaleidoscopic pattern, creating new axess of conflicts and conciliations. Times have changed enormously and the world has become far more complex. Unfortunately, Indian Intelligence has not kept pace with the changes.

It is high time that an Indian Intelligence Reforms Commission is appointed on the lines of the Administrative Reforms Commission to overhaul the old system. There are a whole lot of new paradigms requiring to be considered. If in today's world intelligence has become the first line of defense, there is not a moment to be lost.

The very first reform should be to give Indian Intelligence the backing of legislative enactments. The laws should provide a degree of autonomy which frees intelligence from all bureaucratic restraints and controls relating to financial management, administrative functions, pay scales, recruitment, postings and promotions, hire and fire policies and enforcement of discipline. The laws should spell out the charters and authorize the Central Government to fix broad targets within the charter. This will prevent the misuse of the institutions by those in authority. The laws should hold intelligence accountable to the Cabinet or its Committee for national Security but also create a parliamentary committee for oversight. Detailed rules can be worked out to determine the parameters of oversight and areas of intelligence work over which it will be exercised in consultation with the Parliament. Absence of legislative cover is a serious lacuna for Intelligence. All intelligence work is carried out under executive instructions but foreign intelligence operations would involve breaking of local laws of the country concerned. Neither those who give instructions for such operations nor those who carry them out are protected legally under the Indian laws. Institutions like the CIA of US are created by laws of the US Congress. All activities which CIA may be required to carry out are directly or indirectly identified in the charter legally given. Their operations are thus safe under US laws but no such protection is available to Indian operatives, carrying out intelligence tasks in a foreign country.

Autonomy is essential for non-conventional organisations to do their jobs. They should be free to hire the best talent available which will be possible only if a very superior compensation package is on offer to the recruit. Today's intelligence needs require Engineers, Management Specialists, Economists, Scholars, Scientist, Sociologists among others, of supreme quality but only the inferior type wants to make a career in intelligence because the better type finds the existing compensation packages totally unattractive. Intelligence services of other countries are usually the best paid organizations in those countries. This is the reason why CIA serves as a magnet drawing in large numbers of PhDs from the best schools in the US. In recent years the threats from International terror has grown exponentially. There are threats of mass destruction of population and property through use of weapons of mass destruction, mass disruption of communications through manipulation of cyberspace and of mass doctrinal madness through clever selective religious indoctrination. Such a range of offensive tactics cannot be countered by keeping intelligence on the defensive. Intelligence has to be provided teeth to bite with. It should therefore develop its own cadre of offensive operators or learn to do so in the company of select uniformed services. While the major countries of the world have for long practiced the offensive mode of Intelligence work, we have lagged behind in India. Intelligence reforms should open up the possibilities of covert actions. Use of non state actors by state actors effectively takes away India's options to stay neutral to covert operations. A redefinition of nation's security interest will shout loudly for India to give up its self created soft image and to move out to meet challenges boldly as they should be.

Intelligence has to acknowledge appearance of new perspectives following globalization. Fast moving technologies have made borders meaningless. There is a new competition for economic penetration. Sovereignties of nations are at a discount because of these trends. In the times ahead India will face acute competition from the other two rising powers of the Asia, China and Japan. Issues of land, water and climatic changes, all of which singly or together, lead to mass migrations, creating demographic imbalances. Who else should study such phenomenon holistically if not intelligence? Their database and sharp analysis can contribute to keep the nations interests secure.

The rising complexity calls for another reform – the operations and analysis cadres in the intelligence should be made distinct and separate. When intelligence needs were few, there may have been a justification for the two streams to flow as one, but not any longer. Indian Intelligence has to grow much larger than what it is today. The value of an analyst lies in the depth of his studies of his field. The longer he specializes, greater is the intuitive insight he acquires. Such knowledge will go waste if he moves to operations. Naxalism has been identified as the nation's most serious problem in the field of national security. Starting from a single village, Naxalbari, in West Bengal in 1965, Naxalism is now present in 16 states, affecting 160 districts. In the context of intelligence reforms, one must examine why such a growth has taken place. It would seem that our constitutional scheme by dividing powers between states and centre has prevented the latter from formulating and executing a cohesive policy for the country to battle this problem. If this situation is not rectified, mere reforms in intelligence will not take us anywhere.

REGARDED AS INTELLIGENCE REFORM

'Nothing should be as favourably regarded as intelligence; nothing should be as generously rewarded as intelligence; nothing should be as confidential as the work of intelligence.'

It is possible that had the state paid any attention to Sun Tzu's principles, our systems might have been better equipped to handle events that led to and occurred on 26/11. In India we have violated all these principles, more or less consistently but especially in these last few years, since after the time of Rajiv Gandhi. In the aftermath of the Mumbai massacres, and even before that, throughout 2008 questions about intelligence failures have been raised after each major terrorist act. However, Mumbai was more than just intelligence failure. Like Kargil it was also a systemic failure but the starting point is inadequate intelligence, the failure to connect the dots within the system and then the rest just happened as the world saw on TV.

Intelligence reforms without police reforms are pointless because the local policeman develops the strategic intelligence given by the central agencies. Police reforms without civil service reform are equally meaningless. And civil service reform without political reform is similarly meaningless. It is unfortunate that for a country like ours that has had to deal with insurgencies and unending terrorism for sixty years, the political leadership and a civil bureaucracy has viewed the business of intelligence collection with disdain. Efforts to control have usually meant putting roadblocks and reducing intelligence functions to bureaucratic practices.

Any state that seriously wants to preserve or enhance its national interests needs statecraft that is a mixture of diplomacy, intelligence, military technology and economic power. No single instrument is powerful enough in the pursuit of national interests and all instruments have to be sharp and powerful but intelligence is an important function at all times, peace or war or between the two stages. Unless leaders equip themselves with a strong intelligence arm, they will continue to be surprised and making wrong choices.

In understanding the role of external intelligence we must first accept few basic truths. Even the best intelligence will not be a guarantee against all terrorist attacks or other nasty surprises but it will make the price higher, will be a deterrent and of immense help in investigations, instead of what happens at present where the investigating agencies are blindsided. Secondly, intelligence is not just by the IB or R&AW or DIA; in case of terrorism it is the local state units in the district and the sub-division that have to perform.

Third, since external intelligence operates on foreign soil, it is an extra-legal or even illegal activity. That is why governments need the cover of plausible deniability since relations between sovereign powers could get adversely affected even ruptured because of clandestine activities. That is also why preserving an intelligence operative's identity becomes vital but is often not understood. It is not a quirk of personality or a desire for mystery that makes an intelligence operative uncomfortable when he is exposed as so often happens in India. In fact the best intelligence operatives are those who have a passion for anonymity although in the Indian system this is impossible.

IT-driven globalisation also covers the criminal world. Interaction between narcotics smugglers, arms merchants, human traffickers and terrorists is that much easier, faster and safer. They all have access to sophisticated denial and deception techniques. Further, intelligence is often an amalgam of information and data from various sources — technical of various kinds and human sources, all of which is converted into knowledge by skilled analysts. But all this is not enough because intelligence is as good as the process that converts this information into knowledge and the ability of the ultimate user to assimilate this intelligence.

Intelligence is generally considered evil because it is secret, therefore it must be controlled by transients who are either biased or ignorant about the methods and needs. There is therefore an absurd expectation among some wise people that intelligence agencies and their methods should be made transparent. At the other end of the spectrum is the declining professionalism among the agencies where they have been resorting to leaks to protect themselves. Presumably in an atmosphere of uncertainty and a highly politicised bureaucracy, this is another way to save one's gaddi — when sycophancy ceases to work.

There are other things that are wrong today within the agencies. The first aspect is to consider whether the present system of recruitment and manning the intelligence organisations is the best that is possible given the present nature and level of threats. National threats have changed. There are other transnational threats that no single agency or a single country can handle. Besides, there is no knowing how the new threats will evolve. The rapidly changing technological applications bring their own threats. Catastrophic terrorism, cyber terrorism, remote control missile attacks and virtual wars are the other new threats. International trade and commercial transactions have become faster and more intricate; banking transactions move at the speed of lightning.

IT-driven globalisation also covers the criminal world. Interaction between narcotics smugglers, arms merchants, human traffickers and terrorists is that much easier, faster and safer. They all have access to sophisticated denial and deception techniques. Add to this, radical religious terrorists who are affecting India most dramatically and are supported by Pakistan in every way. The normal civil servant however bright just does not have these skills or the aptitude.Within organisations there has been an increasingly greater reliance on techint in preference to humint capabilities. No amount of techint is a substitute for an intelligence operative or an astute and experienced analyst. Techint will give facts but not intentions

Within organisations there has been an increasingly greater reliance on techint in preference to humint capabilities. No amount of techint is a substitute for an intelligence operative or an astute and experienced analyst. The best techint is of little use if this is not preceded or accompanied by effective and sound humint capacities. Techint will give facts but not intentions and particularly in the case of counter terrorism, humint is an absolute must. Intelligence collection and operations are increasingly highly specialised skills. This is not something that can be handled by men and women who seek to join an intelligence agency as a temporary haven or as an opportunity to treat the organisation as a secondary foreign office with no commitment to the profession. These are jobs meant for lifetime committed professionals who acquire their skills in tradecraft, languages, areas and issues over a long period of time. Besides relatively small organisations like the R&AW cannot have a revolving door where officers come and go every few years. The R&AW is the only major external intelligence organisation in the world that has a fixed quota for seconded officers to man its clandestine and analysis desks. In an era of specialisation this means that these very skills are lacking; so is the commitment. This means a loss of talent every few years apart from other drawbacks that an officer has walked away with many operational secrets and can be vulnerable once he leaves.

The R&AW was not conceived as a Central Police Organisation. It was Prime Minister Indira Gandhi and the organisation's founding fathers, Rameshwar Nath Kao and Sankaran Nair, who repeatedly stressed that the R&AW should not become just another police organisation, and should have talent from wherever they could find, including other services of the Government of India. Recruitment to what would be a new service began in 1971 and many other lateral entrants later got absorbed in a service that became their new life.

Since personnel of intelligence agencies seek promotion within their own agencies there is need to change the nomenclature of their ranks, to break free from the system of equivalence with the hierarchy, and strike out on one's own. It was during the watch of Garry Saxena that the service rules were formalised and later other lateral entries were possible. The underlying principle of this was intelligence collection and operations were not assumed to be the preserve of any particular service but unfortunately the IPS still assumes it should have primacy in the R&AW and the result has been a constant and a debilitating battle between the in-house service and the IPS.

The result has been that apart from calamities like Morarji Desai that befell R&AW in the ninth year of its existence, the organisation has been subjected to periodic attempts at reforms which have been a little better than merely reorganising quotas among various services or creating more promotional avenues. These reviews and committees have attempted to exercise external control and succeeded in creating only road blocks. This has only meant increasing bureaucratisation of a profession which by nature has to be unconventional, and needs imaginative and flexible handling far away from stodgy bureaucrats who feel at home only in carefully structured and rigid systems. For this mindset, the process and not the result, is an end in itself.

Drawing the right talent has been an increasing challenge in the government. It is more so in the R&AW. The UPSC route may have been the more transparent, but now seems increasingly unimaginative and irrelevant to the needs. This is not to overlook that the IPS has contributed some truly outstanding intelligence officers but these officers would have been outstanding anywhere. It is just that the requirements have changed today. Besides that an exam passed five, ten or twenty years ago does not qualify a man or a woman as an intelligence officer.

The former Naval Chief Admiral Arun Prakash highlighted the kind of problem that exists in his recent article "The clear and present danger from 6th CPC". He pointed out the difficulties R&AW had in accommodating Naval officers on secondment because of the equivalences laid down by "the Kafkaesque Department of Personnel."

It is estimated that today outsourcing is a 50 billion dollar business annually and consumes about 70 percent of the budget of the US intelligence community and this includes those working on covert operations. This comment underscores the problem of manning that afflicts both the intelligence agencies and the armed forces because as with the Navy, so with the Army and Air Force. There are other problems in a world where the threat perceptions are changing rapidly and where the terrorist is invariably a step or two ahead of the counter terrorist. There is a need to break out of the hierarchical system introduced in intelligence agencies where promotions within the organisations must lag behind the superior service, the IAS. Since personnel of intelligence agencies seek promotion within their own agencies there is need to change the nomenclature of their ranks, to break free from the system of equivalence with the hierarchy, and strike out on one's own. The same principle could apply to the Armed Forces who do not have to be bound down by archaic principles of equivalence. They can still be answerable to the civil authority of the government.

The regular UPSC recruit, however bright, will not suffice. The brightest no longer join the civil service. And an intelligence agency needs language skills, in depth knowledge about the target country and its cultural mores, computer whizz kids, technology experts, military men, financial experts and bankers who can help trace the financial trails of the terrorist, the ability to link the terrorist with the arms and drug smuggler. It needs economists, scientists, area experts, political analysts, university dons, journalists and those with the skills like those of Connie Sachs in John le Carre's "Tinker, Tailor, Soldier, Spy." Ideally, therefore, an external intelligence agency should be able to pay its personnel well but be able to hire and fire for non-performance.

It cannot afford to carry disgruntled men and women in its ranks. Promotions throughout will have to be performance based not linked to seniority. There has to be a fast track for those who excel. Since everybody cannot climb the ladder and there has to be some sidelining of even the bright ones, it is best for the government to consider the system of flexible pay bands so that officers can at least hope to end up with a better pay packet at the end of the day.

Intelligence is not just by the IB or R&AW or DIA; in case of terrorism it is the local state units in the district and the sub-division that have to perform. This means having to break out of the iron cage of the bureaucracy. It also means recruiting in the open market from colleges and universities as all the well known agencies of the world like the CIA, the SIS and Mossad do. Catch them young and then mould them is the motto. In the present system, the man joins an organisation when he may be in his mid-twenties or if he is seconded, even much later. Most have got accustomed to the frills of bureaucracy, are married and have children. They are just too rigid to learn anything new and too old to take any risks or gamble, so essential for an intelligence operative.

It is of course unrealistic to expect any banker or finance wizard to give up his fancy job and work for a still lowly paid government assignment. The CIA faced with budget cuts in the Clinton era got over this problem by outsourcing which has now become an Intelligence-Industrial Complex rather like the Military-Industrial Complex that has typified US capitalism. It is estimated that today outsourcing is a 50 billion dollar business annually and consumes about 70 percent of the budget of the US intelligence community and this includes those working on covert operations.

The CIA, the National Security Agency and the Pentagon now have partnership arrangements with giants like Lockheed Martin, IBM, CACI and Booz Allen Hamilton. This may not be the model for India to follow but there is no way that there can be any effective functioning of intelligence agencies in the future without some involvement and reliance on the private sector. This involvement is going to be inevitable and necessary chiefly because it could be in the interest of the private sector to be participatory in the security of the country and it has the means and the resources to do so. The private sector could provide the technological inputs in battling terror.

In a fast changing world with a rapidly changing threat perception, intelligence agencies have not been nor allowed to be flexible to meet the evolving threat. There is hardly any surge capability where the agency can, on its own, shift manpower and resources to meet the new threat.

In a fast changing world with a rapidly changing threat perception, intelligence agencies have not been nor allowed to be flexible to meet the evolving threat. There is hardly any surge capability where the agency can, on its own, shift manpower and resources to meet the new threat. The present system is far too cumbersome and slow to allow any rapid redeployment and by the time the new system is put into place the quarry has moved on, either morphed into something different or has just become too big so that the changes originally proposed become inadequate. The head of an intelligence organisation must have the flexibility and authority to move men and material around. None of these freedoms would be available without checks and balances and accountability or oversight. We are perhaps not yet ready, as a people, to have the US system but the British system is better for us where accountability is to the Cabinet. A great deal would depend on the Prime Minister who needs to choose his chiefs of intelligence with great care. Past experience, career performance and integrity should be the main guiding factors and not seniority.

All this is meaningless unless there is a systemic overhaul. Both Mumbai and Kargil were as much systemic failures, yet the target always is the intelligence systems. Mumbai occurred because the lessons of Kargil were not adequately learnt. Intelligence reforms without police reforms are pointless because the local policeman develops the strategic intelligence given by the central agencies. Police reforms without civil service reform are equally meaningless. And civil service reform without political reform is similarly meaningless.

Given the needs of the hour, the threats that we face and will continue to face in the future, the country can no longer afford to have nothing but the best.

8

Anatomy of Indian Intelligence Services and Alliances

Master strategist, Chanakya alias Kautilya's (literally meaning 'crooked') taught the art of dishonesty,cunning, insincerity,plot and plan,and stabbing and was adopted in Toto by India and its chief intelligence agency, the Research and Analysis Wing (RAW). While laying the foundation stone of RAW, India's late Prime Minister Mrs. Indira Gandhi approvingly quoted Louis F Hallis, when she said that its objectives should be the, "Ability to get what one wants by whatever means: eloquence, reasoned arguments, bluff, tirade, threat or coercion, as well as, by arousing pity, annoying others, or making them uneasy".

RAW is basically a Secret Service established to perform secret operations based on the Chanakyan principles of deception and cunningness. It has successfully destabilized neighboring countries, disintegrated independent states and backed the most notorious guerrilla organizations to achieve its ends.

If it is compared to other intelligence agencies of the region, it emerges as an aggressive, cold-blooded and ruthless institution, engaged in the most chilling deeds.

Modes & Method of Espionage

Chanakya advocated that "the weak should be subjugated

by means of conciliation and gifts, the strong by means of dissension and force".

Motivation and Recruitment

Motivation of persons to cater intelligence is directly proportionate to their weakness for sex and money, besides the burning desire of revenge or voracious hunger for power. The Spymasters of ancient India exploited these weaknesses to their fullest advantage, and even the modern intelligence agencies heavily depend on these considerations.

Selection of Targets

Chanakya, in a very understated manner and with an intimate knowledge of human psychology, selected his targets in foreign lands depending on their weaknesses and motivation. His selection and target area were,

Those who are dissatisfied with the rulers or had been humiliated or exiled.

Who have not been compensated for their expenditure?

Those that have been deprived of their rightful inheritance to office.

Whose women have been molested by force?

Who were wrongly imprisoned?

Whose property had been confiscated?

Who are prone to blackmail due to some weakness?

Double Agent

Chanakya suggested that secret agents should not refuse pay from the targets for working with them as their employees.

A 'Double-Agent' is a spy who works for the opposition while pretending loyalty to those who employ him.

'Double-Agents' were used to winning over the confidence of their adopted masters by sacrificing a few exposed, treacherous, disaffected or inefficient spies.

'Double-Agents' were used for creating open conflict and confusion among the confederates of the enemy.

They floated false documents, got them seized from the possession of the enemy's army and thus weakened the enemy.

This technique is an indispensable facet of agent-running and was extensively practiced in ancient India.

Payment & Emoluments

Encouragement of secret agents with money and honor was considered an imperative necessity.

The sources were paid both in cash and kind, besides receiving extraordinary courtesies and favors.

It was also recommended that secret agents not only be rewarded for the job done by them but, also, in the event of repeated mistakes, silent punishment-death-be awarded to them.

Communication of Intelligence

Intelligence not properly and promptly conveyed, cannot be acted upon thereby loses its value and validity.

Interception of Mail

Interception of messages, signals and letters by postal censorship, monitoring, tapping telephones, and breaking codes is the standard practice of modern intelligence agencies.

In the ancient period, since intelligence was communicated through pre-determined signals and with the assistance of pigeons, secret agents must have made elaborate arrangements to intercept these messages.

Assessment of Information

Caution against the placing of reliance on agents without proper validation has always been the ethical mode of information.

The Arthasastra emphasized that all aspects of a report

must be gone through, including the source of information, the mode of its collection and the past performance of a source before it is accepted.

Briefing and debriefing of secret agents was an elaborate exercise, and they were trained to be precise, accurate and truthful in reporting.

Working Under 'Cover'

The institution of espionage in ancient India, like modern times, required secret agents to work under some kind of 'cover' to preserve secrecy.

Chanakya institutionalized the art of working under the most imaginative 'covers'.

The most common disguises recommended by him were those of frugal, beggar, merchant, artisan, wandering minstrel, artiste, cook, barber and shampooer, bath and toilet attendant, deaf, dumb, eunuch and prostitute.

Chanakya recommends the use of women as effective tools of espionage particularly those who were engaged in prostitutism.

Counter Intelligence

A counter-intelligence operation is directed at discovering the identities and methods of foreign spies and intelligence officers working for the opposition.

One of the most important duties of the Secret Service in ancient India was to counteract the activities of such agents operating within the country.

Chanakya recommends that secret agents should discover foreign spies by operating at the places of entertainment, conclaves of people, among beggars, in gardens and public places, and the houses of prominent citizens.

Disinformation and Dissension

Manipulation of public opinion is as important an object of the State today as it was in ancient India.

It is used to create disharmony and distrust among the enemy's friends, ill-will among his allies, loss of confidence in their leadership and disruption by psychological means his capacity and will to fight.

Chanakya had perfected the technique of disinformation and highly praised the use of conflict in enemy's ranks for winning a battle without any military action.

Sabotage

The technique of sabotage, which the political strategists consider as the second to last means to crush an enemy, had been greatly perfected in ancient India.

Secret practices for sabotage were advocated by Chanakya to ensure victory.

He suggests the creation of an atmosphere nice to arousing terror, fear, demoralization, disappointment and loss of confidence among the enemy ranks.

Prior to launching a full-scale assault on the enemy fort, Chanakya suggests implementation of secret measures to weaken its defenses not only physically but in all respects. These include prevention of sowing the fields, destruction of the standing crops and cutting of the enemy's supply lines.

He also advises free and uninhibited use of poison in the articles used by the enemy.

His detailed and scientifically valid knowledge of the subject has earned for him a place in Arabic medical literature, which knows him as Ibn Shanaq (son of Chanak).

Some of the secret stratagems advocated by Chanakya include the use of smoke with properties seriously affecting the vision, and, arson or setting fires within the enemy fort.

The Employment of Poison-damsels

Visakanya is a unique feature of the Indian genius to poison the monarch.

These venomous beauties are,

A damsel,whose body is saturated with gradual doses of poison, and who is likely to transmit poison from her body to another person coming in contact with her.

A woman, who treacherously captivates the heart of a person and then mixes poison in his "food or drinks",.

A girl, who is, one way or the other, so much poisoned or infected with disease that she is likely to convey her poison or disease to the person coming in contact with her.

A woman suffering from Venereal disease or, in the latest situation one suffering from Aids is a Visa kanya of this kind.

Secret Agencies in ancient India had perfected very ingenious techniques to sub serve the interests of their crowned heads.

Besides using the promising technological advancement available to them, they exploited human weakness for sex to achieve royal objectives.

'In the work of espionage, all methods are admissible Ñ snooping, lying, bribing, poisoning, using women's charm and the assassin's knife.

To a weak king menaced by strong neighbors, Chanakya advice was to rely chiefly on spies and remuneration what he described as a 'battle of intrigues'(mauvering) (mantra yuddha) and 'secret wars' (kuta yuddha).

The spies, in order to achieve their objective, were to practice all kinds of fraud, tricks, arsons and robbery.

Their objective was to demoralize the enemy's troops by circulating false news, and seduce the allegiance of his minister and commanders.

The underlying idea seems to have been to keep the strong neighbors preoccupied with domestic troubles thus making it impossible for him to launch a foreign expedition.

Transformation of Predecessors in to Successors

The rules of business of espionage have not changed; at least the basic principles remain as before, from the days of Chanakya.

It was towards the end of 1966 and the beginning of 1967 that the concept of a separate foreign intelligence agency began to take concrete shape.

In 1968, after Indira Gandhi had taken over, it was decided that a full-fledged second security service was needed.

R. N. Kao, then a deputy director of IB, submitted a blueprint for the new agency.

He was appointed as the chief of India's first foreign intelligence agency named as 'the Research and Analysis Wing' or RAW'.

Shaping the Organization

Starting humbly as a Wing of the main Intelligence Bureau with 250 personnel and an annual budget of Rs 2 crore (estimated), in the early seventies, its annual budget had risen to Rs 30 crore while its personnel numbered several thousand.

In 1971, Kao had persuaded the government to set up the Aviation Research Centre (ARC) for aerial reconnaissance.

By the mid-70s, RAW, through the ARC, had high quality aerial pictures of the installations along targeted borders countries.

In 1976, Kao was promoted to the rank of a full-fledged Secretary responsible for Security directly reporting to the Prime Minister.

With this rise of appointment RAW became India's premier intelligence agency.

Reference: abstract from, Raw at War-Genesis of Secret Agencies in Ancient India Columnist Gp. Capt SM HALI,the historical capacity of Research & Analysis Wing (RAW) of India to conduct clandestine operations/(Sisupala-vadha, 2.112)

"R............A ....W"

Research & Analysis Wing"

Country: India

Area of expertise: Destabilizing Pakistan

Activities: Founded in, 1968, specifically, to counter Pakistan.

Over the years it has grown into one of the world's most formidable intelligence services, with wide-ranging activities in Pakistan, Sri Lanka, Nepal, Bangladesh, and elsewhere.

It is particularly active in Bangladesh and Pakistan, where it played a key role in that country's movement for independence from Pakistan.

Research and Analysis Wing [RAW]

The Cabinet Secretariat Research and Analysis Wing [RAW], India's most powerful intelligence agency, and is India's external intelligence agency.

RAW has become an effective instrument of India's national power, and has assumed a significant role in formulating India's domestic and foreign policies.

Since its creation, R.A.W. has been a vital, though unobtrusive, actor in the Indian policy-making apparatus.

Engagements

RAW has engaged in disinformation campaigns, espionage and sabotage against Pakistan and other neighboring countries.

Federation of American Scientists website comments on RAW in these words,

"RAW has engaged in disinformation campaigns, espionage and sabotage against Pakistan and other neighboring countries. RAW has enjoyed the backing of successive Indian governments in these efforts.

Working directly under the Prime Minister, the structure, rank, pay and perks of the Research & Analysis Wing are kept secret from Parliament."

Organization & Reporting

RAW has enjoyed the backing of successive Indian governments in these efforts.

R.A.W.'s boss works directly under the prime minister.

It is worth mentioning here that in other democratic countries, the external intelligence services have to report to parliamentary committees that scrutinized their activities, evaluate their performance and audit their accounts.

There are no such checks for RAW.

An Additional secretary to the government of India is responsible for the Office of Special Operations.

The additional secretary as well as the director general of security is also under the director of R.A.W.

The director of security has two important sections:

The Aviation, Research Center, and The Special Services, Bureau.

The joint director has specified desks with different regional divisions/areas (countries)

Area one, Pakistan

Area two, China and Southeast Asia

Area three, the Middle East and Africa

And area four, other countries.

The Aviation Research Center (A.R.C.) is responsible for interception, monitoring and jamming of a target country's communication systems.

It has the most sophisticated electronic equipment and also a substantial number of aircraft equipped with state-of-the-art eavesdropping devices.

These aircraft can reportedly fly at an altitude of 52,000 feet and have an operating range of 5,000 kilometers.

A.R.C. also controls a number of radar stations located close to India's borders.

Its aircraft also carry out oblique reconnaissance, along the border with Bangladesh, China, Nepal, and Pakistan.

Structure of Organization

The structure of the RAW is a matter of speculation, but brief overviews of the same are present in the public domain.

Attached to the HQ of RAW at New Delhi are different regional headquarters, which have direct links to overseas stations and are headed by a controlling officer who keeps records of different projects assigned to field officers who are posted abroad.

Intelligence is usually collected from a variety of sources by field officers and deputy field officers; it is either pre-processed (vetted) by a senior field officer or by a desk officer.

The desk officer then passes the information to the Joint Secretary and then on to the Additional Secretary and from there it is disseminated to the concerned end user.

The Director RAW is a member of the JIC Steering Committee and is authorized to brief the Prime Minister should the need arise.

List of Indian Intelligence agencies, sister concerned:

Research and Analysis Wing (R.A.W)

The Research and Analysis Wing (R&AW) of the Cabinet secretariat was formed on September 21, 1968 and handles India's external covert intelligence gathering.

Although its budget is unknown, some estimates peg it at $160 million.

It is believed to have about 10,000 agents in its payroll.

The Chief of R&AW is designated as Secretary (R).

The first to hold this post was R. N. Kao of the IB.

Intelligence Bureau

The IB was established in 1947 to assume responsibility for India's domestic security.

The IB is shrouded in secrecy and there is little public information concerning its main operations.

Defence Intelligence Agency

This agency was established on 5 March 2002 with the appointment of Lt. General Kamal Davar as the first Director General (DG).

It is supposed to be the nodal agency for all defense related intelligence.

Joint Cipher Bureau

The Joint Cipher Bureau works closely with the IB and RAW.

It is responsible for cryptanalysis and encryption of sensitive data.

All India Radio Monitoring Service

The Central Monitoring Service of All India Radio monitors all radio broadcasts in India as well as all foreign radio broadcasts which can be received in India.

Joint Intelligence Committee

The JIC is entrusted with the tasks of coordinating intelligence between all government agencies, civilian and military.

It consists of experts on several issues who analyze intelligence inputs.

Signals Intelligence Directorate

The Signals Intelligence Directorate is a joint service organization, manned by personnel from the Army, Navy and Air Force.

It has a large number of WEUs (Wireless Experimental Units) that carry out the task of monitoring military links of other countries.

Aviation Research Centre

The ARC is the (signals intelligence) arm of the RAW.

It has stations in Palam Airport in Delhi and at the Farkhor Air Base at Farkhor/Ayni in Tajikistan.

It reports to the Director General of Security and RAW.

Directorate of Air Intelligence

Directorate of Air Intelligence (India).

The DAI is responsible for air and satellite reconnaissance missions.

Directorate of Naval Intelligence (India)

This is the Indian Navy's intelligence arm.

References:Military Intelligence in India: An Analysis Bhashyam Kasturi: The Indian Defence Review, 1997 Cryptography Technology and Policy Directions in the Context of NII Gulshan Rai, R.K.Dubash, and A.K.Chakravarti. Information Technology Group Dept. of Electronics Govt. of India December, 1997.

Mission & Objectives

"What is not possible by deployment of force is possible by the use of stratagem. The black cobra was defeated by the stratagem of the crow and the golden chain". (Chanakya)

In 1968 India established this special branch of its intelligence service specifically targeted on Pakistan.

India's intelligence agency Research and Analysis Wing (R.A.W.), has assumed a significant status in the formulation of the country's domestic and foreign policies, particularly the latter.

Its internal role is confined only to monitoring events that have a bearing on the external threat.

Working directly under the prime minister, it has over the years become an effective instrument of India's national power.

Having been given virtual carte blanche to conduct destabilization operations in neighboring countries inimical to India, R.A.W. seriously undertook restructuring of its organization accordingly.

The Daily Mail findings reveal that the RAW, established in 1968, was given the special assignments to launch a multi-dimensional secret war against Pakistan.

The formation of RAW was created with the specific purpose that Pakistan should not be given enough room to strengthen itself and incapacitate it to broaden its relations with different influential countries by creating occasional internal unrest and anarchy.

The experts believe that the Indian agencies cause this act of terrorism, as an attempt to achieve a number of goals, including halting of Pakistan's foreign collaborated Defence projects, blocking the flow of foreign investment etc.

The other aim behind its formation was to destabilize Pakistan's economy and cripple its nuclear program.

Numerous missions were assigned to RAW upon its creation. These included monitoring political and military developments in neighboring countries that affects Indian national security.

Consequently, considerable attention is paid by RAW to Pakistan and China, countries that are traditional rivals of India.

Target Countries

R.A.W. was given a list of seven countries-Bangladesh, Sri Lanka, Nepal, Sikkim, Bhutan, Pakistan, and Maldives-that India considered its principal regional protagonists.

It very soon systematically and brilliantly crafted covert operations in all these countries to coerce, destabilize, and subvert them in consonance with the foreign policy objectives of the Indian government.

Central to the operations was the establishment of a huge network inside the target countries.

It used and targeted political dissent, ethnic divisions, economic backwardness, and criminal elements within these states to foment subversion, terrorism, and sabotage.

Having thus created conducive environments, R.A.W. stage-managed future events in these countries in such a way that military intervention appears a natural concomitant of the events.

Doctrine and Perception

In consonance with (Kautilya's) precepts, R.A.W.'s espionage doctrine is based on the principle of waging a continuous series of battles of intrigues and secret wars. (Kautilya's, or more popularly, (Chanakya) was an ancient Indian political theorist.)

But it is the massive international dimensions of R.A.W. operations that merit a closer examination.

To the credit of this organization, it has in a very short span of time mastered the art of spy warfare.

To suit her much publicized Indira Doctrine (India Doctrine), Gandhi specifically asked R.A.W to create a powerful organ within the organization that could undertake covert operations in neighboring countries.

It is this capability that makes R.A.W. a more fearsome agency than the superior K.G.B., C.I.A., M.I.6, B.N.D., or Mossad.

Skill: R.A.W.'s operations against the regional countries were conducted with great professional skill and expertise.

In most cases, R.A.W.'s hand remained hidden, but more often than not target countries soon began unearthing this "hidden hand."

RAW in Pakistan

RAW has an extensive network of agents and anti-government elements within Pakistan, including dissident elements.

Pakistan's size, strength, and potential have always overawed India.

It has always considered Pakistan to be the main opponent to its expansionist doctrine.

India's animosity toward Pakistan is psychologically and ideologically deep-rooted and unassailable.

India's 1965 and 1971 wars with Pakistan over Kashmir, which resulted in the dismemberment of Pakistan and the creation of Bangladesh, is just two examples.

Pakistan remains RAW's primary concern.

It runs thousands of agents and spends millions of rupees in its operations against Pakistan.

It has made a three-pronged attack against Pakistan in an attempt to destabilize it.

Propaganda Espionage, and Subversion

RAW is totally committed on all these three fronts and is engaged in launching covert operations in consonance with India's hostile foreign policy.

All aspects of Pakistani activities, economic, military, industrial and cultural receive a close scrutiny of RAW.

The 'Indian Doctrine' spelt out a difficult and onerous role of RAW.

It goes to its credit that it has accomplished or at least continued in a motivated manner its assigned objectives.

The Indian government spelling out the task for RAW in this regard has stated,

'Pakistan should be so destabilized internally that it could not support the 'Kashmir cause even morally, diplomatically or politically'.

RAW in Provinces

R.A.W. considers Sindh and Balochistan province and now FATA as well to be Pakistan's soft underbelly.

It has made it the prime target for sabotage and subversion.

R.A.W. has enrolled an extensive network of agents and antigovernment elements and is convinced that with a little push restless things will revolt.

Taking full advantage of the agitation in Sindh in 1983, and the periodic ethnic riots, which have continued to today, R.A.W. has deeply penetrated Sindh and cultivated dissidents and secessionists, thereby creating hard-liners unlikely to allow peace to return to Sindh.

R.A.W. is also similarly involved in Balochistan.

R.A.W. has successfully accomplished its target for confusing the ground situation in Kashmir so as to keep the world's attentio away from the gross human rights violations in Indian-occupied Kashmir.

RAW and ISI Phobia

Pakistan's Inter-Services Intelligence agency (I.S.I.), being almost 20 years older than R.A.W. and having acquired a much higher standard of efficiency in its functioning, has become the prime target of R.A.W.'s designs.

The I.S.I. is considered to be a stumbling block in R.A.W.'s operations and has been made a target of massive misinformation and propaganda campaigns.

The tirade against I.S.I. continues unabated.

The idea is to keep I.S.I. on the defensive by alleging in multi factorial issues whatsoever.

R.A.W.'s fixation on I.S.I. has taken the shape of I.S.I.-phobia, as in India every one traces the origin of all happenings and shortcomings to the I.S.I.

Whenever and wherever there is a kidnapping, a bank robbery, a financial scandal, a bomb blast, or what have you, the I.S.I. is deemed to have.

Ashok A Biswas, a Delhi-based research scholar, in his recently compiled study RAW-An Unobstructive Instrument of India's Foreign Policy, (as quoted by Pakistan Observer in 'A RAW deal for South Asia, 03 May, 1998) states that 'the aim of RAW is to keep internal disturbances flaring up and the ISI preoccupied so that Pakistan can lend no worthwhile resistance to Indian designs in the region.' He concludes, 'RAW over the years has admirably fulfilled its task of destabilizing target states through unbridled export for terrorism had a hand in it.

Infiltration

Data reveals by published reports allegedly that as many as 35,000 RAW agents entered Pakistan between 1983-93, with 12,000 are working in Sindh, 10000 in Punjab 8000 in North West Frontier Province and 5000 in Balochistan.

Training Camps

As many as 40 terrorist training camps at Rajasthan, East Punjab, Held Kashmir, Uttar Pradesh and other parts of India are run by the RAW's Special Service Bureau (SSB).

Belief

The formation of RAW was based on the self assumed belief that Pakistan was supplying weapons to Sikh terrorists, and providing shelter and training to the guerrillas in Pakistan.

Pakistan has accused the Research and Analysis Wing of sponsoring sabotage in Punjab, where RAW is alleged to have supported the Siraiki movement, providing financial support to promote its activities in Pakistan and organizing an International Siraiki Conference in Delhi in November-December 1993.

The objectives of RAW include: The objectives of RAW is to monitor the political and military developments in all the adjoining countries, which have, direct bearing on India's national security and in the formulation of its foreign policy.

To, seek the control and limitation of the supply of military hardware to Pakistan, mostly from European countries, the USA and China.

And last but not the least, the presence of a large ethnic Indian population in foreign countries, provide a powerful lobbying. These countries could back a favorable policy in international councils, motivated by the ethnic Indian group.

Aggressive Intelligence

The primary mission of RAW includes aggressive intelligence which comprise espionage, psychological warfare, subversion, sabotage, terrorism and creating dissension, insurgency and, ultimately, insurrection to destabilize the target country.

Modus Operandi

RAW operatives find good covers in Multinational organizations. NGOs and Cultural programmes are also popular screens to shield RAW activities.

International media centres can easily absorb RAW operatives and provide freedom of movement.

Collaboration with other Agencies

RAW maintains active collaboration with other secret services to meet its ends in a particular target country.

Its contacts with KGB of the former Soviet Union, KHAD, and the erstwhile Afghan agency, Mossad, CIA and MI6 have been well-known. A common interest being, the Pakistan's Nuclear Programme.

Third Country Technique

RAW has been very active in obtaining information and operating through third countries like the Middle East, Afghanistan, UK, Hong Kong, Mayanmar and Singapore.

Spotting and Recruitment

RAW operatives are on the lookout for local recruits to serve their ends. Acting on the Chanakyan principles, they tend to exploit human weaknesses for wine, women and wealth, and, at times resort to blackmail.

Separatist tendencies and ethnic or sectarian sensitivities are also well-known grounds for manipulation.

Armed Forces personnel remain a primary target. Journalists, intellectuals and politicians harboring and preaching goodwill and better Indo-Pak relations also make suitable targets for inadvertent and unconscious recruitment by RAW agents.

RAW and Afghan War

Throughout the Afghan War RAW was responsible for the planning and execution of terrorist activities in Pakistan to deter Pakistan from support of Afghan liberation movement against India's ally, the Soviet Union.

The assistance provided to RAW by the KGB enabled RAW to arrange terrorist attacks in Pakistani cities throughout the Afghan War.

KGB

Country:Russia

Area of expertise: Officially-counterterrorism, and protecting, Russian, commercial interests abroad.

Unofficially-consolidating, political power back home.

Activities: Russia has a formidable spying tradition that dates back to the czarist-era Cheeka.

After the collapse of the Soviet Union, KGB was broken up into several smaller organizations with vastly limited powers.

Since ex-KGB man Vladimir Putin took power, however, the SVR, or Sluzhba Vneshney Razvedk as it's known in Russian, has recovered much of its swagger.

Russian spying within the United States is now back to Cold War levels, U.S. officials believe.

Peter Earnest, the executive director of the International Spy Museum in Washington, who matched wits with the KGB as a CIA operative for over three decades, shared this assessment.

"They are as important today as they ever were, if not more," he said.

"Russia has not eased off at all on its espionage activity.

President Putin in May 2000 amended the presidential announcement on nuclear exports to allow Russia to export nuclear materials, technology and equipment to countries that do not have full-scope IAEA safeguards, and it supplied India, that do not have full-scale safeguards, with material for its civilian (nuclear) Programme in 2001," it says.

Russia,also continues to be the main supplier of technology and equipment to India' sties."

In addition, Russia has discussed leasing nuclear-powered attack submarines to India, the CIA says.

Russian entities, it says, during 2001 supplied a variety of ballistic missile-related goods and technical know-how to countries such as India

Besides, Russia was the primary source of advanced conventional weapons for India in 2001..

Despite progress in creating a legal and bureaucratic framework for Russia's export controls, lax enforcement and insufficient penalties for violations "remain a serious concern" to the United States, the CIA Washington, January 9: Russia has significantly supported in developing India's nuclear programmes with technology and equipment, and become a main source of arms for the country, the CIA has said.

The defeat of the Soviet Union in Afghanistan did not end the role of RAW in Pakistan, with reports suggesting that India has established a training camp in the town of Qadian, in East Punjab, where non-Muslim Pakistanis are trained for terrorist activities.

Since December 1979, throughout the Afghan War, the K.G.B., K.H.A.D. (W.A.D.) (a former Afghan intelligence outfit), and R.A.W. stepped up their efforts to concentrate on influencing and covertly exploiting the tribes on both sides of the Pakistan-Afghanistan border.

There was intimate coordination between the three intelligence agencies not only in Afghanistan but also in Pakistan, where destabilization was sought through a subversion and sabotage plan related to Afghan refugees and mujahideen in the tribal belt and inside Pakistan.

The joint coalition organized, spotted and recruited the hostile tribesmen and trained them in guerrilla warfare, infiltration, subversion, sabotage, and the establishment of saboteur forces/terrorist organizations in the pro-Afghan border tribes of Pakistan in order to carry out bombings and unrest in the Northwest Frontier province (NWFP), Balochistan, Punjab and sindh provinces to threaten and create pressure to accomplished the mission.

They also carried out bomb blasts in populated areas deep inside Pakistan to create panic and hatred in the minds of locals against Afghan refugee mujahideen to pressure Pakistan to change its policies on Afghanistan.

Research and Analysis Wing also conducted execution of

sectarian violence between Shias and Sunnis which has resulted in thousands of deaths during these years.

RAW and Terrorist Activities

Apart from launching the propaganda, the economy and psychological warfare the RAW has been indulging in a series of terrorist activities in Pakistan. Many of the major terrorist attacks, carried out in Pakistan by RAW have been acknowledged by independent international observers such as Foundation of American Society (FAS), owing to the overwhelming evidences left by the agency behind.

The Government of Pakistan frequently assigns responsibility for terrorist activity to the Indian Government, even when no evidence can be verified. Terrorist activities in Pakistan attributed to the clandestine activities of Indian and Afghan intelligence agencies that have credibly been vested are and include,

A car bomb explosion, in Saddar Area, Peshawar, on 21 December, 1995, causing death of 37, innocent people and injuring over 50 others.

An explosion at, Shaukat Khanum Cancer Hospital, Lahore, on 14 April 1996, claiming the lives of 7 persons and injuring some 34 others.

A bomb blast near Bhaipheru in a passenger bus, traveling from Lahore to Sahiwal on 28 April 1996, killing 44 people on the spot and wounding another 30.

A bomb explosion in a bus near Sheikhupura on 8 May, 1996, killing 7 people and injuring 29.

A bomb explosion near Alam Chowk, Gujranwala, causing a significant number of casualties on June 10, 1996.

A bomb explosion in a passenger bus near Kharian on 10 June, 1996.

A bomb explosion outside Madrassah Faiz-ul-Islam Rawalpindi on 10 June, 1996.

A bomb blast at Faisalabad railway station on 8 July, 1996.

A bomb blast in Rawalpindi.

A bomb blast in Lahore.

A bomb blast at Sabzi Mandi of Islamabad on 19 September, 2000, killing 20 people and injuring nearly 80 others etc.

Apart from these blasts the RAW has carried out a number of other subversive activities including sniper' firing and grenade attacks on Mosques, Imam Bargahs, and other religious places, printing and distribution of inflammatory religious literature.

Punjab has remained the main target of RAW activities during the past few years where 224 bombs were exploded by RAW agents during the past 13 years or so resulting in the killing of 554 innocent citizens and injuring 2958 others.

During the year 2000 there have been 18 bomb attacks in Punjab, eight in Punjab alone killing 13 persons.

In May, 1999 the US State department, in its annual report on terrorism, spared three lengthy paragraphs for Pakistan (as a victim of terrorism and sectarian strife).

It is learnt that the US authorities strongly believe that RAW and some other Indian intelligence agencies have been the only source of terrorism in Pakistan.

It is learnt that experts are of the firm view that RAW, India's external intelligence agency, is not the only secret agency of India, assigned the duties to carry out subversive activities in Pakistan but in fact several other Indian agencies have also been given similar assignments.

According to The Daily Mail findings, a Joint Intelligence Committee (JIC) at Delhi assigned terrorist and sabotage duties to the Intelligence Bureau, RAW, Military Intelligence, Naval Intelligence, Air Intelligence, Special Frontier Force, Joint Cipher Bureau etc. All these agencies have been actively executing plans of terrorism formulated by the succeeding governments in many countries of the region, particularly Pakistan.

RAW allegedly executed a hijacking of an Indian Airliner to Lahore in 1971 which was attributed to the Kashmiris, to give a terrorist dimension to the Kashmiri national movement. However soon the extent of RAW's involvement was made public.

RAW during Partition and Thereafter

RAW has a long history of activity in Bangladesh, supporting both secular forces and the area's Hindu minority.

The involvement of RAW in East Pakistan is said to date from the 1960s, when RAW promoted dissatisfaction against Pakistan in East Pakistan, including funding Mujibur Rahmanh's general election in 1970 and providing training and arming the Mukti Bahini.

Indian intelligence agencies, were involved in East Pakistan now, Bangladesh, beginning, in the early 1960's.

Its operatives were in touch with Sheikh Mujib for quite some time. Sheikh Mujib went to Agartala in 1965.

The famous Agartala case was unearthed in 1967.

In fact, the main purpose of raising R.A.W. in 1968 was to organize covert operations in Bangladesh.

As early as 1968, R.A.W. was given a green light to begin mobilizing all its resources for the impending surgical intervention in erstwhile East Pakistan.

When in July 1971 General Manekshaw told Prime Minister Indira Gandhi that the army would not be ready until December to intervene in Bangladesh, she quickly turned to R.A.W. for help.

R.A.W. was ready. Its officers used Bengali refugees to set up the guerilla force Mukti Bahini. Using, this outfit as a cover, the Indian military sneaked deep into Bangladesh.

The story of Mukti Bahini and R.A.W.'s role in its creation and training is now well known.

R.A.W. never concealed its Bangladesh operations.

The creation of Bangladesh was masterminded by R.A.W. in complicity with the K.G.B under the covert clauses of the Indo-Soviet Treaty of Friendship and Cooperation (adopted as the 25-Year Indo-Bangladesh Treaty of Friendship and Cooperation in 1972).

R.A.W. retained a keen interest in Bangladesh even after its independence.

R.A.W. was involved in training of Chakma tribes and Shanti Bahini, who carried out subversive activities in Bangladesh.

It also unleashed a well-organized plan of psychological warfare, created polarization among the armed forces, propagated false allegations of the use of Bangladesh territory by Pakistan's Inter-Services Intelligence agency, created dissension among the political parties and religious sects, controlled the media, denied the use of river waters, and propped up a host of disputes in order to keep Bangladesh under constant political and socio-economic pressure.

International RAW

Foreign Missions provide an ideal cover and RAW centres in a target country are generally located inside the Embassy premises.

The RAW and the Ministry of External Affairs are provided Rs 25 crore annually as "discretionary grants" for foreign influence operations.

An extensive network of Indian operatives is controlled by the Indian Embassy in Washington DC.

The Indian embassy's covert activities are reported to include the infiltration of US long distance telephone carriers by Indian operatives, with access to all kinds of information, to reverse blackmail of relatives of US residents living in India.

In 1996 an Indian diplomat was implicated in a scandal over illegal funding of political candidates in the US.

Under US law foreign nationals are prohibited from contributing to federal elections.

The US District Court in Baltimore sentenced Lalit H Gadhia, a naturalised US citizen of Indian origin, to three months imprisonment.

Gadhia had confessed that he worked as a conduit between the Indian Embassy and various Indian-American organizations for funneling campaign contributions to influence US lawmakers.

Over $46,000 from the Indian Embassy was distributed among 20 Congressional candidates. The source of the cash used by Gadhia was Devendra Singh, a RAW official assigned to the Indian Embassy in Washington.

Illicit campaign money received in 1995 went to Democratic candidates including Sens. Charles S. Robb (D-Va.), Paul S. Sarbanes (D-Md.) and Reps. Benjamin L. Cardin (D-Md.) and Steny H. Hoyer (D-Md.).

Raw-Mossad-Connection

Janes information group, the world's foremost source on intelligence information, reported in July 2001 that the Indian spy agency RAW and the 'Israeli spy agency Mossad have create" four new agencies to infiltrate Pakistan to target important religious and military personalities, journalists, judges, lawyers and bureaucrats.

In addition, bombs would be exploded in trains, railway stations, bridges, bus stations, cinemas, hotels and mosques of rival Islamic sects to incite sectarianism. Pakistani intelligence agencies also said that RAW had constituted a plan to lure Pakistani men between 20 and 30 years of age to visit India so they could be entrapped in cases of fake currency and subversion' and then be coerced to spy for India. This was high point of cementing an unholy alliance which began much earlier and which continues to tighten its noose around the neck of Pakistan, Iran, Afghanistan and Central Asia.

It appears that RAW and Mossad-either singly or jointly, either covertly or overtly-have been making efforts to penetrate sensitive circles of top echelon in Pakistan.

What is clear right now in RAW-Mossad connection is that Indian RAW and Israeli Mossad are collaborating extensively to curb the freedom movement of Kashmir and destabilize Pakistan.

Pakistani intelligence agencies also said that RAW had constituted a plan to lure Pakistani men between 20 and 30 years of age to visit India so that they could be entrapped

"In cases of fake currency and subversion and then be coerced to spy for India."

It appears that RAW and Mossad-either singly or jointly, either covertly or overtly-have been making efforts to penetrate sensitive circles of top echelon in Pakistan.

Qutbuddin Aziz, former minister in Pakistan embassy in London, wrote an excellent article, titled 'Dangerous Nexus between Israel & India.' It was published by a prominent Pakistani newspaper on April 1, 2001.

Aziz writes:

"Top secret details of Indian Home Minister LK Advani's visit to Israel in June 2000, show that the deals he has struck with the Israelis would make India and Israel partners in threatening the Muslim world with diabolic conspiracies to fragment and cripple it as a political force in the world. The details of his meetings with Israel's rulers, particularly the heads of the Israeli Home Ministry and its intelligence agencies, Mossad and Sabak, reveal that the arrangements he has made for joint Indo-Israel espionage operations in key areas of the Muslim world would make the Indian embassies in these Muslim countries the eyes and ears of the worldwide cloak-and-dagger Israeli spy network.

"Under the euphemism of 'counter-terrorism,' India is allowing Israel to establish a huge spy establishment in India which will, inter alia, unearth and monitor 'Islamic fundamentalist' individuals and groups for elimination by extra judicial process or by cold-blooded murder and kidnapping.

"The Indian side showed a keen interest in learning from Israeli security experts how they had run the slice of Lebanon which Israel ruled for 18 years and gave up recently.

Some information about the Israeli torture and investigation methods was gathered by the Indian side from the Israelis with regard to dealing with Arab dissidents within Israel and in the Palestinian Authority region.

"The Indians gave the Israelis a long shopping list of spying, torture and surveillance equipment such as electronic fencing of sensitive sites, laser systems, short-range rockets, eagle-eyed long distance snipers, observation blimps, giant shields, night vision device, unmanned aircraft of the MALAT wing of the Israeli Aircraft Industries Limited, special protective dress and gear for security personnel, cross border snooping devices and gadgets, training and deployment of spies and the special gear for them, use of computers and Internet for espionage and disinformation, code-breaking, tailing of enemy agents and their elimination, nuclear espionage, purloining state secrets of hostile countries and pooling them for the good of India and Israel and their mutual friends.

"The Israelis were interested in having access to the secret reports of Indian undercover RAW diplomats from certain Muslim countries of special interest to Israel (especially Pakistan, Libya and Iran). India is apparently willing to grant access to Israeli agents to the Indian Home Ministry's

Central Intelligence Processing Unit (CIPU) in New Delhi. This was set up under Advani's direction with Israeli and US help. A handpicked RAW officer, trusted by Advani's, heads this unit. Israel wants full access to its information data. The Indian government has already allowed access to it by American intelligence agencies now working with the Indian government on so-called anti-terrorist assignments.

Tarek Fatah, a Turkish scholar settled in Canada, wrote: "Britain's authoritative and respected defense publication, Jane's Terrorism & Security Monitor, reports that Israel and India have formed a military relationship and that Israeli intelligence is active in Occupied Kashmir.

"Israel has several teams now in Kashmir training Indian counter-insurgency forces to fight the dozen separatist guerrilla groups operating in the Indian-controlled sector of the disputed state.

Ed Blanche writes in Janes' Security on 14 August 2001: "Israeli intelligence agencies have been intensifying their relations with India's security apparatus and are now understood to be heavily involved in helping New Delhi combat Islamic militants in the disputed province of Kashmir, India's only Muslim-majority state which lies at the core of the conflict with neighboring Pakistan.

Israel: It has several teams now in Kashmir training Indian counter-insurgency forces to fight the dozen separatist guerrilla groups operating in the Indian-controlled sector of the disputed state.

"The exact extent of the involvement in Kashmir by Israel s intelligence agencies is far from clear, but it fits into Israel's increasing focus on events in Central Asia, and as far field as Indonesia, the world's most populous Muslim state, to counteract Islamic fundamentalism, which it perceives as a major threat.

We have been reading the name MOSSAD.

Mossad and its role in destroying Muslims around the

world and especially in South East Asia with the help of India RAW wraps, in a fascinating plot, full of intrigue and betrayal.

It is said that it is the joint venture of the trigone that is the core point of consideration.

Mossad, RAW and Israeli Russian Ukrainian drug mafia have been performing these functions as coalition partner previously.

The Mossad

Country: Israel

Area of expertise: Combating Islamist terrorism, evacuating Jewish refugees.

Activities: "We're all students of the Mossad," says Earnest.

Since it was founded in 1951, "the Institute," as it translates in English, has acquired a reputation for extraordinary skill and aggressiveness in combating Israel's enemies.

Some of its notable achievements include the abduction of Nazi leader Adolf Eichmann from Argentina in 1960, the assassination of the planners of the 1972 Munich Olympics killings, and the assassination of a senior Hamas operative with an exploding cell phone in 1996.

The Mossad has also been active over the years in efforts to assist Jewish refugees who seek to immigrate to Israel, including the secret airlifting of thousands of Ethiopian Jews in "Operation Moses" in 1984.

The Mossad made some moves toward greater transparency and openness in the 1990s, including revealing the name of its director for the first time, but under Ariel Sharon it turned back toward the clandestine operations for which it is best known.

Reports indicate that the Mossad may have had either an agent or an informant at the Syrian military installation that Israel bombed in September 2007.

Mossad is the nickname of,

'The Institute for Intelligence and Special Tasks'

(Ha-Mossad le-Modiin ule-Tafkidim Meyuhadim)

It is a compact body of about 1500 regular employees; Mossad relies on Jews and sympathizers worldwide forits operations. During years it has begun paying special attention to Pakistan, Iran and Central Asia.

Hi-Tech Mossad Dan Yahkin, a Jewish analyst, wrote an article which was published on 19 April 2001 in Globes, a Tel Aviv publication.

He narrates the story of 'Gil' and 'Or', pseudonym of two former operatives of Mossad.

The contention behind his narrative is that Mossad is as hi tech as any outfit in the world, military or otherwise.

"Political Action and Liaison Department conducts political activities and liaison with friendly foreign intelligence services and with nations with which Israel does not have normal diplomatic relations.

In larger stations, such as Paris, Mossad customarily had under embassy cover two regional controllers

One to serve collection department and the other the Political Action and Liaison Department.

"Special Operations Division, also known as Metsada, conducts highly sensitive assassinations, sabotage, paramilitary, and psychological warfareprojects.

"LAP (Lohamah Psichlogit) Department is responsible for psychological warfare, propaganda and deception operations.

Research Department is responsible for intelligence production, including daily situation reports, weekly summaries and detailed monthly reports.

The Department is organized into 15 geographically specialized sections or "desks", including the USA, Canada and Western Europe, Latin America, Former Soviet Union, China, Africa, the Maghreb Morocco, Algeria, Tunisia, Libya, Iraq, Jordan, Syria, Saudi Arabia, the United Arab Emirates and Iran.

A "nuclear" desk is focused on special weapons related issues.

Recently the makings of a plot for a 7/7 style terrorist attack by Israeli Mossad terrorists against Montreal's Metro was exposed. Posted by anarchore on March 29, 2008,with the heading Montreal 911 Truth Movement Averts Mossad Metro Terror Plot.

Pro-Israel Zionists placed by treasonous Canadian politicians now hold important posts in Canada's Parliament(the Isreali allies caucus), Supreme Court, and the CBC.

Fox News has allegedly reported that Terror state Israel Involved in 911 Posted by anarchore on March 30, 2007 Updated: June 27, 2007. Accordingly Israeli were arrested in connection with 9/11 but were then released under pressure by ADL.

You tube has pulled the video of the Fox News reports exposing Israeli involvement in 9/11.

9/11 having all the signs of having been an "Operation Northwood" type event. Flag operation (Northwood) was called through a remotecontrolled "airliner" purportedly carrying American "students", but inreality was empty of passengers and was to be detonated in close proximity to Cuba. The Cuban MiGs would be blamed for "shooting" it down, thereby"justifying" an American invasion of that country.

What's even more incredible about "Northwood" was that the plan called forgangs of paid "terrorists" toactually run wild through Miami's streetsshooting innocent American civilians in order to exacerbate the effect ofCuban "hostility" by terrifying innocent American citizens and therebygalvanize maximum support at home for the planned invasion.

There have been numerous firsthand reports of car bombs going off in thestreets on 9/11 as panic caused by the aircraft impacts rapidly spread across the city.

If there is still any doubt as to the real intentions of Israel, then please see this statement issued by David Ben Gurion, the first Israeli Prime Minister. His words, as printed in the Jewish Chronicle, 9 August 1967, leave nothing to imagination:

"The world Zionist movement should not be neglectful of the dangers of Pakistan to it".

"It is essential that we...strike and crush Pakistanis, enemies of Jews and Zionism, by all disguised and secret plans."-David Ben Gurion, the first Israeli Prime Minister.

With, the permission, of Mr. Saeedi Tariq, to reprint excerpts, from his special report, that appeared first in The Balochistan Post. "This lover of the Arabs is more dangerous to us than the Arabs themselves."

"For that matter, it is most essential for the world Zionism that it should now take immediate steps against Pakistan."

"Whereas the inhabitants of the Indian peninsula are Hindus"

"Whose hearts have been full of hatred towards Muslims?"

Therefore,

"India is the most important base for us to work there from, against Pakistan".

"It is essential that we exploit this base and strike and crush Pakistanis"

"The enemies of Jews and Zionism, by all disguised, and secret plans."

"First target, for this ideological State is a threat to our existence."

"And Pakistan, the whole of it, hates the Jews and loves the Arabs."

Previous war against religious extremists could have been a laudable goal but it seemed to target only those elements which could have brought a semblance of moderation to the religious swatch cutting across Pakistan society.

Thus leaving, the entire, field, wide open, for, the extremists.

India and Pakistan have routinely accused each other of responsibility for organizing bombings and sponsoring civil unrest in the other country.

The allegations are always strongly rebutted.

This brings us to the other reason for the Jewish Hindu friendship.

Israel knows that the Hindus are the dominant group, at least numbers wise, in the Middle East.

In UAE, Oman, Qatar, Bahrain and Kuwait they are very strong businessmen and hold strategic positions in many institutions.

In Medina in Saudi Arabia, the best hotel closest to the Prophet's mosque is owned by a Hindu-the Oberoi.

These Hindus are a very effective third column in these Gulf States providing a wealth of information and ready for subversive action when required.

One of the greatest abilities of Mossad is that it can mobilize US resources anywhere to protect Israeli interests.

Jewish Michael Savage. Zionofascist radio host at Neocon talk radio pitbull says

We are all in danger of annihilation by the Islamic hordes, to describe a fundamentalist Islamic ideology of conquest. Mr. Savage has recently been calling for nuclear strikes against Iran.

Summary: In summary, R.A.W. over the years has admirably fulfilled its tasks of destabilizing target states through the unbridled export of terrorism.

It goes to its credit that it has accomplished its assigned objectives due to the endemic weakness in the state apparatus of these nations and the failures of their leaders.

The Daily Mail has credibly cited and as written by Isha Khan, Dhaka, Bangladesh September 12, 2007.

"Highly informed sources revealed that the US, the French and the British counter terrorism specialists, who were constantly keeping a very vigilant eye on the affairs of the Indian intelligence agencies, particularly Research and Analysis Wing (RAW), very strongly believe that while the Indian Government and its political leadership has constantly been claiming to be the champion of the cause of anti-terrorist campaigns, its own intelligence agencies have been causing first degree terrorist activities not only in the neighboring countries but even beyond the regional ambits, making India a Numero Uno state, sponsoring organized terrorism in different parts of the world mainly targeting Pakistan, either covertly orovert

It It is learnt that the investigators are convince on killing of the French Naval engineers,in Karachi as an activity carried out by a very cunning enemy of Pakistan who desires to strongly harm Pakistan's foreign collaborated Defence projects and its further enhancements in this field.

They are of the view that the attack might have been planned by the Indians when they started their new Naval ventures with Russian and Israeli collaboration, which includes the assembling of a powerful electro accelerating machine i.e. Kilo-Ampere Liner Injector(KALI)etc.

It is learnt that after September 11 incident RAW is mainly using ex-KHAD operators to carry out subversive activities in different parts of the world particularly Pakistan.

The intelligence officials of the above mentioned countries are of the firm view that even if the terrorists behind incident are of different origins, they are surely having a full backing of a highly organized agency who prepared a fool-proof plan for them. The Daily Mail findings indicate that there is a great resentment and disliking for RAW among the International Intelligence community as RAW operates in a Mafia style, each time overstepping the limits of Intelligence operations.

The RAW has not only indulged in cross border terrorism, it has also played a very significant role in creating and funding militant and terrorist political and under cover extremist religious parties within India and other countries of the region.

It plays a key role not only in the national politics but also tries to have an impact on the political life of other regional countries.

According to the Daily Mail findings,

RAW is the godfather of some hostile and terrorist political and fundamentalist parties of India including the Hindu Dharma Raksha Samiti (HDRS), Bajrang Dal (BD) Rashtria Sawayamsevak Sankh (RSS) Shiv Sena (SS) etc.

RAW not only played a vital role in establishing and organizing these parties but it constantly financing and patronizing them with full strength.

The agency uses these parties not only to carve out a role for itself in the internal politics but to divert the international focus from its terrorist activities.

9

Indian Intelligence Organization: Knowledge Management, Strategy and Policy

In India the highest body in the intelligence structure is the Cabinet Committee on Political Affairs (CCPA). It functions under the Prime Minister, and comprises Ministers of Defence, External Affairs, Home and Finance. This body is assisted by a high powered committee of secretaries, the chairman Chiefs of Staff Committee, directors Research and Analysis Wing (RAW) and Intelligence Bureau (IB) and the chairman Joint Intelligence Committee (JIC).

Next in the multi tier intelligence system is the Joint Intelligence Committee (JIC) in which senior representatives of the ministries of Defence, Home and External Affairs, the RAW, the IB and the three directors of intelligence of the Defence services, are integrated under a full time Secretary. This committee is the highest intelligence assessment body chartered to prepare national intelligence estimates and perspectives on short and long term basis.

The real task of collection and collation, analysis and dissemination of intelligence rests with the large number of Intelligence agencies functioning in the country. Intelligence Bureau (IB) is the oldest intelligence agency, functioning under the Union Home Ministry, which is tasked to provide inputs on developments affecting internal security and counter intelligence. Research and Analysis Wing (RAW) established in 1985 is organized to gather and analyse external intelligence inputs that affect national security. The aim of military intelligence in our country is primarily to collect information and assess the capabilities of foreign military establishments that directly or indirectly threaten the security of the country. The intelligence gathering apparatus includes a wide variety of surveillance and intelligence gathering systems including space based surveillance systems, air borne surveillance-manned and un-manned, signal intelligence (SIGINT), electronic intelligence (ELINT) and vital human intelligence HUMINT sources. In India the three arms of the defence service have their own intelligence formations, headed by directors of intelligence from the respective service, under whom there is a directorate which collects intelligence and processes it for further dissemination to the operators in the field as well as service commanders.

Besides the two primary civilian intelligence organisations and the military intelligence infrastructure, there are a number of other organisations, which carry out the task of intelligence gathering and analysis, mainly oriented towards security, vigilance, enforcement and policing functions. These agencies have their defined sphere of activities concerning their specific organisations. Some such organisations in the country are-Central Bureau of Investigation, Narcotics Control Bureau, Directorate of Revenue Intelligence, Enforcement Directorate, field level intelligence units of the Police Organisations of different states. Besides these, field level intelligence units of para-military organisations which include-Border Security Force, Indo Tibetan Border Force, Central Reserve Police Force, Territorial Army, Central Industrial Security Force, Assam Rifles and Railway Police.

Need for Knowledge Management

In such a large and diverse Intelligence organisation, often there would be diverse groups or agencies flung across the organisation collecting and collating similar intelligence information. In the existing system of communications and integration, neither of these groups would have any clue about the other's work or efforts, unless there is an effective knowledge management infrastructure.

In today's knowledge driven military environment, the Indian Intelligence organisation needs to be integrated, responsive, innovative, competent and efficient. It can not depend on the current abysmally low levels of intra-organisational interaction and coordination to contribute towards the flow of appropriate information at the appropriate time. To effectively function as an efficient Intelligence structure there is a need to utilize the currently available technology and expertise to set up an integrated communication network based on a comprehensive national Intelligence Knowledge Management (IKM) strategy.

Components of Intelligence Knowledge Management

Over the years that these varied organisations have been in existence, their operatives and sensors have collected large amounts of data. This includes knowledge of enemy assets, his dispositions, economic, political and military activities, political ideologies etc. These data are recorded at different places in the organisation. Till date the data has probably been recorded in registers, Intelligence folders, files or lately in specific information systems that the specific department uses. However, just the intelligence data is not Intelligence by itself. Proper analyses of the data would yield useful information. Information is power. This has never been more relevant than in today's cutting edge technology driven military warfare. Therefore, it is imperative for the Intelligence organisation to harness the available information for it to be used by the 'right people at the right time'.

What is Knowledge?

Knowledge is a fluid mix of framed experience, values, contextual information, and expert insight that provides a framework for evaluating and incorporating new experiences and information. It originates and is applied in the minds of knowers. In organisations, it often becomes embedded not only in documents or repositories but also in organisational routines, processes, practices and norms.

What is Knowledge Management?

It is a discipline that promotes an integrated approach to identifying, managing, and sharing all of an enterprise's information assets. These information assets may include databases, documents, policies and procedures, as well as previously unarticulated expertise and experience resident in individual workers. Knowledge Management or Information Management has a vital role to play in the defence of the country. An initiative by the US DOD towards effective management of knowledge systems is the Information Technology Management (ITM) Strategic Plan. This plan provides overall direction and guidance for managing the Department's information resources. The mission as defined in this strategic plan is to provide, in a secure fashion, the right information, at the right place and time from the right sources, in a form that users can understand and reliably use to accomplish their missions and tasks effectively and efficiently.

Tangible Knowledge Base. The information that is collected by the numerous agencies and stored in various forms for collation, analyses and subsequent dissemination forms what is known as the tangible knowledge base or explicit knowledge. It is essentially the knowledge that can be easily recorded, stored and hence shared.

Intangible Knowledge Base. Besides this quantifiable and recordable information, there is this collective knowledge base that comes from experience and rests in the heads of the operatives, the analysts, the area experts, the issue experts and the field users. This is the knowledge base that is more difficult to identify, record or share within the organisation. Usually this knowledge is shared through informal sources and not in a well defined or structured manner. Normally when a crisis comes up the organisation is found looking towards its employees for an expert who has had previous experience or knowledge in handling a similar crisis. If such a person happens to be available at hand, his expertise is utilized towards diffusion of the crisis. However, what happens when this expert cannot be identified or is not available when required. More often than not the organisation is not aware that they have these tremendous assets in the form of experts within their own organisation who have grown out of experience provided by their own very organisations.

Therefore, it is important for the IKM strategy to address the issue of management of this intangible or tacit knowledge base as much as the issue of tangible knowledge management.

March towards an Informated Organization

Indian Armed Forces as well as other organisations in the Indian Intelligence structure are being transformed into informated organisations.

There are individual attempts at developing MIS (Management of Information Systems and decision support systems by the individual components of the intelligence structure. There is increasing use of information in these organisations with operators and end users having more and more access to information. Most organisations today have indeed started to pay some attention to the important aspect of information management.

However, it is important to realize that though this effort at transitioning to an era of networked information systems is laudable, at individual levels, it is still a maze of plethora of organisations often working at cross-purposes and often resulting in considerable duplication of effort with little synergy or coordination of effort. Instead of a "System of systems" eventually materialising to unify the fighting forces under one information umbrella, facilitating economy of force on the battlefield, there is a plethora of competing IT systems which may not be able to talk to each other. Let us therefore, have a look at the main requirements of an effective Intelligence setup and a setup for command and control system.

Intelligence. The intelligence community needs to be an agile enterprise.

- Information from the best sources needs to flow into multi-disciplined, cross-organisational teams of analysts that respond quickly and effectively to continuing threats and immediate crises.
- The astonishing volume of information that is gathered through all source collection methods, needs to be assessed, and in many cases further enriched to assure its relevance to national policy issues, mission planning and operational use.
- A system set up wherein data is fed into models and simulations so that options can be realistically assessed.
- Information must easily flow across security levels.
- Information security capabilities must ensure the protection of sensitive material and sources.

Command and Control. The proverbial "fog of war" needs to be lifted through integrated intelligence, surveillance and reconnaissance (ISR) capabilities. A common operating picture would let joint commanders see the three-dimensional battle space in near-real time.

- The command and control (C2) systems must develop courses of action and executable plans in minutes, after simulation and analysis of all options.
- C2 systems should seamlessly link the national, theater, operational and tactical levels to ensure vertical and horizontal integration of forces.
- Where reaction time must be in seconds, sensors must be able to acquire targets and pass that information directly to smart weapons over high bandwidth communications pipes.

- We must be able to use information warfare against our enemies, while protecting our own vital information resources.
- All our systems must be interoperable integrating all the three armed forces and the civilian intelligence and decision making process by interoperable and integrated systems and infrastructure.
- Information superiority could then form the basis of a decisive edge in regional dominance in South Asia.

Knowledge Management

Tangible Knowledge Management. This explicit or tangible knowledge base needs to be worked upon in a joint manner keeping the basic tenets of Revolution in Military Affairs in mind. There is a requirement to work out a hierarchical and well-defined Communication and Information structure for the management of this tangible knowledge base. This should essentially allow for:

- Coordinated and centralized definition of goals and objectives.
- Sharing of sectional responsibilities for intelligence gathering in overlapping domains.
- Making Intelligence analyses and estimates available across the organisation through an access based sharing system between different agencies.
- Systems for appropriate "notification" and "Requests for Information" between agencies.
- Coordinated collection, analyses, sharing and dissemination of information.
- A responsive system for two way communication for effective and timely delivery of critical information and feedback.

This can only be achieved by setting up a secure and reliable Intelligence sharing and distribution network encompassing both the civilian and military intelligence structure. The realisation of such a countrywide information infrastructure and command and control net is an inescapable necessity. This net would need to have all necessary protection and security measures installed to ensure reliability, safety and redundancy and the time to put these measures and checks in place is now and not after the net has been established and compromised.

However just achieving what has been outlined in the preceding paragraphs would yet amount to completing only half the picture. For gaining the competitive edge over the adversary it is essential to tap the large storehouse of tacit knowledge base that is residing in the heads of the people who constitute this intelligence framework. It is towards capturing this intangible knowledge base that we need to develop a comprehensive Intelligence Knowledge Management strategy and put the infrastructure in place to implement this strategy using the KM tools available in the market today or by developing our own custom defined IKM tools.

Knowledge Management Imperatives

In order to enmesh the requirements of effective Intelligence and Command and Control setup using knowledge management tools, the Intelligence Knowledge Management strategy would be shaped by the following KM imperatives:

Intelligence Gathering deals with the explicit knowledge base. It is based upon examining and filtering the large volumes of data that are generated or acquired by the various intelligence agencies. This data needs to be analysed and at times it may need to be enriched with background information to make the information relevant to the issue under analysis. Only when some sense is made out it is classified as Information and fed to the users. It is thus the data processed and filtered, which constitutes the explicit usable knowledge base.

Collaboration is about creating an environment in which users and different agencies can interact and share information and knowledge more freely. Here knowledge would include both explicit and tacit knowledge. All the various reports and analyses could be made available to the appropriate agencies. Besides individual agencies need to identify the experts within their organisation and have their talent pool listed on their information systems which will enable other agencies to have access to this intangible resource pool.

Knowledge Transfer is the area that actually takes into consideration the formalisation of the transfer of the tacit knowledge base. This encompasses the handing down of the experience within the organisation through inter departmental exposure, training sessions classroom sessions etc.

Knowledge Mapping deals with the identification of the body of knowledge within the organisation. Its main role is to identify the tacit knowledge base and making a repository of all those skills and expertise in the organisation. For example, we could have expert groups on Pakistan, on nuclear proliferation, on Northeast whose analyses and estimates could be called for by various intelligence agencies on 'as required' basis.

Expertise Management is based on the fact that a very small percentage of the tacit knowledge in any organisation can be made explicit because of the very nature of tacit knowledge.

This brings out the importance of identifying a talent pool, organising it and facilitating others across the organisation to find it when required.

Knowledge Management Strategy

- *Identify the knowledge needs in the overall Intelligence Organisation*. Who needs what knowledge and at what time? How much knowledge needs to be made available to which level? Who needs to be given a knowledge edge over others? Whether this knowledge edge is likely to contribute to a power base within the organisation or no. All these issues need to be considered.

- *Knowledge Acquisition.* How is the knowledge going to be acquired? What kind of intelligence going to be acquired by which specific departments. Are they equipped to acquire the needed intelligence?
- *Knowledge design* would require:
  - — Designing the network. The entire infrastructure must be able to manage the internal data and its modulation and also manage the external information flows. This phase is often referred to as the *Knowledge Absorption* phase.
  - — Choosing the right technologies. This is where the important activities of Information Warehousing and Data mining would come into play. *Information Warehouse* is an information repository containing storage areas for similar set of information broken down into smallest meaningful structures for easy retrieval. This is the stage wherein the interface of IT comes into the KM initiative in the form of *different software and hardware solution*. This needs to be clubbed with a *data mining* operation in order to churn out intelligent information which greatly impacts on the operating parameters of the organisation and in turn helps in attaining the defined objectives.
  - — Establishing collaborative working and knowledge sharing mechanisms. This phase, the next logical step in the KM initiative is termed as *Information Retrieval*. This has more to do with system designing and database applications so that the information pools synchronize with the user requirements.
  - — Training all users and operatives in the tools, techniques and processes.

  Basically this phase would provide a technical solution for implementing the IKM strategy. The logical solution would need to be mapped with the various KM technologies (like document management, information flow management, and collaboration) and also designing the technical architecture for the solution.

- *Knowledge Implementation*. This involves:
  - — Implementing the network. Build a framework to determine the value of information. Our military capabilities are heavily dependent on focused information. The value of information is a primary discriminator in military decisions and information assurance protection strategies that focus on priority targets. This strategy requires developing and applying knowledge management methods and tools for helping an end user determine the value of information to their missions and tasks (and the risks of not having the information). This methodology, if successful, can help reduce the "glut" of information and enable the Intelligence community to treat information itself as a commodity.
  - — Developing and Refining a knowledge performance index for the activity.
  - — Measuring improvements on an ongoing basis.
- *Development of a Knowledge-Based Workforce*. Effectively utilize existing personnel processes, collaborate with other organizations to create new policies, and implement a multi-faceted approach to acquiring, retaining, and maintaining highly skilled personnel in the Information/Knowledge Management and IT fields. Use the recruitment process to acquire skilled personnel based on core competencies.
- *Identify relationships between KM/IT activities in different domains*. Identify the relationships between KM/IT applied in different domains to ensure that overarching objectives such as interoperability, information security, and efficiency are met; and

mission threads, such as sensor-to-shooter, are effective. Dependencies such as those between IT activities in support missions (e.g., procurement, personnel) and the common infrastructure are described and strategies for managing them established. Interoperable IT is integral to the effectiveness of our weapon systems.

- *Ensure that the Intelligence Network's vital information resources are secure and protected.* In today's environment of sophisticated weaponry and fast pace of the modern battlefield, the ability to provide timely accurate information is vital to all aspects of military operations. Information Assurance (IA) and security is essential to achieve and maintain information superiority which would enable free and timely flow of information to the end user.
- *Establish an Integrated Security Management Infrastructure.* Integrate a broad spectrum of network services (e.g., audit, intrusion detection, operational network monitoring and control) into the Intelligence network security management infrastructure. Confidence in the secure operation of the Intelligence network must be grounded in a real-time understanding of network-wide activities. Further, the ability to identify when network users have gained access to unauthorized areas or information or to be able to attribute specific network activity to specific users of the network is an important factor in dealing with the insider threat.

To support its users as they improve mission performance, the IKM community must continue to reengineer its internal processes to be more effective and efficient. There are certain checklists, which must be complied with when managing Intelligence Knowledge Management networks and systems. These are:

- The IKM community must maintain a user-oriented focus and must measure user satisfaction through regular feedback.

- Systems and technical architectures must be applied to ensure interoperability and integration.
- The IT acquisition process must use prototypes, demonstrations, and exercises to evolve IT capabilities in full collaboration with end users.
- IT services and products must be benchmarked to achieve "world-class" performance at the lowest possible cost.
- IKM organisations must continually improve their internal processes, such as software design and technology insertion.
- IKM must empower its people and embody the principles of a "learning organisation".
- The IKM community, working in partnership with its end users, must streamline the processes and the infrastructure to eliminate unnecessary headquarters staff.
- Individuals must be empowered and accountable.
- Vertical stovepipes and hierarchical thinking must give way to horizontal teaming and cross-functional integration.

New paradigms for IKM must fully realize the value of information as a resource. Information needs to be managed by and for users. Information specialists must help users to find the information they need, assess and assure its fitness for use, and provide professional knowledge as needed through the network to assure end user satisfaction. The entire intelligence dissemination network must be seamlessly integrated and transparent to user. Procedures to ensure new capabilities are continually transitioned into the infrastructure without any disruption in ongoing operations. Advanced technologies such as data mining, intelligent agents, and mobile computing must be made available to appropriate users regardless of their location or activity.

It is time the National Security Council and the JIC consider this important aspect which would have a telling impact on any future conflict. India is in a unique position with a talent resource, which is the envy of most nations in the world. If we do not tap the requisite human resources and do not assign adequate funds to put in place the necessary infrastructure we would have no one else to blame but ourselves for not paying heed to the winds of RMA which are sweeping the armed forces the world over. Mission processes, information uses and services must be clearly understood and communicated to drive Knowledge management planning and resource decisions. The link from doctrine, strategy, goals, measures, and architectures to IT must be clear and compelling. The time to act is now and not after the gaping holes in our (Intelligence) Knowledge Management strategy is exposed.

EMOTIONAL INTELLIGENCE AND LEADERSHIP IN ORGANIZATIONS

Ever since the publication of Daniel Goleman's first book on the topic in 1995, emotional intelligence has become one of the hottest buzzwords in corporate World.. For instance, when the Harvard Business Review published an article on the topic two years ago, it attracted a higher percentage of readers than any other article published in that periodical in the last 40 years. When the CEO of Johnson & Johnson read that article, he was so impressed that he had copies sent out to the 400 top executives in the company worldwide.

Emotional intelligence is defined as a person's self-awareness, self-confidence, self-control, commitment and integrity, and a person's ability to communicate, influence, initiate change and accept change (Goleman, 1998). Studies have shown that emotional intelligence impacts a leader's ability to be effective (Goleman, 1998). Goleman identified the five 'domains' of EQ as:

1. Knowing your emotions.

2. Managing your own emotions.
3. Motivating you.
4. Recognizing and understanding other people's emotions.
5. Managing relationships, i.e., managing the emotions of others

Three of the most important aspects of emotional intelligence for a leader's ability to make effective decisions are self-awareness, communication and influence, and commitment and integrity. Managers who do not develop their emotional intelligence have difficulty in building good relationships with peers, subordinates, superiors and clients (Goleman, 1998).

Emotional Intelligence embraces and draws from numerous other branches of behavioural, emotional and communications theories, such as NLP (Neuro-Linguistic Programming), Transactional Analysis, and empathy. By developing our Emotional Intelligence in these areas and the five EQ domains we can become more productive and successful at what we do, and help others to be more productive and successful too. The process and outcomes of Emotional Intelligence development also contain many elements known to reduce stress for individuals and organizations, by decreasing conflict, improving relationships and understanding, and increasing stability, continuity and harmony.

Leadership

Leadership is a legacy that prepares others to carry on with courage, determination and the ability to see the larger picture. True leadership is the ability to be a catalyst for change, to inspire and persuade people to follow the righteous path. Empowering one's followers rather than controlling them is the hallmark of a true leader.

What makes a person a leader is still debated, but according to Warren Bennis (1994) all leaders seem to share some common traits. The first is a guiding vision or purpose. A leader has a clear idea of what she or he wants to do professionally and personally, and will pursue the goal regardless of the setbacks. The second characteristic is passion or enthusiasm and the ability to communicate that passion to others. Third, is integrity, consisting of three ingredients: self-knowledge, candor, and maturity. Self-knowledge is knowing one's strengths and weaknesses. Candor is being honest with yourself and is the key to knowing yourself. Maturity is the result of the lessons learned through following, while observing others, learning to be dedicated, and working with others. It is being truthful and never servile. The last two traits go hand in hand: curiosity and daring. A leader wants to learn as much as possible and is willing to take risks.

"Emotional Intelligence has an enormous impact in the Workplace..."

In a new book,' Working with E.I." (Bantam), Goleman focuses on the need for E.I at work, an area often concerned more head than heart. Not only do the bosses and corporate need high need of E.I., but every people-oriented job demands it too. Goleman says cognitive skills 'get you in the door' of a company, but emotional skills helps you thrive once you are hired.

For some time we have recognized the importance of these components of emotional intelligence to those who go about their 'work' on the sporting field and intuitively we have understood their importance in the more traditional workplace. However, it has only been in recent times that strong empirical evidence has been gathered which highlight the enormous impact high emotional intelligence can have in the workplace. Researchers have gathered data from hundreds of companies and thousands of executives measuring the importance of individual emotional intelligence competencies, as well as the clusters of emotional intelligence competencies that make up each domain. Goleman's own findings are typical. When he compared star performers with average performers in senior leadership positions, he found that nearly 90% of the difference in their profiles was attributable to emotional intelligence factors.

" EI is the sine qua non of leadership..."

Bosses and leaders in particular, need a high EQ because they represent the organization to the public, they interact with the highest number of people within and outside the organization and they set the tone for employee morale, says Goleman.

'E.I. affects just everything you do at work,' says Goleman. Even when you work in a solitary setting, how well you work has a lot to do with how well you discipline and motivate yourself.

As Mr. Goleman wrote in the Harvard Business Review 1998, 'it's not that IQ and technical skills are irrelevant. They do matter, but mainly as threshold capabilities, that is they are entry-level requirements for executive positions. My research, along with other studies, clearly shows that emotional intelligence is the sine qua non of leadership.'

If the ultimate leader does not champion the effort, it won't be perceived as important.If it's not perceived as important, it's not likely to get done.

Emotional Intelligence does not fit the classic historical models of leadership. The latter are usually associated with great figures of military history and conjure up charismatic and sometimes despotic images. However, people often use the same language for leadership today-bold, brave and tough with a strong sense of purpose and resolve. However, this does not fit today's needs, because:

- today's workforce does not accept the autocratic style often adopted by leaders following historical models of leadership.
- leadership has had to evolve to match a growing sense of democracy and independence in the workforce

- employees now have far more options and choices than the foot soldiers of yesterday

Leaders now need to manage and lead an "empowered" workforce and go beyond the consultative, co-operative and democratic styles of today. These new demands include:

- consultation and involvement – *but leaders still get criticised for not having and communicating a compelling vision and purpose*
- autonomy and freedom – *but leaders are still expected to take full responsibility when things go wrong*
- opportunities for growth, challenge and glory-*but leaders must be on hand to coach and mentor us so that we develop our potential*
- inclusion and team spirit – *but we still want our leaders to give us individual recognition and acknowledgement.*

A Leader With Emotional Intelligence

These findings are consistent with Patricia Pitcher's (1999) description of a company led by one CEO with high emotional intelligence that was succeeded by a CEO without emotional intelligence. She began with a description of the high emotional intelligence CEO (the artist) who took over a medium-sized company. He had a vision to build the company into a global corporation "operating in general and life insurance, banking, trust and investments services" spanning the world. This dream of his was during the time when most people believed banking and insurance would never meet. After 15 years, the company was worth $20 billion dollars and was an integrated service company in Europe, Asia and North America. The CEO's colleagues described him as a warm, generous, people-oriented, imaginative, daring and funny person.

Patricia Pitcher explains the generous, people-oriented attributes helped him attract and keep great colleagues and investors. His emotional and inspiring traits allowed his enthusiasm to spread. The visionary, daring, intuitive and unpredictable qualities helped him to keep focused on the goal, avoid short-term gratifications and achieve his goal. His open-mindedness helped the company and himself to develop and retain different kinds of people. This ensured new ideas and fresh approaches to problem solving. The CEO surrounded himself with the best talent he could find. He decentralized the power structure allowing his talented staff to express themselves in their own way. He sat on the independent boards and asked questions, but did not interfere with his staff. The other executives included artists and six craftsmen.

The craftsmen were described as being well balanced, trustworthy, reasonable, sensible and realistic. They were complementary to the artists. These craftsmen knew what worked and what did not. They understood that people made mistakes, but they learned from them, and if you drove out error, you drove out innovation. These people dealt with the day-to-day operations.

There were six other people in the company whom Pitcher calls the technocrats. These people were described as being "intense, determined, uncompromising, hardheaded, cerebral and analytical." They were often called "brilliant, stiff and distant." Their interpersonal relationships lacked depth, and they misread the people around them. She described the technocrats as people who thought they were "realistic and sensible, even imaginative, but no one else did". Technocrats erred in their judgments of others, markets and situations. They did not learn from the mistakes because they thought others were at fault. Those who made errors would be fired. The article goes on to describe what happened when the CEO felt it was time for him to leave and let 'fresh air' into the company.

A Leader Without Emotional Intelligence

In 1980 the company leadership was given to the second-in-command, a technocrat. This leader was analytical, uncompromising and brilliant. Patricia Pitcher believes such a person would find decentralization a sloppy way of doing business. So, the new CEO started to centralize the decision-making processes. He created a new head office that replaced the subsidiaries' authority. All of the craftsmen and artists running the subsidiaries were gradually fired and replaced by 'competent professionals' or technocrats by 1992. Within three years the "organization was dead." If the 'professionals' where so brilliant, what caused the company to fail?

Pitcher suggests that the company failed because "If you [do not have] respect for the emotional qualities that come in the imaginative package, you drive out the peculiar vision of an Artist. If you equate experienced with outmoded or old-fashioned, you drive out the Craftsman, who inspires the loyalty and the dedication, and who knows what making widgets is all about. If you fire people for making one mistake, nobody's going to go out on a limb to make any. Innovation stops. An organization without loyalty, dedication, skill, and dreams can go downhill very fast". She points out that running a modern company requires "all kinds of perspectives – even the cerebral, analytical and uncompromising. The Artists and Craftsmen can live with those different perspectives, but the Technocrat cannot". What does this perspective reveal about the relationship between emotional intelligence and leadership effectiveness?

To answer the question, an examination of the influence of emotional intelligence on the two leaders is required. The first chief executive officer demonstrated most of the attributes associated with emotional intelligence. Accurate self-assessment (self-awareness) was demonstrated by his ability to know his limits and his strengths. He surrounded himself with people who had abilities he did not, e.g. the craftsmen, other artists and technocrats. Daring to follow his dream demonstrated self-confidence (self-awareness) and innovation (self-regulation), aspects of emotional intelligence (Goleman, 1998). His openness to new ideas, decentralization of power and his constant learning (shown by asking questions at board meetings and listening to the responses), demonstrated empathy.

Empathy is being aware of the feelings of others, their concerns and needs. It can be broken down into seeking understanding, development of others' abilities, leveraging diversity to allow new ideas and opportunities to be heard, and being politically aware of a team's needs and power structure (Goleman, 1998). The CEO's social skill, another aspect of emotional intelligence, was demonstrated by cultivating relationships with investors, colleagues, and his employees. These aspects lead to trust which is the second most important characteristic of emotional intelligence (Cooper, 1997).

Trustworthiness is an important element in a leader's makeup as shown in the previously described study. Without trust, much time and effort is spent on non-productive activities because leaders feel compelled to draw up procedures in great detail, even for simple transactions (Copper, 1997). Innovation will stop when subordinates do not trust the leaders. Creativity will vanish if the sense of trust in an organization is lost and if people are preoccupied with protecting their backs. (Cooper, 1997). The second CEO probably lost the trust of his employees as a result of his lack of emotional intelligence.

Because the new CEO was not aware of how his actions and emotions were affecting others, he could be considered to be lacking in emotional intelligence (Ryback, 1998). Pitcher said that he blamed others for problems and did not look at the situational forces people were reacting to. In order for the technocratic leader to be able to see the situation realistically he must be aware of his own influence on the situation and the motives of others involved. According to Manfred F R Kets de Vries "to be able to decipher these deeper motives-to tease out the emotional, cognitive, and experiential components...requires the capacity to "listen with the third ear... an awareness about our own feelings, the knowledge and skill to handle those feelings, and an appreciation of emotions in other people (empathy)" (1999, p. 752). Mike Miller's (1999) opinion is that many managers fail because they are too rigid and have poor relationships. As a consequence they are unable to adapt to changes in the business environment, organization, culture, work processes, and technology. Managers unable to receive or respond to feedback are unable to determine how they need to change their approach to leading others. This will alienate the people they work with by "being overly harsh in their criticisms, manipulative, insensitive, unethical, and untrustworthy. They cling to autocratic, outdated methods of direction and control. These managers demonstrate clearly that being technically talented is not enough to drive success".

It is apparent the second CEO was ignoring how his emotions influenced his actions in favor of an analytical or autocratic approach to management. Without emotional intelligence, the technocrat CEO was limited in his ability to influence people in a positive way, e.g. he did not help people to develop their potential. Being able to influence people is an important part of being an effective leader. It is easy to assign a project. It is another matter to persuade a colleague or superior to change his or her mind about a policy decision (Church, Waclawski, 1999). Clearly the major difference between the first and second CEOs was the level of emotional intelligence shown by each. While IQ serves as the entry-level requirement for executive positions, "emotional intelligence is the sine qua non of leadership". An example of how emotional intelligence is used to express leadership is in the book "Seven Habits of Highly Effective People" by Stephen R. Covey (1989).

According to Covey the effect of developing the first three habits significantly increases self-confidence. You will come to know yourself in a deeper, more meaningful way. Understanding of one's nature, deepest set of values and unique contribution capacity becomes clearer. This is the foundation of emotional intelligence as defined by Daniel Goleman – self-awareness. It is also the building of motivational ability. Covey continues, saying that as the first three habits continue to be developed, one's sense of identity, integrity, controls and inner-directedness will increase. There will be an increase in caring about what others think of themselves and their relationship to you. This is the development of the self-regulation and empathy aspects of emotional intelligence. The next three habits describe the social skills of emotional intelligence. They help a person to heal and rebuild important relationships. Good relationships will improve, becoming more solid, more creative and more adventuresome. The seventh habit is developing one's self through the use of the first six habits. It is taking the time to reflect or further develop self-awareness.

The paper suggests that managers who don't feel a responsibility to others, can't handle stress, are unaware of their own emotions, lack the ability to understand others, or erupt into anger easily are viewed as likely to derail due to problems dealing with other people. High scores from direct reports on Difficulty Changing or Adapting were related to EQ-i scores on stress tolerance, and impulse control. Managers who resist change and growth, as high scores on this derailment factor imply, may be plainly visible to direct reports. Self-Awareness is key to leadership development and is a skill to handling stress. The more accurately we can identify and monitor our emotional upsets, the faster we can recover. Self-awareness can be developed through the practice of seeking on-going feedback. Ask supervisors and co-workers who know you well for honest feedback on how your behavior is impacting them. Use opportunities to self-reflect upon adversity – business failures, demotions, missed promotions, unchallenging jobs, and personal trauma. Consider what you learned as a result of these hardships. Participate in a leadership development program that features self-awareness and reflection and ask for feedback on a multilateral assessment.

The ability to demonstrate yourself as a cooperative, contributing, and constructive member of the group, is critical for long-term career success. Consider managing an inexperienced work team or employees who are resistant. Think about what you can do to contribute positively to group and organizational goals through new job assignments, existing jobs, role models or coaches. If maintaining self-control is a developmental area for you, consider leading a task force or project team made up of diverse members, taking calls on a customer hot line, negotiating a high profile case, or representing your organization to the media or influential outsiders. Seek a job assignment such as a project or task force headed by someone known for his or her high since of integrity and crisis management strength.

A leader has to have emotional intelligence to align personal and subordinate goals to accomplish company goals. James A. Belasco and Ralph C Stayer (1993) suggest four responsibilities a leader must implement at all levels of an organization. First, transfer ownership for work to the people who do the work. Second, create the environment where the transfer of ownership can take place, where each person wants to be responsible for his or her own performance. This entails painting a clear picture of what the company believes great performance is, for the company and each person; focusing individuals on the few great performance factors; developing in each person the desire to be responsible for his or her performance; aligning organization systems and structures to send a clear message as to what is necessary for great performance; engaging each individual's heart, mind and hands in the business of the business; and energizing people around the business focus. Third, develop individual capability and competence. Fourth, create conditions in the organization that challenge every person to continually learn, including him or her self. These four principals align personal and company goals through emotional intelligence.

10

Bureau of Police Research and Development

INTRODUCTION

The police personnel have a vital role in a parliamentary democracy. The society perceives them as custodians of law and order and providing safety and security to all. This essentially involves continuous police-public interface. The ever changing societal situation in terms of demography, increasing rate and complexity of crime particularly of an organized nature and also accompanied by violence, agitations, violent demonstrations, variety of political activities, left wing terrorism, insurgency, militancy, enforcement of economic and social legislations, etc. have further added new dimensions to the responsibilities of police personnel.

Of late, there has been growing realization that police personnel have been functioning with a variety of constraints and handicaps, reflecting in their performance, thus becoming a major concern for both central and state governments. In addition, there is a feeling that the police performance has been falling short of public expectations, which is affecting the overall image of the police in the country. With a view to making the police personnel more effective and efficient especially with reference to their, professionalism and public interface several initiatives have been launched from time to time. The Ministry of Home Affairs, Govt. of India, the Bureau of Police Research and Development (BPR&D), the National

Crime Records Bureau (NCRB), the SVP National Police Academy (NPA) have initiated multi-pronged strategies for the overall improvement in the functioning of police personnel. The major focus is on, to bring about changes in the functioning of police personnel to basically align their role with the fast changing environment. Some of the steps suggested by the National Police Commission in this direction are:

- To bring about a change of attitude of police personnel so that they become people friendly.
- To bring about more transparency and openness in police working.
- To improve public image and public participation in police working.
- To make the police more efficient and effective.

In order to achieve the above mention direction, the Ministry of Home Affairs with the support of UNDP has taken up an experimental project covering nine police stations in Rajasthan, Tamilnadu and Assam. One of the major aims of this project is to revise the curricula for training of police personnel at State Police Training Institutions.

It is in this context the Director, Training. BPRD. Ministry of Home Affairs, Government of India vide his letter dated 30th September 1998 approached the Administrative Staff College of India (ASCI) to undertake an assignment to carry out Training Needs of Constable/Head Constable/ASI/SI/ Inspector/Dy.SP. Based on the details provided in the above-mentioned letter, a comprehensive proposal spelling out the scope of the study, approach and methodology, cost, time frame, etc. was submitted. Subsequently the BPR&D authorised the ASCI to undertake the study with the following scope.

a. to assess the existing curricula for induction and in-service training for police officers of the level of Constable/Head Constable/ASI/SI/Inspector and Dy. S.P. in view of the Training Needs Analysis.

b. To assess the existing gaps and future needs in the training curricula of police personnel.

c. To produce model curricula for the above different level of training.

d. To identify the training methodologies compatible with the model curricula and Project objectives.

e. To identify individuals/institutions who can produce the requisite training material including texts, work books, case studies, audio visuals training films, simulation, role play, etc.

APPROACH AND METHODOLOGY

The ASCI had spelt out the details of the approach and methodology to carry out the Training Needs Analysis and Development of Training Curricula for police personnel in the proposal submitted to BPR&D. As part of the methodology, the following information was provided by BPR&D.

- Model description of roles of different levels of police personnel.
- Existing-training curricula of different programmes for different levels of police personnel and methodology used in training.
- Sample feedback reports of different programmes.
- Changes introduced in curricula in the last five years.
- Typical profile of faculty.
- List of training-related facilities available in Police Training Institutions.

The ASCI study team consisted of Shri K. Vijayarama Rao (IPS-Retd.), Former Director of Central Bureau of Investigation (CBI) besides Dr A A Firdausi and Prof Umeshwar Pandey, Faculty Members, Human Resource Area. The team was actively supported by S/Shri A K Mohanty, IPS and Navneet Rajan Wasan, IPS both working as Inspector Generals of Police in Andhra Pradesh.

The ASCI study team along with functionaries of BPR&D and UNDP consultant and some of the senior Police Officers of AP cadre formally met at ASCI on 20th April, 1999 to basically share the broad approach and methodology to be followed for undertaking the study. Several suggestions were made to further enrich the methodology of the study. It was decided not only to interact with the officers in the Training Colleges and other Police Training Institutions but also seek the views of a wide cross-section of the officers of Police Department at various levels in different locations including retired police personnel, senior citizens, NHRC activists, victims of the crime etc. This was primarily to understand the issues and concerns that affect the police in relation to the training as faced in various situations.

Various documents, data and information with regard to training provided by BPR&D were analysed by the study team to basically apprise themselves of the status of various induction programmes.

The ASCI team conducted structured workshops separately for Constables/Head Constables, ASIs/SI/Inspectors and Dy. S.Ps. level personnel with the Delhi Police, Police Training College at Delhi, Police Training College at Madhuban, Haryana and at different Police Stations at Kurshketra and Panipat in Haryana, CBI Academy, Ghaziabad, some police stations in Delhi, UP and Andhra Pradesh. The ASCI team organised separate Workshops with the top-level police personnel of Delhi police as well as AP Police at Hyderabad.

The primary purpose for this differentiation was to ensure that there is a level of comfort and openness in bringing forth and discussing issues related to training needs which in some cases were of a sensitive nature. Further, this grouping also facilitated retaining the number of officers attending each workshop within a manageable size, whereby equitable opportunity was provided to each individual attending the workshop. The workshop approach provided a good opportunity to the study team to interact directly with a large number of a wide cross section of police personnel at their respective locations.

In addition to the workshops, the team also had specific focused in-depth discussion with the officers in charge of Police Training Colleges, Heads of the states police organisation and also in a few cases officers in other specific locations to understand the nuances of their work *and work structure and update the perceptions of the team* members.

The team also developed two detailed structured questionnaire, (Annexure I & II) designed to elicit data on work patterns, personal skills and behavioural training, police functioning with reference to their training, views on changes likely to occur as a consequence to environmental changes which he/she feels would need to be strengthened to enhance his/her on-the job effectiveness and also increase efficiency of himself/herself, his/her department and of the police as a whole.

While the workshops provided the team an exposure to the perspectives and views expressed by the police personnel, the questionnaire provided specific in-depth data regarding the individual's work and training related needs.

The study team also visited the training establishments, looked into the teaching and living facilities and infrastructure of training establishments at Police Training College Delhi, Police Training College Madhuban, and Andhra Pradesh Police Academy Hyderabad. Exclusive discussions were also held with members of the faculty and administration at the Training Centres.

The data/information thus collected were analysed and issues concerning training and related areas were identified.

Subsequently during the month of August the study team made a presentation before the International consultant for UNDP at BPR&D, Delhi. Following the above methodologies the draft curricula have been finalised and presented in this report, which is divided in three parts.

FUNCTIONS AND POWERS OF POLICE (DUTIES, FUNCTIONS AND ROLE)

The National Police Commission has incorporated in its report, a draft Police Act that details the functions and duties of the police. Subsequent to this report many changes have taken place particularly in relation to internal security, terrorism, organised crime, financial crimes, Public order situations etc. In the area of science and technology particularly information technology, the revolutionary changes have had their impact on crime and its prevention and detection. There has been an increasing focus on weaker sections, gender discrimination, human rights and functional autonomy in investigation. The role, functions, duties and powers of the police are identified in this context with the National Police Commission report as the main source.

Main duties and responsibilities of Police are to:

- Promote and preserve public order,
- Enforce of laws especially conferring exclusive jurisdiction on Police.
- Collect and communicate intelligence affecting public peace, national integrity, security and crimes in general, including organized crime, terrorist, environmental, social and economic offences.
- Prevent the commission of offences and public nuisances.
- Investigate, detect offences and bring offenders to justice.
- Apprehend, where appropriate, all persons whom they are legally authorized to apprehend.
- Prevent to the best of their ability, if necessary by use of force, the wanton destruction of any property by violence.
- Protect if necessary by use of force, individuals who are in danger of physical harm.

- Prevent such conduct in public places as might prove to be dangerous to the persons indulging in such acts or others.
- Ensure that a person is not denied his rights and privileges while under detention.
- Counsel and resolve conflicts other than property disputes and promote amity.
- Arrange for food and shelter for every person in custody.
- Ensure compliance with the provisions of the Police Acts or any rule or regulation or order made there under.
- Obey any lawful order given by any superior officer in relation to any employment in connection with services declared as essential services by the State Government or Government of India.
- Perform such other duties as may be enjoined on them by the laws for the time being in force.

The Duties of the Police in public places are to:

- Facilitate orderly movement of people and vehicles.
- Regulate and control the traffic in the streets, and prevent obstructions therein.
- To prevent the contravention of any rule, regulation or order made under the Police Acts or any other Law in force.
- Keep order in the streets and at public places including places of public worship.
- Regulate the public at public bathing or washing places and in all other places of public resort.

Duties of the Police towards women, poor persons and general public are to:

- Behave courteously towards all persons, particularly the women, the children, the poor, the weaker sections and the senior citizens.

- Refrain from causing avoidable inconvenience to members of the public in the discharge of his duties.
- Inform the poor people in custody of the Legal Aid Schemes.
- Provide immediate medical aid to victims of road accidents or victims of other crimes or Police action and inform their families about the accident or incident.
- Advise the victims of road accidents about their rights and privileges and assist accident victims or their heirs or their dependents with such information and documents as would facilitate the compensation claims.
- Prevent harassment of women, children, and weaker sections.
- Take charge of intoxicated and mentally ill persons at large, who may cause harm to themselves or others or property.
- Prevent ragging in educational institutions and hostels.

It is the duty of Police to ensure compliance with the provisions of the Various Acts in force, Police Acts or any rule, regulation or order made there under and for that purpose give appropriate publicity and to warn, arrest or prosecute as per law. In the discharge of these duties all police personnel are ordained to uphold the human rights as prescribed by law.

Exercise of Powers

The important powers of the Police relate to arrest, custody, search, seizure, bail, surveillance and use of force under certain circumstances. There are certain regulatory powers relating to traffic, Arms, Explosives etc. All these powers are to be exercised to achieve the objectives of prevention, detection of crime and other tasks indicated in the above paragraphs.

All these powers are specifically provided and are subject to fundamental rights guaranteed in the constitution. The training of police officers at all levels has to provide for a proper awareness of this situation and inculcate ability to be effective within the framework of the limitations to exercise of such powers. The induction courses have to provide for professionalism of highest order coupled with the right attitude to achieve this objective.

EXISTING AND EMERGING POLICING PROBLEMS.

The problems and situations that the police will encounter and have to deal with are summarized below.

i) Emergence of organized (mafia) crime, economic offences, terrorism, drug trafficking and criminalisation of politics.

ii) Offences involving social, environmental, and cultural phenomena.

iii) Mass violence and destruction arising out of communal, other social economic and political frictions.

iv) Violent conventional crimes.

v) Safety of Neighbourhood.

vi) Security related problems.

vii) Human Rights violations.

viii) Science, Technology, particularly Information Technology Revolution and changing concepts of time and space, freer interaction between regions and nations.

ix) Mutual help and coordination.

x) Trained personnel, professional equipment and infrastructure for police.

xi) Morale, Skills and training of police personnel.

xii) Community Policing, Public interface and co-operation.

The training has to create understanding of the existing and emerging problems as also the concerns of modern policy.

ISSUES AND CONCERNS

As mentioned in the approach and methodology, several techniques were used to analyse and review the current status of induction programmes with reference to the above. This section covers various problem-areas and opportunities culled out of the data; information and opinions expressed by different level of police personnel through the workshops, Questionnaires, individual discussions and analysis of records and reports made available to the study team. While some areas of concern culled out are system-related, some others are directly training-related. Considering the interdependence, it would be appropriate to list out the areas of concern, both related to systems as well as training.

SYSTEM-RELATED CONCERNS

During our visit to different police stations across the country, invariably most of the functionaries, especially constable, head constable, Sub-Inspectors and SHOs at the police stations, opined that they are asked to put in consistently 16 to 18 hours of duty on a continuous basis. They also reiterated that fatigue caused by long hours of duty is reflected in their general behaviour towards public, thus affecting their public relations. Majority of the functionaries at the police stations have pointed out that they are being denied the weekly off as well. This may, perhaps, be due to shortage of manpower with reference to situations they have to deal with every day there is no provision of reliever, which is a normal practice in any shift operation.

Sub-standard Physical Facilities

Poor physical facilities in all most all the police stations are one of the major areas of concern, which is also resulting in a variety of perpetual behavioural consequences of police personnel. This was brought to our notice by most of the police personnel when the study team visited several police stations in Delhi, which are being organized in tents. Even in those police stations, which are housed in pucca buildings, the facilities such as toilets and drinking water were of sub-standard. In many places, it was noticed that many of the functionaries at the lower level do not have any office facilities. Even the furniture was inadequate and the stationery items were not provided to the police stations.

Poor Housing Facilities

While some of the police stations have got housing facilities, these are not available to most of the police personnel. Inadequate housing facilities coupled with low compensation and insufficient House Rent Allowance forces them to hire houses at far away places, which create a serious commutation problem. During the Workshop, especially with the Constables and Head Constables, it was pointed out that the Department also takes advantage of such a situation by continuously putting them on longer hours of duty. This affects their normal family life to a great extent and results in behavioural consequences.

Inadequate Growth Opportunities

Majority of the police personnel joining at the Constable level either retire as Constable or Head Constable. Very few reach the level of Sub-inspector or Inspector, this has got serious repercussions on motivation level of police personnel and works as a hindrance factor in discharge of their normal duties.

Frequent Change in the Nature of Duties

It is a fact that most of the police personnel are expected to perform a variety of duties pertaining to maintenance of law and order in different situations. Of late, deployment of police personnel on VIP security and bandobust duties especially in Metro Cities result in too frequent changes in the nature of duties which not only brings the constraint on them but also affect their normal discharge of duties at the police stations. In addition, several factors listed above in paragraph 4 also affect morale and motivation level of the police personnel.

TRAINING-RELATED CONCERNS

During our interactions, time and again as well as our perception the present training approach is more militaristic in nature having less compatibility with the job responsibilities of the police personnel, particularly in the context of civic society. Also, it was pointed out that the present training especially in certain areas is far short and is unable to keep pace with the type and nature of modern crime taking place in the society. The existing curricula have not been able to effectively address these prime issues. For example, the use of the latest weapons in crime, computer related crime, financial crime and other white collared crimes are not adequately covered in the existing induction training programmes

Selection of Instructors

The process of selection of Instructors does not take into account the intellectual and academic aptitude of the candidates. More often than not, Instructors are selected on the basis of availability and/or proximity to the training institute. There are hardly any faculty development programmes, where the Instructors can improve and enrich their training skills. There are no incentives worthmentioning for good police officers to opt for the training colleges.

Course Materials

Course materials provided to the trainees are seldom revised and updated. There is no in-built system, which takes care of revision of reading materials. The course kit does not contain relevant case studies or exercises such as role-play.

Course Content

In contemporary management training, the behavioural traits and use of scientific aids are the most important ingredients. These two aspects are, generally, referred as software and hardware, part of the training. Areas such as public relations, interpersonal effectiveness, attitudinal framework, etc are the software component, while the computer applications, forensic science, correct reflexes use of modern weapons, etc. constitute the hardware part of the training. The existing course contents run short of both software and hardware components.

Training Infrastructure

Many basic facilities for conducting training courses are lacking at the training colleges. The quality and setting of classrooms, number of ceiling fans, poor quality of blackboards, overhead projectors, etc. is below standard. Added to these are the poor maintenance of the hostels and the mess in many training colleges.

Inadequate Honorarium to Guest Faculty

As the training colleges do not pay sufficient honorarium to the Guest Faculty, not many experts do come to share their practical experience with the trainees.

Lack of Sufficient Funds

The budgetary allocations for the police training colleges are less than what it should have been. As a result, the physical and academic development of the colleges has to suffer. A significant portion of the financial allocation is earmarked for staff salaries alone; hence very little resources are available for professional activities.

In Service Courses

The most serious gap in training is found in the matter of in-service courses, promotion courses and on the job training. Rarely does a constable get a chance to attend a training course after initial training. The updating of skills, briefing on specific duties, use of available modern scientific aids, changes in the attitudes and expectations of the people, changes in the laws, new and sophisticated methods of committing crimes, changes needed in traditional methods to meet the present day challenges more professionally are not absorbed by the constables and no opportunity exists for such improvement.

The situation is only marginally better for sub-inspectors and in more recent times, somewhat better for DSPs and IPS Officers. Even in the existing courses, the content, duration and purpose is not well defined or focused. These yawning gaps have to be filled by designing a comprehensive package for each level. While the package is indicated, the content has to be drawn up for each course and mechanism to update the same in each state as per the requirement.

On the job courses

The old system of catechism and classes during weekly periods were intended to update the knowledge of the personnel and daily briefing was to be done. This has fallen to disuse completely and on the job training is not replaced by utilizing the new technology now available. There is always a better way for performing a particular duty. It defers from place to place and depends on changing Laws, dynamic situations, psychology and the temperament, intelligence and resources available. This is best achieved within the framework of a general law and procedure made specific to a situation and imparted interactively to those entrusted with various tasks. The designing of these courses is vital to give a full meaning and success to the inductive courses that are now designed in this project.

Distance Learning

The expense and sometimes large-scale difficulties make institutional training difficult and at times unnecessary. Distance learning techniques using available IT methods are advantageous in running certain in service courses. These courses have to be structured and positioned to complement the institutional inductive course. Right now there are no distance learning courses worth the name for any rank in the country. This gap has to be filled up to derive maximum benefit and impart high degree of professionalism.

TRAINING SKILLS REQUIRED AS PERCEIVED BY POLICE OFFICERS

The strengths of the existing training programmes as perceived by police officers consist of some parts of induction, some short/long term in service courses and special courses workshops on scientific issues. The course and their content, which in their opinion constitute an important part of their professional equipment, are enumerated (these vary from state to state). However they are perceived on the strengths of the existing courses even though they are not uniformly run in all training institutions. They also indicate what police officer consider as relevant.

As pointed out earlier, two questionnaires were developed to-elicit the views of a cross section of the functionaries on multiple aspects of training. We received responses from *95* functionaries belonging to different levels; we also had overwhelming response from trainees at Delhi and Haryana Police Training colleges, as well as A.P Police Officers. The following table reflects their considered views on strength and short comings of the existing training courses and their suggestions so further improve the content of the training courses.

The Policeman and the officers above him require certain attributes to be able to handle the job effectively and to inspire confidence in the people whom they deal with. Courage, self esteem, sympathy for victims of crime and weaker sections, capacity to withstand long hours, stress management, respect for Law, and cool temper are some of the attitudes needed. These have to be in some measure innate to the person and they should be nurtured and enhanced in the course of training. It is important that the trainee first discovers or made to realize what extent he possesses these attributes and made through appropriate training exercises to further build on them

The skills essentiality consist of understanding basic law, physical fitness, capacity to handle assault, self defence, observation, computer application relevant for his job, handling of weapons, knowledge application of science to police work, particularly capacity to observe and preserve clues, lift and pack finger prints and collection of information. These cannot be taught in induction course fully, but a thorough introduction and grounding is essential, while in service on job training and practical experience shapens *these skills* further.

EXISTING TRAINING SYLLABI

The training syllabi for induction courses are confined to training institutions, with duration of six to nine months. The course is divided into out-door training and Indoor classes. In the out door training P.T, foot drill, Arms drill, including squad, platoon drill and ceremonial parades form the main part. In many States only Rifle training is given with only one field firing practice. Lathi drill is also taught. The words of command and practices are completely based on the Infantry drill of the Army. The Indoor syllabus consists of class room lectures on various laws, investigation, police duties, police organization, Scientific aids to investigation, Medical jurisprudence. For constables the emphasis is mostly on outdoor drill and very elementary classroom lecturing on law and police regulations. In recent times, there has been improvement with addition of some more subjects and practical training in the field and emphasis on unarmed combat etc.

FUTURE TRAINING NEEDS

1) Practical training, physical fitness, skills, attitudes and behavior required for a professional policeman in the contemporary society.
2) The methodology adopted should retain the syllabus to the extent necessary. Such methods as distance learning, role-play, hand on experience, acquisition of skills relevant to detection and prevention are to be introduced.
3) Modification of police behaviour in the context of human rights and the role of protecting citizens of all categories

is to be given due weightage The methodology also aims at preparing them to face boldly the organized criminal activities.

4) Exposure to use of information technology is introduced as all future operations are closely linked with the computers

TRAINING MODULE FOR SUB-INSPECTOR OF POLICE

The training module presupposes and contemplates a recruitment process, aimed at selection of candidates having Bachelors Degree (in any discipline), prescribed physical standards, physical efficiency tests, and qualifying in a written examination aimed at testing mental ability, aptitude, attitude, general awareness and knowledge of elementary law and sociology. The selection process presupposes provision of distance learning material to prospective candidates to facilitate their preparation on appropriate lines for the written examination. The distance learning materials are to be supplied along with call letter for the written examination after they qualify in the prescribed Physical Efficiency Test (PET) and possess the required physical standards.

The Training Module: The training module is structured and designed as follows:

Pre-Institutional Training Module: This scheme of training contemplates an informal pre-institutional training system through distance learning material like text books, reference books on law, police manual, Police Sciences and other connected subjects which are required to be prepared by a group of experts with reference to the functions & responsibilities of the Sub-inspectors/S.H.Os. A bench mark standard for physical fitness is also to be prescribed to the selected candidates who would be required to equip themselves with the standard so prescribed before they join training institution. This system will save quality training time in training institutions and facilitate appropriate focus on practical training, physical fitness, skills, attitudes and behaviour required for a professional police officer in the contemporary society.

Institutional Training Module: Phase 1: The first phase of institutional training module will be for a period of 7 months over 168 working days consisting of 840 periods, each period having a duration of 45 minutes. During this period following subjects are to be covered.

I. Republic of India-Role of the Police
   a) The Indian Constitutional Frame Work and Indian Polity
   b) Socio Economic Environment
   c) Role of Police

II. Administration and Police Organisation
   a) Administrative set-up and Central Police organisations
   b) Police Organisation in the State/Union Territory
   c) Police Administrative and Service Matters
   d) The State Police Manual

III. Human Behaviour and Relationship Management
   a) Human Behaviour
   b) Relationship Management
   c) Relation with Groups and Institutions
   d) Police and Human Rights
   e) Community Policing

IV. Law
   a) Jurisprudence and Legal concepts
   b) Indian Penal Code 1860
   c) Code of Criminal Procedure 1973
   d) Indian Evidence Act 1872
   e) Special and Local Laws

V. Criminology
   a) Concepts of Criminology
   b) Criminological Factors
   c) Deviance & Delinquency
   d) Emerging Trends in Crime
   e) Penology
   f) Victim logy

VI. Crime Prevention
   a) Study and History of Crime
   b) Beats and Patrols
   c) Surveillance & Collection of Intelligence
   d) Crime Records and use of computers

VII. Public Order Traffic & Security
   a) Maintenance of Law & Order
   b) Traffic Regulation and Management
   c) Security & Protective Duties
   d) Relief & Disaster Management

VIII. Investigation and Trial-Methods and Skills
   a) Investigation
   b) Forensic science & Forensic Medicine
   c) Scientific Aids & Methods of Investigation
   d) Trial of Cases and Court Management
   e) Computer Appreciation and Introduction to other Office Automation Devices

Practical Training Module in field and operational areas: This training module will be for a period of 2 months spreading over 48 working days after the first phase of institutional training. This training will be imparted to the trainees in the field and operational areas with reference to the duties of S.H.Os, which would be performed by them on completion of training. This is also a module for application of the knowledge imparted to them in the first 6 months in the training institution. During this period the trainees would remain in the training institution and would be attached to the local police stations of the district in which training institution is located or Police Stations of other Districts. In this context, it would be useful that the Police Station selected for practical training are brought up to a level both in matter of personnel and infrastructure as experimented and recommended in Rajasthan, Tamil Nadu and Assam as part of UNDP Project. The trainees will have perform various duties of S.H.O. On the field they will be observed and guided by the instructors from the training institutions. The training institution would assess their field performance and review the work under taken by them once in a week to ensure immediate correction and give guidance at appropriate time. The 2 months period will be apportioned for duties as follows.

1) Prevention of Crime.
2) Investigation of Crime.
3) Maintenance of law & Order.
4) Enforcement of Special and Local Laws.
5) Security Duties.
6) Traffic Regulation
7) Large Scale Bundobast.
8) Community Relationship
9) Collection of Intelligence on Crime, criminal organisations, anti social elements and extremists.

On completion of this phase of training the trainee should return to training institutions for full time institutional training once again for the second phase.

Institutional Training Module: Second Phase: This phase of institutional training is very crucial and extends over a period of 3 months with over 72 working days having 360 periods. This is designed to reinforce and strengthen the training inputs provided through earlier modules. The module includes case studies simulation exercises, practical and field exercises, role-play etc. The trainee would also be exposed to first aid, relief, emergency and fire-fighting, problem solving exercises, hands on training on computers and training in communication skills. During this period final examinations will be conducted for the trainees and the successful candidates will be passed-out from the training institution.

Out door training: Out door training module emphasises development of stamina, endurance and certain practical skills including unarmed combat and weapon training etc. required for the constables during discharge of their duties. Another objective of the Out Door Training will be to inculcate in trainees habit of undertaking physical exercise on regular basis to develop ability to withstand strain and stress of police functioning. The traditional militaristic training has been substantially reduced. The components of drill, which are required to the development of personality and bearing and to create an *espirit de corps*, have been retained. To break the monotony, games like basketball, football, hockey etc., are to be provided us, it helps to enhance the stamina of the trainees. The candidate will also be given opportunity to learn individual games like badminton, lawn tennis etc. The training for unarmed combat and self-defence techniques has been provided for to infuse expertise in trainees for self-defence. Some time is also been earmarked for Yoga/Meditation as part of training for stress management.

During institutional training the trainees will have 3 periods of out door training excluding one period for games. The out door training period would be reduced to only two during their field and operational training. A total number of 816 periods has been earmarked for all types of out door activities.

In-service Training: This training module envisages In-service training subsequent to completion of Induction training with periodical intervals. All the Sub-Inspectors of Police are required to under go pre-promotion training on completion of

Qualifying years of service which could be after 6 or 7 years service The Sub-Inspectors would also be required to under go at least one in-service course once in years on subject of topical interest and relevance in the field. In-service training modules are required to be designed from time to time. The pre-promotion courses and In-service course are to be made compulsory and result of the test will be considered as a perquisite for promotion and award of recognition and medals during their career.

Bridger of gaps and future needs: This syllabus and training module provides for future needs for sub-inspector as frontline police officers closing the gaps existing in earlier modules. The training module is designed with strict reference to the field duties required to be performed by a sub-inspector/ S.H.O. The module prepares the trainees to work in a transparent and professional manner, enlisting partnership of public in police work. While emphasis is on improvement of knowledge, skill and scientific temper the training module is aimed at preparing them to be people friendly and professional during discharge of their duties. The training module also aims at infusing requisite expertise and confidence to keep them away from temptations or shortcut methods. The outdoor trainee is intended to ensure Physical fitness, Weapon training, unarmed combant and other skills needed.

Methodology: The methodology adopted is combination of conventional and contemporary system. The class room teaching methods through talk and chalk, use of teaching aids etc., stands reinforced through various techniques of learning methods such as Group discussions, role play, simulation exercises, practicals, hand on practises and on the field experience in operational duties. All these methodologies have been prescribed to activate the thinking process of the trainees and making the training interactive. This methodology can be standardised for a given period of time by development of case studies, editing of role-plays and designing of simulated exercises through serving and retired police officers that are known for their performance in the field duties. Exposure to use of information technology is introduced as all future police operations are linked with the computers.

Nodal Institution: The State Police Academy has to be a nodal institution to take up the task of production of text books, workbook, case study, audio visual training films etc. The institute has to take up these activities as a package, engages experts for preparation of the materials.

BENEFITS OF OSINT

We need to rethink the distinction between open sources and secrets. Too many policymakers and intelligence officers mistake secrecy for intelligence and assume that information covertly acquired is superior to that obtained openly. Yet, the distinction between overt and covert sources is less clear than such thinking suggests. Open sources often equal or surpass classified information in monitoring and analysing such pressing problems as terrorism, proliferation, and counterintelligence. Slighting open source intelligence (OSINT) for secrets, obtained at far greater expense when available at all, is no way to run an intelligence community. Also, we must put to rest the notion that the private sector is the preferred OSINT agent. In the end, I would contend, the Intelligence Community (IC) needs to assign greater resources to open sources.

Mistaking Secrecy for Intelligence

Judging from their words, too many policymakers and intelligence officers mistake secrecy for intelligence. President Nixon, for example, once belittled the Central Intelligence Agency (CIA) in words that capture the common mistake: "What use are they? They've got over 40,000 people over there reading newspapers." The president's remarks, reflecting a persistent misperception, echo even now within the Intelligence Community. Recent CIA recruiting literature suggests to applicants: "You can be on the sidelines, reading about global events in the newspaper. Or you can be at the heart of world-shaping events... " in the CIA. The brochure proposes a world divided between those who read newspapers "on the sidelines" and those with access to "intelligence" within the Agency. George Tenet, a recent director of central intelligence, was fond of defining the CIA to audiences both within and outside the Intelligence Community with a curt phrase: "We steal secrets." Neither from reading the CIA's recruiting brochure nor listening to its chief would one learn that the Agency includes an OSINT service that produces the lion's share of its intelligence.

Deeds also reflect the mistaken notion that secrets are all important. The Intelligence Community now includes large, well-funded agencies for overhead imagery intelligence (IMINT), signals intelligence (SIGINT), and human intelligence (HUMINT). By all accounts, most resources in the Intelligence Community go to such IMINT and SIGINT activities as developing reconnaissance satellites, collecting signals, and analysing the take. OSINT, the stepchild of the Intelligence Community, lacks its own agency. The Foreign Broadcast Information Service (FBIS), the largest IC organization devoted to open sources, resides in the CIA. Other OSINT units are scattered within the Department of Defense and the State Department. Alone and in the aggregate, OSINT organizations have few people and little funding. Despite numerous surveys putting the contribution of open sources anywhere from 35 to 95 percent of the intelligence used in the government, OSINT's share of the overall intelligence budget has been estimated at roughly 1 percent.

Indistinct Categories of Intelligence

Those who swear that secrets are the only true intelligence, in contrast to mere "information" found through open means, would do well to consider the indistinct character of the categories of overt and covert in intelligence. Information hidden behind walls of classification and special access programs may prove no more than equal in value to material available to the public. Overt and covert streams of intelligence are by no means completely parallel and distinct; they often mingle and meander over one another's territory. Covert reports at times are amalgams of press clippings. And newspaper editors, for their part, frequently publish stories based on accurate leaks of classified material. Examples abound. Veteran CIA case officer James Lilley learned early in his career how Chinese agents had "swindled" his office with supposedly inside information on Chinese developments that later proved to be "embroidered versions of articles from provincial Chinese newspapers." Similarly, European con men reportedly passed off Soviet newspaper articles as intelligence from behind the Iron Curtain to operatives of the CIA and the West German Gehlen Organization in the 1950s. More recently, journalist Bill Gertz of the *Washington Times* has leaked classified information in his stories. His published photocopies of actual intelligence documents underscore how the overt and covert streams mingle.

The more one considers the problem, the less distinct appears the distinction between open information and secrets. Let us consider the case of the B-29 bomber aircraft, whose use in the Second World War was reportedly classified. Samuel Halpern, an officer of the Office of Strategic Services (OSS), recalled how he once surprised an admiral by referring in his briefing to the B-29 Super Fortress bombers. When the admiral demanded to know how Halpern knew of the "highly classified" aircraft, the OSS officer replied that he had learned of the bomber through monitored Japanese radio broadcasts. In short, what is classified to some is open information to others. This can lead to the absurd situation where foreigners learn details of US intelligence operations in their country through their national media, while the American public and Intelligence Community remain unaware of the overseas exposure. Perhaps "unilateral secret" would be the proper term for this phenomenon!

The Value of Open Sources

Not only are open sources at times indistinguishable from secrets, but OSINT often surpasses classified information in value for following and analysing intelligence issues. By value, I am thinking in terms of speed, quantity, quality, clarity, ease of use, and cost.

Speed: When a crisis erupts in some distant part of the globe, in an area where established intelligence assets are thin, intelligence analysts and policymakers alike will often turn first to the television set and Internet.

Quantity: There are far more bloggers, journalists, pundits, television reporters, and think-tankers in the world than there are case officers. While two or three of the latter may, with good agents, beat the legions of open reporters by their access to secrets, the odds are good that the composite bits of information assembled from the many can often approach, match, or even surpass the classified reporting of the few.

Quality: As noted above, duped intelligence officers at times produce reports based on newspaper clippings and agent fabrications. Such reports are inferior to open sources untainted by agent lies.

Clarity: An analyst or policymaker often finds even accurate HUMINT a problem. For example, when an officer of the CIA's Directorate of Intelligence (DI), reads a report on a foreign leader based on "a source of unproven reliability," or words to that effect, the dilemma is clear. Yet, the problem remains with a report from a "reliable source." Who is that? The leader's defense minister? The defense minister's brother? The mistress of the defense minister's brother's cousin? The DI analyst will likely never know, for officers of the Directorate of Operations (DO) closely guard their sources and methods. This lack of clarity reportedly contributed, for example, to the Iraqi WMD debacle in 2002-03. The DO reportedly described a single source in various ways, which may have misled DI analysts into believing that they had a strong case built on multiple sources for the existence of Iraqi weapons of mass destruction. With open information, sources are often unclear. With secrets, they almost always are.

Ease of use: Secrets, hidden behind classifications, compartments, and special access programs, are difficult to share with policymakers and even fellow intelligence officers. All officials may read OSINT.

Cost: A reconnaissance satellite, developed, launched, and maintained at a cost of billions of dollars, can provide images of a weapons factory's roof or a submarine's hull. A foreign magazine, with an annual subscription cost of $100, may include photographs of that factory's floor or that submarine's interior.

Beyond this general argument for open sources, I would maintain that OSINT often equals or surpasses secrets in addressing such intelligence challenges of our day as proliferation, terrorism, and counterintelligence. When a nation develops a weapon of mass destruction, for example, hundreds or even thousands of engineers, scientists, and manufacturers may join the program.

Bureaucrats and traders may sell the weapons abroad. The OSINT target is immense. Engineers attend conferences; scientists publish scholarly articles; manufacturers build production lines; bureaucrats issue guidelines; and traders print brochures for prospective clients. Many paper trails wind around the world beyond whatever may surface in the media.

Before terrorists act, they issue warnings, religious leaders of their community deliver sermons, and political leaders plead their cause. Open sources, while they may not tell us where the next bomb will explode, do allow us to understand the terrorist agenda and act thereby to address grievances or launch competing campaigns for hearts and minds.

When foreigners seek to tap US technology abroad or on our soil in order to evade embargoes or leapfrog the R&D process at our expense, open sources may alert counterintelligence officers to their activities. For example, the National Counterintelligence Executive has published reports based on Korean media from both sides of the DMZ to bring to light North and South Korean efforts to acquire Western technology both abroad and in the United States.

The Cost of Slighting Open Sources

Arguing that we need to rethink the distinction between open information and secrets, which is more blurred than many think, and that OSINT is often more useful in addressing intelligence challenges, it would be further maintained that Washington's slighting of open sources is no way to run an intelligence community. In earmarking only one of every hundred dollars in the intelligence budget and assigning some similarly meager percentage of IC personnel to OSINT, our policymakers and intelligence executives are learning less than possible about our nation's challenges while paying a higher price than necessary. DO officers without access to foreign media published uncounted numbers of bogus reports based on Chinese, Soviet, and other newspaper articles. We are also almost certainly spending large sums today to obtain covertly information similar or identical to that openly available. Rather than learn through HUMINT or SIGINT that a scientist of interest attended an international conference, for example, would it not be better simply to acquire, then print or report the contents of the conference proceedings? Open acquisition would likely be less expensive, and all policymakers and analysts would have access to the information.

Policymakers and intelligence executives would also do well to resist the siren call of those who argue that we should simply privatize OSINT. Private corporations are an excellent source of dictionaries, software, and contractors for our government. But private companies alone are no substitute for accountable, dedicated OSINT professionals in government offices. Let us take the vital issue of translation as an example. Contractors— whether individuals, translation agencies, or research companies (the latter generally subcontracting with translation agencies or independent translators for the talent they lack in house)—today translate most of the foreign newspapers, scientific journals, and other open information for the Intelligence Community. They do so under the lead of cleared OSINT officers who, knowing both the requirements of the Intelligence Community and the mysteries of the foreign media, manage the translation flows to provide answers to intelligence questions. Staff officers are also available to translate priority items themselves on a crash basis when contractors are unavailable. Staff officers serve one master. Contractors, busy with a mix of assignments from corporate and government customers, often are unavailable when most needed.

Ideally, in my view, the government should develop its own sizeable cadre of translators. Yet, that would be much more expensive than the present system. Some would argue for the opposite path of privatizing OSINT, which would mean intelligence analysts, case officers, and others buying their translations directly from the private sector without OSINT officers to apply their general requests against the appropriate media for the right information or to edit, often heavily, contractor translations that are frequently of poor quality.

The above logic, which applies to media analysis, targeting, and other OSINT functions as well as to translation, suggests that the government should retain its OSINT capabilities. The Intelligence Community requires staff officers to lead the contractors. To use an analogy from history, private corporations may have supplied the aircraft, landing craft, and rifles for D-Day, but General Eisenhower, his military staff, and soldiers in uniform took the beaches at Normandy.

11

Need for New Intelligence System

Indian intelligency system is not fit for the current size of our system. We need to urgently upgrade, it, restructure and modify it. Considering his experience as a researcher to few government bodies in Europe on commercial and economic interests intelligence and espionage, he says we are not prepared for the kind of system we are growing into, which is complex, global and where we are going to interact with the world on open door policy. We need to work on our system to protect Indian people's interests.

Before we go further into the details let us analyse what is intelligence and the current structure of world intelligence that is ON SURFACE. There is much more to dig below the surface. IF we published the data on certain things you will be surprised at the naivete and ill preparedness of Indian government and our intelligence and analysis system.

The espionage in the US is now being focused on commercial interests, besides the enemies of humanity, communists and other species. The Chinese have copied entire nuclear, advanced weapons development of USA and now saving 50 years of research done by thousands of American scientists. The US system has failed in this respect and they are not able to coop with it. The Chinese have also copied all intelligence on space research. Most US and EU research is shared yet some countries simply copy and steal but do not share their own research. This is obviously on very high level but the world's security is paramount considering that we are sitting on the biggest arsenal of human history. EVEN a slight mistake can blow entire continents. We will write more about this issue in a later thread.

The People's Republic of China (PRC) has stolen classified information on all of the United States? most advanced thermonuclear warheads, and several of the associated reentry vehicles. These thefts are the result of an intelligence collection program spanning two decades, and continuing to the present. The PRC intelligence collection program included espionage, review of unclassified publications, and extensive interactions with scientists from the Department of Energy's national weapons laboratories.

The stolen U.S. secrets have helped the PRC fabricate and successfully test modern strategic thermonuclear weapons. The stolen information includes classified information on seven U.S. thermonuclear warheads, including every currently deployed thermonuclear warhead in the U.S. intercontinental ballistic missile arsenal. Together, these include the W-88 Trident D-5 thermonuclear warhead, and the W-56 Minuteman II, the W-62 Minuteman III, the W-70 Lance, the W-76 Trident C-4, the W-78 Minuteman III Mark 12A, and the W-87 Peacekeeper thermonuclear warheads. The stolen information also includes classified design information for an enhanced radiation weapon (commonly known as the "neutron bomb"), which neither the United States, nor any other nation, has ever deployed.

What is so important about all this? The biggest and foremost aspect is OUR existence. IF you want INDIA and its people to be secure and sound, we must secure our intelligence information and analysis system.

We are way behind. To become just a normal prosper country we need a solid system. Forget the super power syndrome that is merely hogwash, nonsense and unreal myth of media. The real power is only when people can live freely, without fear. India today has more enemies than every before. WHY? Jealousy, dangerous and fake pseudo organized religions, greedy individuals and corporations and many other interests that do not wish India to grow.

Intelligence (Information Gathering)

Intelligence (abbreviated int. or intel.) is information valued for its currency and relevance rather than its detail or accuracy —in contrast with "data" which typically refers to precise or particular information, or "fact," which typically refers to verified information. Sometimes called "active data" or "active intelligence", these typically regard the current plans, decisions, and actions of people, as these may have urgency or may otherwise be considered "valuable" from the point of view of the intelligence-gathering organization. Active intelligence is treated as a constantly mutable component, or variable, within a larger equasion of understanding the secret, covert, or otherwise private "intelligence" of an opponent, or competitor, to answer questions or obtain advance warning of events and movements deemed to be important or otherwise relevant.

As used by intelligence agencies and related services, "intelligence" refers integrally to both active data as well as the process and the result of gathering and analysing such information, as these together form a cohesive network (cf. "hive mind"). In a sense, this usage of "intelligence" at the national level may be somewhat associated with the concept of social intelligence —albeit one which is tied to localized or nationalist tradition, politics, law, and the enforcement therof.

Process

Information collected can be difficult to obtain or altogether secret material gained through espionage ("closed sources"), or it can be banal and widely available, such as newspaper articles or Internet postings ("open sources"). Traditionally, intelligence involves all-source collection, storage and indexing of data, usually in multiple languages, in the expectation that some small portion will later prove important. Intelligence findings or "product" and the sources and methods used to obtain them (tradecraft) are often highly classified and sometimes compartmentalized, and intelligence officers need top level security clearance.

* Government intelligence is usually assigned to clandestine intelligence agencies, often with large, secret budgets. These use a variety of techniques to obtain information, ranging from secret agents (HUMINT) to communications intercepts (COMINT) to spy satellites (IMINT). See surveillance and list of intelligence gathering disciplines. Intelligence agencies often engage in clandestine activities beyond espionage such as political subversion, sabotage and assassination.
* Military intelligence is an element of warfare which covers all aspects of gathering, analysing, and making use of information over enemy forces and the ground. It involves spying, look-outs, high-tech surveillance equipment, and also secret agents.
* Business intelligence denotes the public or secret information that an organization obtains about its competitors and markets.

Intelligence as used here, when done properly, serves a function for organizations similar to that which intelligence (trait) serves for individual humans and animals. Intelligence collection is often controversial and seen as a threat to privacy. While usually associated with warfare, intelligence can also be used to preserve peace.

STRUCTURE OF INDIAN INTELLIGENCE SYSTEM

National Security Council (NSC)

1. Strategic Policy Group,
2. National Security Advisory Board
3. Secretariat represented by the Joint Intelligence Committee (JIC).

A: The Intelligence Bureau.

B: Research and Analysis Wing.

National Security Council (NSC) of India is the apex agency looking into the political, economic, energy and strategic security concerns of India. It was established by the A B Vajpayee government on November 19, 1998, with Brijesh Mishra as the first National Security Advisor (NSA).

Prior to the formation of the NSC, these activities were overseen by the Principal Secretary to the Prime Minister.

Organization

The three-tiered organization of the NSC comprises

1. The Strategic Policy Group,
2. The National Security Advisory Board
3. Secretariat represented by the Joint Intelligence Committee (JIC).

The Strategic Policy Group is the first level of the three tier organization of the National Security Council (NSC) of India. It forms the nucleus of the decision making apparatus of the NSC.

This group consists of the following members:

Military

* Chiefs of Staff of the Army, Navy and Air Force.

Civilian

* Cabinet Secretary
* Foreign Secretary
* Home Secretary
* Defence Secretary
* Finance Secretary
* Secretary (Defence Production)
* Secretary (Revenue)

* Governor of the Reserve Bank of India (RBI)
* Director of the Intelligence Bureau
* Secretary of the Research and Analysis Wing (RAW) of the Cabinet Secretariat
* Secretary of the Department of Atomic Energy
* Scientific Advisor to the Defence Minister
* Secretary of the Department of Space
* Chairman of the Joint Intelligence Committee (JIC).

Other invitees will be brought in as and when required.

The Strategic Policy Group undertakes the Strategic Defence Review, a blueprint of short and long term security threats, as well as possible policy options on a priority basis.

The National Security Advisory Board forms the third element of the National Security Council (NSC) set up in India. It consists of persons of eminence outside the Government with expertise in external security, strategic analysis, foreign affairs, defence, the armed forces, internal security, science and technology and economics.

The board meets at least once a month, and more frequently as required. It provides a long-term prognosis and analysis to the NSC, and recommends solutions and address policy issues referred to it.

The Joint Intelligence Committee (JIC) of the Government of India analyzes intelligence data from * the Intelligence Bureau, * RAW and the Directorates of Military, Naval and Air Intelligence. The JIC has its own Secretariat that works under the Cabinet Secretariat.

It is the third tier of the National Security Council (NSC) setup. The Intelligence Bureau is India's internal intelligence agency.

Origins

It was recast as the Central Intelligence Bureau in 1947

under the Ministry of Home Affairs. The reason for the perception may be because in 1885, Major General Sir Charles Metcalfe MacGregor was appointed Quartermaster General and head of the Intelligence Department for the British Indian Army at Shimla. The objective then was to monitor Russian troop deployments in Afghanistan, fearing a Russian invasion of British India through the North-West during the late 19th century.

In 1921, a new state-run surveillance and monitoring agency — Indian Political Intelligence (IPI) — was established, in reaction the development of Indian anarchist activities in England. IPI was run jointly by the India Office and the Government of India and reported jointly to the Secretary of the Public and Judicial Department of the India Office, and the Director of Intelligence Bureau (DI in India, and maintained close contact with Scotland Yard and MI5.

Responsibilities

Shrouded in secrecy, the IB is used to garner intelligence from within India and also execute counter-intelligence and counter-terrorism tasks. The intelligence bureau is comprised of employees from law enforcement agencies mostly Indian Police Service officers as well as from the military.

The current chief of the IB is Mr. Narsimhan who replaced Mr. Ajit Kumar Doval. In addition to domestic intelligence responsibilities, the IB is particularly tasked with intelligence collection in border areas, following the 1951 recommendations of the Himmatsinhji Committee (also known as the North and North-East Border Committee), a task entrusted to military intelligence organizations prior to independence in 1947. The IB was also tasked with other external intelligence responsibilities as of 1951

Activities

Understanding of the arcane workings of the IB is largely speculative. One known task of the IB is to clear licenses to amateur radio enthusiasts. The IB also passes on intelligence between other Indian intelligence agencies and the police. The IB also grants the necessary security clearances to Indian diplomats and judges before they take the oath. On rare occasions, IB officers interact with the media during crises. The IB is also rumoured to intercept and open around 6,000 letters daily.

The Bureau is also authorised to conduct wiretapping without a warrant. This clause is mostly misused by ruling governments to spy on their political opponents, sometimes indicting them on false criminal charges. The IB also has numerous authors who write letters to various newspapers and magazines to support the government's perspective. According to a recent report the government is trying to bring in a restriction on wiretapping without a warrant.

Lapses

The IB was India's external and internal intelligence agency. Due to lapses on the part of the intelligence agencies to predict the Sino-Indian War of 1962, the IB was split up and entrusted with the task of internal intelligence. The external intelligence branch was handed to the newly created Research and Analysis Wing.

Research and Analysis Wing

Indian Intelligence Agency

The Cabinet Secretariat's Research and Analysis Wing (R&AW) is India's premier external intelligence body. It was created as an independent unit in September 1968 from the Intelligence Bureau which at that time handled both internal and external intelligence. Its headquarters are on Lodhi Road in New Delhi. The current director of the organization is P K Hormese Tharakan, who was with R&AW from 1989 to 2001, and is an IPS officer.

PROFILE, STRUCTURE AND FUNDING

Most available information about the R&AW is largely

speculative. Relative to other intelligence agencies of comparable size, the R&AW maintains a very low media profile and is largely ignored by Indian writers, filmmakers and the general public. It reports directly to the Prime Minister's Office (PMO) and its operations and structure are not revealed to Parliament.

The R&AW's budget and funding are not discussed in public forums. According to some reports, part of its funding comes from "discretionary grants" provided to various government bodies, especially Indian embassies and representatives abroad. Estimates of its annual budget vary wildly among experts-from $16 million to $145 million.

One consequence of such a low profile is that it is very difficult to judge R&AW's effectiveness and performance. Reports cover the entire range of judgements from "highly effective and professional" to "inadequate and riddled with internal politics".

The cadre for R&AW is drawn by deputation from state police forces and other intelligence agencies. The Research Analysis Service instituted during the times of Indira Gandhi is the All India Level Service of R&AW.

Founded in 1968, RAW focused largely on Pakistan. Its formation was initially motivated by reports of Pakistan supplying weapons to Sikh militants, and providing shelter and training to guerrillas in Pakistan.

Numerous missions were assigned to RAW upon its creation. These included monitoring political and military developments in neighboring countries that affects Indian national security. In the 1980s RAW played a large role in creating the LTTE in Sri Lanka. Consequently, considerable attention is paid by RAW to Pakistan and China, countries that are traditional rivals of India.

CHANGING THE INDIAN INTELLIGENCE CULTURE

In his R.N.Kao Memorial lecture delivered at the

headquarters of the Research & Analysis Wing (R&AW) on January 19, 2010, Vice-President Hamid Ansari has done well in raising in public issues such as accountability and parliamentary oversight to which the Indian intelligence community is still a stranger.

The concept of an accountable and competent intelligence community, which uses the need for secrecy only for protecting its operations and not for covering up its inadequacies and irregularities, has been accepted and implemented by the intelligence agencies of many democracies——parliamentary as well as Presidential types— of the world during the last three decades. Nobody in those countries has since argued that these concepts have come in the way of the effectiveness of the intelligence process and hence should be re-considered. The overall consensus is that these changes have proved beneficial and hence should be continued and, if necessary, further refined. In India too, these issues have been raised from time to time since the State of Emergency imposed by Indira Gandhi in 1975-77, but follow-up action has been avoided either because of resistance from sections of the intelligence community or because of the reluctance of the political leadership to introduce any changes which might dilute the scope for political misuse of the intelligence machinery for partisan purposes or both.

Accountability of intelligence agencies demands, firstly, that they should have a legal existence and, secondly, that they should have a formal charter of their functions and responsibilities. Forty-two years after its formation in 1968, the R&AW still does not have a legal existence. It was set up by a brief executive order issued on behalf of Indira Gandhi in September 1968. Till today, this order has not been accorded parliamentary sanctity by having necessary legislation authorising its creation passed by the Parliament. No Government, which has held office since 1968, has considered it necessary to have an Act passed by the Parliament providing legal legitimacy to the R&AW. No one has raised the question as to how the various Governments have been incurring expenditure on the R&AW year after year without having its creation approved by the Parliament. In the 1980s, when Indira Gandhi was the Prime Minister, a law was enacted by the Parliament banning strikes in the intelligence agencies. To my knowledge, that is the only Act of the Indian Parliament in which there is a reference to the R&AW by name. When that law was passed, nobody in the Parliament thought it fit to ask: What is this R&AW about? When was it created? Who created it? Has its creation been approved by the Parliament? It goes to the credit of A.K.Verma, who headed the R&AW from 1987 to 90. that he took the initiative in drawing the attention of the Governments of Rajiv Gandhi and V.P.Singh to the fact that the R&AW had been functioning without a legal cover and a formal charter. He wanted the Government of the day to do something about it, but nothing was done.

The fact that the Intelligence Bureau, which was created by the British before 1947, and the Central Bureau of Investigation (CBI), which came into existence after 1947, had been functioning without formal charters of their functions and responsibilities, was highlighted by the L.P.Singh Committee, which was set up by the Morarji Desai Government to enquire into the functioning of these two organisations during the State of Emergency. It not only stressed the need for formal charters to prevent their future misuse, but also prepared for the consideration of the Government detailed model charters for adoption. No action was taken on its recommendations by the Indira Gandhi Government which came back to power in 1980 or its successors. The report was consigned to the Archives—seen, but not read and implemented.

Shri Atal Behari Vajpayee and Shri Lal Krishna Advani were among those who were in the forefront of those who criticised—— during the election campaign of 1977—— the alleged misuse of the intelligence agencies by the Indira Gandhi Government during the Emergency. When Shri Vajpayee became the Prime Minister and Shri Advani the Home Minister in 1998, one naturally expected them to take the initiative in taking the L.P.Singh Committee report out of the Archives and implement it. The expectations were belied. The Task Force for the revamping of the intelligence apparatus set up by the Vajpayee Government in 2000, which was headed by Shri G.C. Saxena, former head of the R&AW, recommended the acceptance by the Government of the principle of formal charters for the intelligence agencies. To give greater meat to its recommendations, it wanted to have a look at the detailed charters for the IB and the CBI proposed by the L.P.Singh Committee. The Home Ministry, then headed by Shri Advani, avoided making available to the Task Force the entire report of the L.P.Singh Committee. However, the Task Force's recommendation for formal charters was accepted and implemented by the Vajpayee Government. One does not know whether the recommendations of the L.P.Singh Committee were taken into consideration while drafting the charters.

The credit for first raising the idea of a parliamentary oversight on the intelligence community should go to Shri Jaswant Singh, who was the Chairman of the Estimates Committee of the Rajya Sabha when Shri V.P.Singh was the Prime Minister. Shri V.P.Singh saw merit in the idea and wanted it to be examined. There was no opposition to the idea from the intelligence professionals then in service including this writer, but when Shri V.P.Singh developed differences with the BJP, he did not pursue it.

Since then, none of the political parties has shown interest in making the intelligence agencies accountable for their performance and integrity and in making their professional performance subject to an independent assessment. Secrecy is an important operational principle for an intelligence agency. Unless an intelligence agency is able to ensure the secrecy of its operations, no source or agent will stick his neck out to work for it. Its capability for collecting technical intelligence will also be affected.

But secrecy should not be allowed to be used as an excuse for covering inefficiencies in performance and irregularities in functioning and financial management. Irregularities do occur in matters such as the personnel policy and diversion of the resources sanctioned by the Government for operational objectives for non-operational purposes. The public and the Parliament have a right to know to what extent the agencies have been producing results and what are the areas of their non-performance. The Parliament has a right to know what kind of financial controls are in place, who exercises those controls and to what extent they are effective. The Parliament has similarly a right to check whether the principle of secrecy in recruitment is being misused to pack the organisations with unsuitable persons, taken not for their qualifications, but for their connections.

It is possible to introduce some of these checks and balances in the functioning of our intelligence community without damaging their operational secrecy. There is reluctance from the political class because it sees the agencies as instruments for partisan exploitation and not for defending national interests. There is reluctance from sections of the intelligence officers themselves because they think that unchecked secrecy gives them an aura of power and influence which they do not want to lose. Ansaris may come and Ansaris may go, but the intelligence agencies will go on functioning in the same manner with the complicity of the political class unless there is sustained public pressure on the political class and the agencies to change the culture of our agencies. I am not very optimistic because I do not see on the horizon any political leader who is genuinely convinced of the need for a change.

Every country gets the intelligence community it deserves. We will continue to have the community which we have deserved unless Shri Ansari's call is followed up.

LAWS AND REGULATIONS

India is a longstanding parliamentary democracy with a bicameral parliament. A parliament sits for 5 years unless dissolved earlier for new elections, except under constitutionally defined emergency situations.

State governments are elected at regular intervals except in states under President's Rule, i.e., rule by the central

Government. On the advice of the Prime Minister, the President may proclaim a state of emergency in any part of the national territory in the event of war, external aggression, or armed rebellion. Similarly, President's Rule may be declared in the event of a collapse of a state's constitutional machinery. The Supreme Court in May 1995 upheld the Government's authority to suspend fundamental rights during an emergency. Although the 25 state governments have primary responsibility for maintaining law and order, the central Government provides guidance and support through use of paramilitary forces throughout the country.

Serious abuses have included extrajudicial executions and other political killings and excessive use of force by security forces combating active insurgencies in Jammu and Kashmir and several northeastern states; torture and rape by police and other agents of government, and deaths of suspects in police custody throughout the country; poor prison conditions; arbitrary arrest and incommunicado detention in Jammu and Kashmir and the Northeast; continued detention throughout the country of thousands arrested under special security legislation; lengthy pretrial detention; and prolonged detention while under trial. The organization and responsibilities of intelligence and security agencies do not appear to be established or regulated by legislative acts of the Parliament of India.

Official Secrets Act (OSA)

Under the Official Secrets Act (OSA), the Government may restrict publication of sensitive stories, but the Government sometimes interprets this broadly to suppress criticism of its policies. Human rights activists state that government pressure caused one national, English-language daily to suppress some stories and transfer a staff reporter.

Newspapers Incitements to Offenses Act

The 1971 Newspapers Incitements to Offenses Act remains in effect in Jammu and Kashmir. Under the act, a district magistrate may prohibit the press from publishing material resulting in "incitement to murder" or "any act of violence." As punishment the act stipulates that the authorities may seize newspapers and printing presses. Despite these restrictions, newspapers in Srinagar regularly publish militant press releases attacking the Government and report in detail on alleged human rights abuses. The authorities allowed foreign journalists to travel freely in Jammu and Kashmir, where they regularly spoke with militant leaders, and filed reports on government abuses.

Special Protection Group Act

The Special Protection Group Act, which received the assent of the President on the 2nd June 1988 provides for the constitution and regulation of an armed force of the Union for providing proximate security to the Prime Minister of India and the members of his immediate family and for matters connected therewith. The SPG Act had an extremely significant fallout with far reaching implications. It legally circumscribed the parameters restricting SPG protection exclusively to the Prime Minister and his immediate family members. This became a controversial issue when the question of providing protection to Rajiv Gandhi was debated after he had ceased to be the Prime Minister of India in December 1989.

Criminal Procedure Code

The Criminal Procedure Code provides for an open trial in most cases, but it allows exceptions in proceedings involving official secrets, trials in which statements prejudicial to the safety of the State might be made, or under provisions of special security legislation. Sentences must be announced in public. The police must obtain warrants for searches and seizures. In a criminal investigation, the police may conduct searches without warrants to avoid undue delay, but they must justify the searches in writing to the nearest magistrate with jurisdiction over the offense.

The authorities in Jammu and Kashmir, Punjab, and Assam have special powers to search and arrest without a warrant. The authorities sometimes require permits and notification prior to holding parades or demonstrations, but local governments ordinarily respect the right to protest peacefully. At times of civil tension, the authorities may ban public assemblies or impose a curfew under the Criminal Procedure Code. There are three classes of prison facilities. Prisoners are not classified by the nature of their crimes, but by their standing in society. Class "C" prisoners are those who cannot prove they are college graduates or income taxpayers. Their cells are overcrowded, often have dirt floors, no furnishings, and poor quality food. The use of handcuffs and fetters is common. Class "B" prisoners—college graduates and taxpayers—are held under markedly better conditions. Class "A" prisoners are prominent persons, as designated by the Government, and are accorded private rooms, visits, and adequate food, which may be supplemented by their families. Class "A" prisoners are usually held in government guest houses.

Indian Telegraph Act

The Indian Telegraph Act authorizes the surveillance of communications, including monitoring telephone conversations and intercepting personal mail, in case of public emergency or "in the interest of the public safety or tranquillity." These powers have been used by every state government. The Union Government also uses the powers of the Indian Telegraph Act to tap phones and open mail.

Armed Forces Special Powers Act of 1958

The Armed Forces Special Powers Act of 1958 remains in effect in several states, i.e., in Jammu and Kashmir, Nagaland, Manipur, Assam and parts of Tripura.

Armed Forces (Jammu and Kashmir) Special Powers Act

Under the Armed Forces (Jammu and Kashmir) Special Powers Act passed in July 1990, security forces personnel have extraordinary powers, including authority to shoot suspected lawbreakers and those disturbing the peace, and to destroy structures suspected of harboring militants or arms.

Disturbed Areas Act

The Disturbed Areas Act has been in force in a number of districts in Andhra Pradesh for more than a year. The Disturbed Areas Act remains in effect in several states, i.e., in Jammu and Kashmir, Nagaland, Manipur, Assam and parts of Tripura. It gives police extraordinary powers of arrest and detention. Human rights groups allege that security forces have been able to operate with virtual impunity in parts of Andhra Pradesh under the act.

Jammu and Kashmir Disturbed Areas Act

Under the Jammu and Kashmir Disturbed Areas Act passed in July 1990, security forces personnel have extraordinary powers, including authority to shoot suspected lawbreakers and those disturbing the peace, and to destroy structures suspected of harboring militants or arms.

Public Safety Act

The Jammu and Kashmir Public Safety Act (PSA) of 1978 covers corresponding procedures for that state. Over half of the detainees in Jammu and Kashmir are held under the PSA. The Government acknowledges that, as of August 1997, it held about 1,600 persons in connection with the insurgency in 5 detention centers in Jammu and Kashmir, compared with 2,070 persons acknowledged held in 1995. Of these 1,298 were held under the Public Safety Act

National Security Act (NSA)

The National Security Act (NSA) of 1980 permits detention of persons considered security risks; police anywhere in the country (except Jammu and Kashmir) may detain suspects under NSA provisions. Under these provisions the authorities may detain a suspect without charge or trial as long as 1 year on loosely defined security grounds. The state government must confirm the detention order, which is reviewed by an advisory board of three high court judges within 7 weeks of arrest. NSA detainees are permitted visits by family members and lawyers and must be informed of the grounds for detention within 5 days (10 to 15 days in exceptional circumstances).

At the end of 1997 approximately 500 persons continue to be detained under the NSA. The NSA does not define "security risk." Human rights groups allege that preventive detention can be ordered and extended under the act purely on the opinion of the detaining authority. Such a subjective decision cannot be overturned by any court.

Terrorist and Disruptive Activities Act (TADA)

Although the law that had been subject to the most extensive abuse—the Terrorist and Disruptive Practices (Prevention) Act (TADA)—lapsed in May 1995, 3,785 persons previously arrested under the act continued to be held in a number of states at year's end, and a small number of arrests under TADA continued for crimes allegedly committed before the law lapsed.

Criminal cases are proceeding against most of those still held under TADA, with more than 3,000 charged under other laws in addition to TADA. In March, the Government asserted that all TADA cases would be reviewed. In February 1996, the Supreme Court eased bail guidelines for persons accused under TADA, taking into account the large backlog of cases in special TADA courts. In reply to a question in the Jammu and Kashmir state assembly in May 1997, the Government reported that 15,826 people were detained under TADA in the state between 1990 and 1995.

The Government acknowledges that, as of August 1997, it held 772 persons under the TADA in Jammu and Kashmir. TADA courts use abridged procedures. For example, defense counsel is not permitted to see witnesses for the prosecution, who are kept behind screens while testifying in court. Also, confessions extracted under duress are permitted in evidence.

Bibliography

Alger, John, *The Quest for Victory: The History of the Principles of War,* New York, 1982.

Arend, A.: *International Law and the Use of Force*, London, Routledge, 1993.

Ayub, Muhammad: *An Army, Its Role and Rule: A History of the Pakistan Army from Independence to Kargil from 1947–1999*. Pittsburgh: RoseDog Books, 2005.

Bamford, James: *A Pretext for War: 9/11, Iraq, and the Abuse of America's Intelligence Agencies*. New York: Doubleday, 2004.

Bellamy, C.: *Knights in White Armour: The New Art of War and Peace*, London, Random House, 1997.

Black, Jeremy, *Introduction to Global Military History: 1775 to the present day*, Routledge Press, 2005

Carpenter, Stanley D. M., *Military Leadership in the British Civil Wars, 1642-1651: The Genius of This Age*, Routledge, 2005.

Chandra, R.: *Judicial System in India, Lucknow*, Print House (India), 1992.

Coll, Steve: *Ghost Wars: The Secret History of the CIA, Afghanistan, and Bin Laden, from the Soviet Invasion to September 10, 2001*. New York: Penguin Press, 2004.

Crile, George: *Charlie Wilson's War: The Extraordinary Story of the Largest Covert Operation in History*. New York: Grove Press, 2003.

Davies.A.: *Telecommunications and Politics. The Secentralised Alternative*, London, Pinter, 1994.

Goleman, D.: *Working with Emotional Intelligence.* New York, NY:Bantam Books, 1998.

Heimanson, Rudolph: *Dictionary of Political Science and Law*, N.Y.: Oceana Publications, 1967.

Henderson, Robert D'A: *Brassey's International Intelligence Yearbook*. Dulles, VA: Brassey's, 2003.

Huntington, S.P.: *The Soldier and the State*, N.Y., Vintage Books, 1964.

Jones, W.H.: *The Government and Politics of India*, London, Hutchinson, 1971.

Kelly, John B.: *Britain and the Persian Gulf 1795-1880*, Oxford, Clarendon Press, 1968.

Lider, Julian, *Military Theory: Concept, Structure, Problems,* Swedish Studies in International Relations, Aldershot, 1983.

Mary, W.: *Asian Power and Politics: the Cultural Dimensions of Authority*, Cambridge, Belknap Press, 1985.

Nair, A. M.: *An Indian Freedom Fighter in Japan*, Bombay, Orient Longman, 1983.

Posen, B.R.: *The Sources of Military Doctrine*, Ithaca, 1984, Cornell Univ. Press.

Rosen, P.: *Societies and Military Power: India and its Armies*, Ithaca, Cornell University Press, 1996.

Savkin, V. Y., *Basic Principles of Operational Art and Tactics,* Moscow, 1972.

Simon, D. : *Public Administration*, New York, Knopf, 1950.

Todd, Paul; Bloch, Jonathan: *Global Intelligence : The World's Secret Services Today*. Dhaka: University Press, 2003.

Victor G. : *Law as a Political Instrument*, New York, Random House, 1955.

Wilden, Anthony, *Man and Woman, War and Peace: The Strategist's Companion*, Routledge, 1987

Index

J

K

L

M

N

O

P

R

S

T

V

W

□□□